CIVIC CENTER

Lewis Maltby

Can They Do That?

Retaking Our Fundamental Rights in the Workplace

PORTFOLIO

PORTFOLIO
Published by the Penguin Group
Penguin Group (USA) Inc., 375 Hudson Street, New York, New York 10014, U.S.A.
Penguin Group (Canada), 90 Eglinton Avenue East, Suite 700, Toronto, Ontario,
Canada M4P 2Y3 (a division of Pearson Penguin Canada Inc.)
Penguin Books Ltd, 80 Strand, London WC2R 0RL, England
Penguin Ireland, 25 St. Stephen's Green, Dublin 2, Ireland (a division of Penguin Books Ltd)
Penguin Books Australia Ltd, 250 Camberwell Road, Camberwell, Victoria 3124,
Australia (a division of Pearson Australia Group Pty Ltd)
Penguin Books India Pvt Ltd, 11 Community Centre, Panchsheel Park, New Delhi–110 017, India
Penguin Group (NZ), 67 Apollo Drive, Rosedale, North Shore 0632,
New Zealand (a division of Pearson New Zealand Ltd)
Penguin Books (South Africa) (Pty) Ltd, 24 Sturdee Avenue,
Rosebank, Johannesburg 2196, South Africa

Penguin Books Ltd, Registered Offices: 80 Strand, London WC2R 0RL, England

First published in 2009 by Portfolio,
a member of Penguin Group (USA) Inc.

1   3   5   7   9   10   8   6   4   2

Publisher's Note
This publication is designed to provide accurate and authoritative information in regard to the
subject matter covered. It is sold with the understanding that the publisher is not engaged in
rendering legal, accounting, or other professional services. If you require legal advice or other
expert assistance, you should seek the services of a competent professional.

LIBRARY OF CONGRESS CATALOGING-IN-PUBLICATION DATA
Maltby, Lewis.
Can they do that? : retaking our fundamental rights in the workplace / Lewis Maltby.
p. cm.
Includes index.
ISBN 978-1-59184-282-8
1. Employee rights—United States—Popular works. I. Title.
KF3319.85.M35 2010
344.7301—dc22   2009031631

Printed in the United States of America
Set in Warnock Pro
Designed by Amy Hill

To my father,

Frederick Maltby,

my first and best teacher

Contents

Acknowledgments   *ix*

Preface   *xi*

Introduction   *1*

1 You Have the Right to Remain Silent:
Freedom of Speech in the Workplace   *5*

2 Smile, You're on *Candid Camera:*
Privacy in the Workplace   *16*

3 Whose Life Is It Anyway?:
Employer Control of Personal Lives   *44*

4 Wrongful Discharge and Employment at Will   *57*

5 No Second Chances:
Background Checks   *68*

6 A Penny for Your Thoughts:
Psychological Testing by Employers   *80*

7 Drug Testing 92

8 Brave New Workplace:
Genetic Discrimination 108

9 Plant Closings 133

10 There's Strength in Numbers:
The Right to Organize 142

11 The Judge Is Not Your Friend:
Obstacles to Justice Even When the Law Is on Your Side 165

12 Tell It to the Arbitrator 175

13 The Rights You Have 196

14 Exporting Human Rights:
The United States and the Third World 210

15 Capitalism and Freedom 215

16 Taking Back Our Rights 230

Appendixes
  A. Model Corporate Privacy Policy 249
  B. Guidelines for IBM Bloggers: Executive Summary 253
  C. Sample Letter to Elected Representatives 254
  D. Sample Letter to Human Rights Organizations 255
  E. Employee Bill of Rights 256
  F. National Workrights Institute Membership Application 259

Index 261

Acknowledgments

I didn't write this book alone. Thank you to the many people who helped me with this book and in acquiring the experience on which it is based, especially:

Bruce Barry	*Ira Glasser*	*Mark Risk*
Jules Bernstein	*Steven Guastello*	*Peter Saucier*
Al Blumrosen	*Jon Hiatt*	*Ari Schwartz*
Kim Bobo	*Frederick Lane*	*Judy Scott*
Norman Brand	*Raj Nayak*	*Nadine Strossen*
Fred Feinstein	*Jules Pagano*	*John Wellemeyer*
Alfred Feliu	*John Philo*	*Adam Wolf*
Matthew Finkin	*James Pope*	

Thanks also to the staff of the National Workrights Institute, upon whose work this book is built:

Jeremy Gruber
Hyunjoo Nam
Sheila Vaidya

Special thanks to Professor Theodore J. St. Antoine, for his wisdom and willingness to share it.

Preface

I didn't always want to be a human rights lawyer.

Growing up, I wanted to practice patent law. It seemed like a safe, comfortable choice for a bright middle-class boy growing up in 1950s Eisenhower America.

Then came college, the civil rights movement, and the Vietnam War. Suddenly I realized, like millions of other students, that America wasn't always the land of the free and the home of the brave. Since being a full-time antiwar protester didn't seem like a promising career plan, I went to law school. The Warren Supreme Court was in full bloom and poor people (who I had just discovered actually existed) were starting to get fair trials for the first time. I decided to join this crusade for justice by becoming a public defender.

Criminal defense law, however, wasn't all it was cracked up to be. On TV, Perry Mason's and Matlock's clients were always innocent. Most of mine were guilty. While the majority of them hadn't done anything so terrible that I felt guilty about keeping them out of jail (which I almost always did), putting a car thief back on the street doesn't give you much of a warm fuzzy feeling at the end of the day. Worse yet are the clients (both innocent and guilty) with families. After closing arguments in a particularly serious case, I was pacing back and forth in the hallway of the courtroom waiting for the jury to return (think of a tiger in the zoo bouncing off the cage walls right before feeding time) when my client's five-year-old daughter pulled on the end of my sleeve and asked, "Mr. Maltby, is Daddy coming home soon?" Daddy came home that day, but if he hadn't, he would have been lucky to get home in time for her high-school graduation. I had to find another line of work.

By this time I had a few private clients, one of which was a small company with some remarkable new technology, big dreams, and not much else. They asked me to come on board as their company lawyer. It sounded predictable, mundane, and unexciting—exactly what I needed while I recharged my batteries and thought about what I wanted to do with my life.

Then a funny thing happened. My countercultural assumptions about business melted away when I saw how exciting starting something new could be. The company was growing like a weed and there was always something new and interesting to do. Soon I found myself (among other things) chairman of the company's Japanese subsidiary and head of its human resources department.

The HR assignment changed my life forever. I had been a civil libertarian my entire life (even before hearing the term) and an ACLU member for many years. I had even become the vice president of the board of directors for the Pennsylvania ACLU. Like all civil libertarians, I believed that random searches of people are wrong; that people should be searched only when there is reason to believe they are doing something wrong and that the search will find evidence of it.

In the corporate world, this opposition extends to random drug tests.

But every other company in the area had a drug-testing program. More important, our company was in the business of preventing toxic chemical tanks from overflowing and killing people. The tragedy at the Union Carbide plant in Bhopal, India, which killed more people than 9/11, occurred because Carbide's local management decided not to install my employer's control systems. Union Carbide has had tanks full of this same deadly chemical (methyl isocyanate) in the United States for forty years using our control systems without incident.

Not conducting random drug testing was right in principle, but people's lives depended upon the quality of our product. What was I going to do? It soon became apparent that this was only one of the dilemmas I would face. I didn't believe it was fair that a long-term employee could be fired at the whim of a new supervisor, but what did I propose instead? Like every company, we had occasional problems with theft. If I didn't believe in spying on people with hidden cameras, how was I going to catch the thieves?

Learning how to run a productive, profitable company without violating employees' human rights became the focus of my life. After ten years in the corporate world, Ira Glasser, the legendary former executive director of the ACLU, asked me to come to New York and start a project focusing on expanding legal protection for free speech and privacy in the corporate world. Ten years later, in 2000, that ACLU office spun off to become the National Workrights Institute.

I haven't got all the answers about running a profitable corporation while respecting employees' human rights, but I've learned quite a bit, and I'm working on the rest. That's why they call it "practicing" law.

Can They Do That?

Introduction

Lynne Gobbell was fired because her boss didn't like the bumper sticker on her car.

During the 2004 presidential election, Gobbell put a "Kerry for President" sticker on her bumper. When her boss saw it, he said Gobbell could "either work for John Kerry or work for me." Gobbell refused to take the sticker off her car and was immediately fired.

Gobbell fell into the black hole of human rights in the United States. The United States invented human rights. People in many countries can only dream about the freedoms we enjoy. In America, you can criticize any government official you want, including the president, even in rude or profane terms, without fear of punishment. Do the same thing in China, Russia, Iran, Kenya, or Guatemala, and you could wind up in prison or worse.

But Lynne Gobbell's freedom, and yours, disappears every morning when you go to work. The United States Constitution applies to the government, not to corporations. A private business, large or small, can legally ignore your freedom of speech. Where your employer is concerned, you have no such right.

Freedom of speech isn't the only right that disappears in the world of work. Privacy disappears too. If the government wants to tap your phone or read your e-mail, it needs to have evidence that you are doing something illegal. In most cases, it needs a court order. But employers routinely monitor telephone calls, e-mail, Web site visits, and virtually every other type of electronic communication.

This surveillance isn't limited to business-related matters; an e-mail you send to your spouse or doctor during your lunch break is just as likely to be read. When you bring your company-issued laptop in for updating or repair, the technician will probably look at anything that appears interesting. Even the contents of your home computer are at risk. Some employers, like Johnson County Community College, in Kansas, have gotten away even with installing hidden cameras in locker rooms and bathrooms.

Under the doctrine of employment at will, your boss can fire you for any reason, or no reason at all. Some employers use this power to control the private lives of their employees. Best Lock Company in Indiana fires workers for social drinking because its president believes drinking alcohol is a sin. Other companies, looking to curtail medical expenses, forbid employees from smoking in their own homes or engaging in risky hobbies like skiing.

You lose your rights before you even get a job. Many employers now conduct extensive investigations into prospective employees. If you've ever been arrested, you probably won't get the job, even if you weren't found guilty. If your credit history is spotty, it can cost you a job, even if the job has nothing to do with handling money. Other employers turn down people because of their driving record, even for jobs that don't involve driving. And even if your background is spotless, you can still lose the job because the information broker gets you mixed up with someone else with a similar name.

If you survive this gauntlet, the drug test is waiting for you. No sensible employer wants to hire a drug abuser, but drug tests can't tell if someone is an abuser, only that someone used drugs at some point in the past. If you've ever smoked marijuana at a party, you could be in for trouble. When your body metabolizes something you ingest, the chemicals it creates (called metabolites) stay in your body for days, or even weeks. Even if you've never touched drugs, you're not safe. Some employers use cheap tests that mistake Advil, Sudafed, NyQuil, and other over-the-counter medications for illegal drugs. Even if proper testing is used, labs often make mistakes. A study by the Centers for Disease Control found that 37 percent of drug test results were wrong; the samples labeled positive were actually clean. And don't count on having any privacy for the test; some employers have "urination monitors" watch everyone while they fill the cup to make sure nobody is cheating.

Finally there are the psychological tests. Some are designed to test your honesty. The only problem with those is that most of the people who fail are honest. Others ask about your sex life, religious beliefs, and other highly personal matters having nothing to do with your ability to do the job.

You may have already lost a job because of one of these pre-employment screenings without even knowing it. The law does not require employers to tell unsuccessful applicants why they weren't hired, and most employers don't. Some employers lie about why you weren't hired. The bottom line is, you'll never know why you were turned down.

As bad as things are, they are going to get worse. All new cell phones are now required by federal law to come equipped with the Global Positioning System (GPS). Some employers who issue company cell phones use this technology to track employees during their private lives, often in secret. Recently developed genetic tests allow employers to determine whether you carry the genes linked to breast cancer, Alzheimer's, and other serious illnesses. Employers are starting to use this knowledge to keep people out of the workforce to save money on corporate medical costs. Some biometric security systems, such as retina scans (which chart the blood vessels in your eye), reveal sensitive medical information such as whether you are diabetic, and facilitate identity theft.

Even in the few areas of employment where you do have legal rights, it can be nearly impossible to enforce them. Almost 20 percent of employers today require all employees to agree in advance not to go to court if the company violates their legal rights, and to take their dispute to a private arbitration system selected (and sometimes run) by the employer. If you don't agree, you don't get the job. Some of these programs are fair. But others are kangaroo courts in which employers may handpick the arbitrators and deny employees the right to have a lawyer, or whose rules don't require the arbitrator to follow the law.

Traditionally, employees who are being treated unfairly have been able to protect themselves by joining a union. Union contracts generally prohibit most of these abuses. But joining a union has become a dangerous undertaking.

Over eight thousand employees are fired every year simply for trying to join one. Technically, this kind of firing is illegal, but the penalties are so trivial that employers just pay the fines and keep breaking the law.

There is something profoundly disturbing, almost schizophrenic, about our approach to human rights. We have fought wars, millions of us have served in the military, and several hundred thousand Americans have died, defending our country and protecting our freedom of speech and other rights. Yet we have created a legal system that leaves those rights in the wastebasket when we go to work.

We could have changed our laws to outlaw these abuses, but we haven't. A handful of states have enacted laws that prohibit employers from firing people because of their politics or putting video cameras in bathrooms. But in most states, all the abuses I've described are completely legal.

As of now, there isn't much you can do to protect yourself from these abuses, but there are some actions you can take, starting with learning more about the company before you accept a job. If you've already accepted the job, you may be able to learn more about the company's practices or even persuade your boss to modify the plan.

In the long run, however, the only answer is to change the law. There is no reason why we should have to give up our rights as American citizens to get a job. Employers that respect employee rights generally outperform competitors that abuse employees. This book will tell you more about how to protect yourself to the extent you can under existing law and how to help change the law to provide better protection for human rights.

Over two hundred years ago, Americans decided that they were no longer going to allow the government to violate their human rights. That decision was a milestone in human history. It is time to make another historic decision: our employers must respect our rights as well.

1

You Have the Right to Remain Silent: Freedom of Speech in the Workplace

Congress shall make no law abridging freedom of speech.

—UNITED STATES CONSTITUTION

Your boss can fire you for your politics, the books you read, or even the baseball team you root for, and there's usually nothing you can do about it.

—PROFESSOR BRUCE BARRY, VANDERBILT UNIVERSITY

Glen Hillier lost his job because he asked a presidential candidate an embarrassing question at a public political rally. During the 2004 presidential campaign, Hillier, who worked at an advertising and design company, attended a rally for President Bush in West Virginia. He attempted to ask Bush a challenging question about the war in Iraq. One of his company's customers, also at the rally, was offended by the implied criticism of Bush and told Hillier's boss. When Hillier came to work the next day, he was fired. When Hillier called his lawyer, he was told that his boss had done nothing illegal.

What happened to Hillier's freedom of speech? What Hillier didn't know is that, where his employer is concerned, he has no right to freedom of speech. The United States Constitution (including the Bill of Rights) applies only to the government. It does not apply to private businesses. A corporation can legally ignore the constitutional rights of its employees.

You don't need to be a constitutional lawyer to understand this. The First

Amendment says that "Congress shall make no law abridging freedom of speech." It says nothing about what private parties can do, including private corporations.*

How could the founding fathers have made such a glaring oversight? The answer is that, at the birth of our nation, the problem didn't exist. The world in 1783 was vastly different from the one we live in today. Most people were self-employed. The few employers that existed were very small, typically farm owners or craftsmen who employed a few helpers. Such tiny enterprises didn't have the power to threaten the rights of citizens en masse. The founding fathers weren't worried about the abuse of power by Paul Revere's silversmith shop, and had no reason to be. The abuses of power they had experienced came from the government, and it was to this threat that they responded.

The world today has changed beyond recognition. Modern multinational corporations dwarf the size of local and state governments. Some are richer and more powerful than most countries. The world's largest corporation, Wal-Mart, has two million employees and an annual budget of more than $400 billion. This is more than the national budget of 197 of the world's 229 countries, including Greece, Austria, Sweden, and Israel.

Wal-Mart has consistently abused its power over workers. It has been found guilty of violating child labor laws, forcing employees to work without pay, and hiring illegal immigrants. Wal-Mart managers have even locked employees inside stores overnight. Injured workers have to wait hours for a supervisor to let them go to the hospital. These abuses are not the fault of a few rogue store managers. Wal-Mart's senior executives set performance goals that are impossible to meet without breaking the law and fire store managers who fail to meet them.

For example, store managers routinely tell employees they must complete a certain volume of work or they will be fired. Both the store manager and the employee know the work can't be completed in forty hours. The manager then

---

* Originally, the Constitution and Bill of Rights applied only to the federal government. Over the course of many years, the Supreme Court gradually expanded the Constitution's reach to include all branches of government, including state and local government. The Court reasoned that this interpretation was more consistent with the principles the Bill of Rights was intended to protect. But the Court has concluded that the term "Congress" could not reasonably be interpreted to include private parties.

tells the employees they are not authorized to work overtime. The result is that employees officially quit work at the end of their shift and then go back to work "off the clock" without pay.

Small employers can be just as abusive. Robert Sprague was a salesman in a carpet store in Oklahoma. His boss, Lee Carroll, a fundamentalist Christian, forced Sprague to attend prayer meetings in his office and constantly berated him in front of his coworkers for his religious beliefs (Sprague was an Episcopalian). When Carroll found out Sprague's grandmother was Jewish, he told him, "Jesus Christ is alive; Moses is dead." When Sprague complained, Carroll gave him a punitive transfer to a store whose sales were so low Sprague couldn't make a living and he had to resign.

Whistle-blowers

> I was working for the Nuclear Services Corporation as a systems application engineer when I became aware of many engineering deficiencies in nuclear power systems that were already on the market. I told my supervisors about these problems, but I was ignored. After a period of indecision about not jeopardizing my career, I presented a paper to a U.S. Senate subcommittee. Three weeks later I was fired.
>
> —PETER FAULKNER, AS QUOTED IN *WHISTLE-BLOWING: LOYALTY AND DISSENT IN THE CORPORATION* (1981) BY ALAN F. WESTIN

If you think voicing your political opinions is dangerous, try talking about your own company. One of the most common reasons people are fired is because they reveal improper conduct by their employer. Corporations consider whistle-blowers traitors and will go to any length to fire them. Even reporting abuse within the company can get you fired.

George Geary worked for U.S. Steel as a salesman. When the company came out with a new type of tubing for high-pressure applications, Geary realized the design was faulty. He didn't tell the media, or government regulators. He quietly brought the matter up with his superiors, who corrected the design mistake. Geary's action saved lives and saved his employer millions of dollars. His reward was being fired. When he sued, the judge dismissed his case. The Pennsylvania Supreme Court upheld the termination.

In 1986, Roger Boisjoly and Bob Eberling, engineers for Morton Thiokol (the company that built the rocket boosters), realized that the rubber O-rings holding the stages of the *Challenger* space shuttle together would not work at the temperature predicted for the launch date. The O-rings must be flexible to work and would become too stiff in the below-freezing temperature on the launch date. They spent six hours on the telephone with their superiors the night before the launch, telling them about the problem and pleading with them to postpone the launch. Their superiors ignored them and gave NASA a green light to launch.

After the shuttle exploded, killing all seven astronauts, Boisjoly was contacted by the presidential commission investigating the disaster and testified about what had happened. The commissioners praised his testimony. Morton Thiokol retaliated by transferring Boisjoly to the worst location within the company and treating him like a pariah. Only the company's fear of offending the federal government (whose contracts keep them in business) prevented it from firing him. Eventually, the harassment got so bad that Boisjoly couldn't take it anymore and quit.

Tom Devine, general counsel of the Government Accountability Project (the leading public interest organization working to protect whistle-blowers) calls telling the truth about your company the most dangerous thing you can do in corporate America today. Devine tells employees who are considering blowing the whistle to expect retaliation. "Retaliation isn't just a risk," writes Devine in *The Whistleblower's Survival Guide*. "You almost surely will suffer some level of retribution."

It isn't only the whistle-blowers who suffer because of corporate retaliation. The public suffers as well. Peter Faulkner (quoted above) warned his employer about the problems that led to the failures at Three Mile Island and other nuclear power plants. But most people with this kind of information keep it to themselves because they are rightfully afraid of being fired. When fear triumphs over truth, public safety suffers and innocent people are hurt.

When employees of the Michigan Chemical Company found out in 1973 that their employer had mistakenly shipped over a thousand pounds of polybrominated biphenyls (PBBs) to the state's farm services bureau instead of magnesium oxide (a cattle feed additive that increases milk production), no one said a word because the company told them not to talk. By that point the PBBs had gone into animal feed consumed by cattle and chickens all over the state, contaminating Michigan's milk and egg supplies with this known carcinogen. Five years later, 97 percent of the people in Michigan had detectable levels of the chemical in their body.

Several states have responded to these abuses by passing whistle-blower protection laws. Sadly, these laws offer almost no real protection. To begin with, the majority of state whistle-blower protection laws cover only government employees; if you work for a private corporation you have no protection. Even for government employees, these laws are almost worthless because public employees are covered by the First Amendment (as discussed later in this chapter).

When the state law actually does cover private-sector employees, there is little actual protection. Some laws protect whistle-blowers only if they report the abuse to their superiors in the company, who are often the people behind the lawbreaking. If you report it to a government agency, or the media, even after your superiors at the company refuse to act, you aren't protected. In other states, it is exactly the opposite. In Alaska, for example, whistle-blowers are protected only if they report misconduct to the government; internal reporting is not protected. No, it doesn't make sense.

Other whistle-blowers lose protection because the misconduct they report isn't covered by the law. In Hawaii, the employer's conduct must be illegal for a whistle-blower to be protected. Unless there is a law on the books specifically prohibiting what the employer did, the employer can still fire the whistle-blower, no matter how unethical the conduct or how much it harms the public. Other states, like Maryland, cover conduct that is unethical, but not technically illegal, but only when it is "a matter of public concern." This means that an employee who reports that the CEO is stealing money from the company is not protected because only the shareholders are hurt, not the general public.

The end result of all these exceptions is that there is often little protection left. It's like a piece of Swiss cheese that is mostly holes. Outten & Golden, the country's largest law firm specializing in representing employees in employment cases, conducted a study of the New York State whistle-blower protection law after it had been in effect for almost ten years and found that not a single person who had brought a case under it had won; the exceptions swallowed the rule.

Blogs

What you write in your blog can also cost you your job. Roughly 26 million Americans have started a blog, and that number increases every day. Another 75 million actively use Facebook. People often vent their frustrations on their blog, including their frustrations about unreasonable policies at work or an unfair boss. Many still think their boss will never read these remarks.

But they do. It's easy to find anyone's blog today using Google or another search engine. Many employers make a habit of tracking employee blog posts and social networking profiles, usually to find out whether they are looking for another job or moonlighting for a competitor. You can't blame employers for wanting to know. Revealing confidential information to a competitor can hurt the company and may be illegal. When an employee leaves without notice, it can make it hard for his or her supervisor to get critical work done. If the boss knows someone is about to quit, he or she can start looking for a replacement. The problem is that, even if you're not doing either of these things, you can still be in trouble. If your boss doesn't like something you say about the company, or about him or her personally, you're likely to get fired. It happens every day.

Meg Spohn from Colorado was fired from her job as a teacher for DeVry University, a technical training school, for complaining about her job. She never got a warning. DeVry never even told her what she said that got her fired. "My blog is just about what's going on in my life," she said afterward. "It never occurred to me that my thoughts could get me fired."

If you think your boss won't fire you for saying something uncomplimentary about him, consider what happened to Dave Steward. Steward posted a *Dilbert* comic on the company bulletin board in which Dilbert asks, "Why does it seem as if most of the decisions in my workplace are made by drunken lemurs?" His bosses at Iowa's Catfish Bend Casino were so angry they reviewed the security tapes to find out who posted it. When they discovered it was Steward, he was fired.

A worker I'll call Charles (he asked me not to reveal his real name) was fired from his factory job in Pennsylvania for calling his boss a "cheapskate" for illegally refusing to pay him overtime. Charles didn't say it to his face; he wrote it in a letter to a friend during lunch. While Charles was away from his desk, his boss came into his office looking for him, saw the letter, and (even though it was clearly personal) read it. When Charles came back to his office, his boss fired him.

Nate Fulmer, from South Carolina, didn't even mention work on his blog. Fulmer and his wife have a Web site (www.nateanddi.com) on which they publish their often critical views of organized religion. This offended Fulmer's conservative Christian boss, who promptly fired him.

Even your creative writing can get you fired. Cameron Barrett, an IT employee from Traverse City, Michigan, liked to write short stories in his spare time, and posted them on his personal Web page. Some of his stories involve sex and violence. When his boss went to Barrett's Web page and found one of his stories offensive, Barrett was fired.

Some people try to protect themselves by not using their real name online. But even this strategy can fail. When a corporate executive in Florida didn't like what someone said about him in a chat room, he demanded that the Internet service provider (ISP) tell him the real name of the person who made the remarks. When the ISP refused, he went to court. The Florida Court of Appeals ruled that the service provider was legally required to release the name.

Fifteen percent of American employers now have formal rules and policies governing what employees can and can't say on their personal blogs. The majority of these policies prohibit personal statements having nothing to do with the employer. According to a survey by the Society for Human Resource Management, 3 percent of employers have disciplined employees for something they said on their blog. Media articles suggest that the actual number may be much higher. Even if you're writing on your personal blog on your own computer and in your own home, many employers think they have the right to censor your speech. The SHRM survey found that almost half of employers with blogging policies make no distinction between posting on company computers and posting on your personal computer at home.

Some of America's most respected companies attempt to control online speech—even those in the technology arena. IBM's policy on employee blogging (see appendix B on page 253) prohibits ethnic slurs, personal insults, and obscenities. It also discourages making statements on controversial subjects such as politics or religion that might be viewed as objectionable.

State Free Speech Laws

A number of states have passed laws aimed at protecting employee free speech. Unfortunately, most of them are virtually useless. New Jersey's statute is typical of such laws. It prohibits employers from "threatening to inflict any loss against anyone in his employ in order to compel such employee to vote or refrain from voting for any particular candidate." This is the one form of protection employees don't need. Every state in the country uses a secret ballot. No one, including employers, has any way of finding out how a person voted. If an employer threatens to fire you unless you vote for the candidate he supports, you can simply tell the boss what he wants to hear and vote the way you want.

A few state laws are even more meaningless. Arizona and several other states prohibit employers from putting statements in employees' pay envelopes telling them how to vote. The only piece of paper in their pay envelope most people look at is the check; the rest goes in the wastebasket. Millions of Americans don't even get a paycheck anymore; their pay is electronically deposited into their bank account.

Missouri has one of the few good state laws. It prohibits employers from making "any rule or regulation to prevent an employee from engaging in political activities, soliciting or receiving funds for a political purpose, participating in a political convention, or subscribing his name to any initiative, referendum, or recall petition." If Lynne Gobbell or Glen Hillier had lived in Missouri, they would have been protected.

But even the better laws have their shortcomings. William Niess was an executive in a Wisconsin company. His boss, the vice president of sales, was eager to make a name for himself in local politics and told the executives on his staff to contribute to the Republican Party. Niess, who was a Democrat, declined to contribute and was fired. He could do nothing about it under Wisconsin state law. Even had he lived in Missouri, he would have been out of luck because he wasn't punished for something he did do, but rather for something he didn't.

Laws in some states, such as New Jersey, make employer interference with free speech a criminal offense. This may sound like a good idea, but it isn't. Unlike a civil suit, which can be brought by a private individual, charges under a criminal statute can be brought only by the police and the district attorney. Private citizens cannot charge someone with a crime and bring them to trial. Most police departments are far too busy trying to catch murderers, rapists, burglars, and other dangerous criminals to spend time enforcing free speech laws. Asking the police to arrest your boss for interfering with your freedom of speech is a complete waste of time; you'd be better off wishing on a star.

Fortunately, a few states have strong laws that give their citizens the protection they need. California's law states that "no employer shall make any rule controlling or tending to control the political activities or affiliations of employees." Employees whose rights under this law have been violated have the right to sue their employer for damages. Unfortunately, only four other states have comparable laws. The rest of us are out of luck.

Government Employees

Public employees have some right to freedom of speech because they work for the government. The government, whether federal, state, or local, is bound by the Constitution, including when it acts as an employer.

This freedom, however, is very limited. In *Connick v. Myers*, the Supreme Court laid out the guidelines. Sheila Myers was an assistant district attorney in New Orleans. The district attorney—Harry Connick, father of the famous singer—fired Myers for circulating a questionnaire to the other lawyers in the office asking about their morale, confidence in their superiors, whether they felt pressured to work on political campaigns, and whether they felt the need for a grievance committee.

The Court dismissed all but one of Myers's free speech arguments on the grounds that her issues were not matters of public concern. There is nothing in the Constitution that restricts free speech to matters of public concern. The Court has established circumstances under which speech isn't protected. You can't yell "fire" in a crowded theater, threaten to hurt someone, or commit slander. But there is nothing about "public concerns." The Court just made up this requirement.

One could argue that the morale and confidence in their superiors of the attorneys who protect the public by prosecuting criminals is very much a matter of public concern. The more important problem, however, is that the Court ruled that the thing government employees (like private employees) most want to talk about—whether they are being treated fairly at work—is not protected.

The Court did recognize that the issue of whether prosecutors were being pressured to work on political campaigns was a matter of public concern. But even here Myers lost her claim. Justice Byron White's opinion stated that the impact of Myers's questionnaire on the functioning of the prosecutor's office must also be considered. Connick admitted that circulating the questionnaire had not interfered with Myers's performance of her job, nor had it interfered with the performance of anyone else in the office. But the Court upheld her firing anyway because her questioning of management could adversely impact her working relationship with her boss. Justice White seems to have missed the "Catch-22" quality of his rule. You don't need to question management when you agree with them, and you can't question management when you disagree with them because the very act of questioning could hurt your working relationship.

Over the years, many public employees have attempted to escape the Scylla and Charybdis of White's opinion. A few have succeeded, such as Ardith McPherson, who lost her job as a clerk in a Texas county sheriff's office for criticizing President Reagan in incendiary terms. The Supreme Court found that expressing one's opinion of the president is a matter of public concern and ordered the county to reinstate her. Far more, however, have ended up like a public schoolteacher in Connecticut named Gilbertson who was fired for criticizing decisions of the school board, and lost his case because the court disapproved of the acid tone of his language.

When all is said and done, the sad reality is that freedom of speech is a myth where your employment is concerned, whether you work in the public or private sector.

Employer abuse of the right to freedom of speech does more than hurt individual employees. It undermines our democratic system. Democracy works only when people are free to discuss their opinions, political or otherwise, in public. Letters to the editor, signs on the lawn, and bumper stickers are part of the democratic process. When people can't express their thoughts out of fear of retaliation, democracy suffers.

2

Smile, You're on *Candid Camera:* Privacy in the Workplace

The right of the people to be secure in their persons, houses, papers, and effects shall not be violated.

—UNITED STATES CONSTITUTION

Privacy is dead. Get over it.

—SCOTT MCNEALY, FORMER PRESIDENT, SUN MICROSYSTEMS

"I always know what you're doing," Tim Johnson, the general manager of Atlas Cold Storage of Pendergrass, Georgia, told his employees. "There is nowhere in this plant where I can't see you."

Pamela Allen and the other employees at Atlas took Johnson seriously. They knew he watched them like a hawk and seemed to know about everything that happened in the facility. But they didn't know how true his words were until a female employee who was using the bathroom noticed something strange in the ceiling. When the employees investigated, they found a hidden video camera aimed straight into the stalls. A cable attached to the camera led to a television set in Johnson's office.

Allen and her coworkers were stunned. "I felt violated," said Joyce Bavar, another female employee. "I couldn't believe something like this could happen to me."

Outraged, Allen and eighteen other women sued. Atlas's response made them feel as though they had been violated again. The company couldn't deny that the women had been spied on; Johnson had been caught red-handed. Instead, the company argued that what their manager had done was not illegal and filed a motion to have their case dismissed.

The women thought this argument was preposterous. But their lawyer explained that it wasn't far-fetched at all. Their constitutional right to privacy hadn't been violated because they didn't have any constitutional rights where their employer was concerned. Moreover, there was no law in Georgia prohibiting secret video surveillance, even in bathrooms. They could try to convince the judge to let the case go to a jury on a general theory of privacy, but there was no guarantee that they would be successful. Faced with the prospect of defeat, Allen and her coworkers accepted a modest settlement. Tim Johnson kept his job.

You might think that the outcome would have been different in another state, but you'd be wrong. Only two states, California and Rhode Island, have laws banning video cameras in workplace bathrooms and locker rooms. In all other states, victims of video voyeurism at work must overcome the same legal minefield as the women from Atlas Cold Storage.

William Thompson found a hidden video camera in the locker room at Johnson County Community College, in Kansas, where he and other employees changed clothes. When the employees went to court, the judge dismissed their case. He ruled that since heating and air conditioning equipment in the locker room might someday need maintenance, the area was public and the employees had no legal expectation of privacy. By this definition, there is no such thing as a private space; everything is open to surveillance.

Meanwhile, if the video surveillance takes place anywhere other than a locker room or bathroom, you have no legal protection at all. Most of the time, this practice isn't very intrusive, especially when the cameras are visible. But sometimes it can be humiliating.

Gail Nelson worked at Salem State College in suburban Boston, and frequently exercised after work. There was no locker room, and using the bathroom was inconvenient, so she waited until work was over and everyone else went home before changing clothes in her cubicle. What Nelson didn't know was that the college had installed a hidden camera in the office because it suspected misconduct by another employee. The first day they reviewed the tapes, they found that they had recorded Nelson taking her clothes off.

The college could have thrown the tape away and changed the camera angle slightly so it would have covered the suspect's cubicle but not Nelson's. It could have quietly suggested to Nelson, without explanation, that she not change clothes in her cubicle for a while. But the college didn't do either. Instead, it continued to tape her every afternoon taking her clothes off. The men on the security team undoubtedly enjoyed this a great deal.

When Nelson found out about the taping, she was mortified. "I'm a very modest person," she explained. "The idea of strange men watching me undress makes me physically ill." She asked her boss why they had continued to tape her, rather than reposition the camera. She got no answer. She asked how many tapes there were, who had seen them, and where they were. Salem State wouldn't tell her.

Finally, she went to court. The judge dismissed her case. He ruled that she had no right to privacy in a "public" area, even if she had done everything possible not to be seen by others. Even if the college had videotaped her on purpose she wouldn't have had a case. Nelson appealed the decision to the Massachusetts Supreme Court. The National Workrights Institute filed an amicus brief in support of her position. But the answer was the same. Because she wasn't in a locker room or bathroom, she had no right to privacy.

Most victims of video voyeurism are women, but men are sometimes humiliated too. The Boston Sheraton secretly filmed the men's locker room because management heard a rumor that some employees had been smoking marijuana there. The cameras found no one doing anything wrong, only employees dressing and undressing. But that didn't stop management from keeping the camera rolling. The situation came to light only when management carelessly left one of the videos lying around where it was found by a female employee. Franklin Etienne, a worker who had recently immigrated from Haiti, said, "I left Haiti to escape this kind of abuse. I can't believe this happened to me in America."

Consolidated Freightways, a California trucking company, installed two-way mirrors in both the men's and women's bathrooms with video cameras on the other side. As in Boston, management claimed that employees were using drugs. And, again, as in Boston, nobody was. The only misconduct in the bathrooms was the employer's spying. The employees were shocked when they found out. Fortunately for the employees, they worked in one of the two states with a law against video surveillance of bathrooms. If they had worked anywhere else, they might well have been unable to stop the surveillance.

What makes this practice especially frightening is that the use of video cameras has exploded. Until recently an employer who wanted to spy on his employees had to hire a private investigator to install an expensive video system. Many employers might have been tempted to spy, but few were willing to pay the expense.

Today the landscape has changed. A boss who wants to spy can buy a video camera in his local Radio Shack. If that is too much trouble, he can buy it for fifty bucks on the Internet without leaving his office. He doesn't have to pay a private investigator to install the camera; it's so easy he can do it himself. Plus there's little chance that anyone will notice; modern pinhole cameras require only a three-sixteenths-inch opening, barely larger than the holes in the ceiling tile. The camera can even be disguised as a clock, or a smoke alarm. When I appeared on *Donahue* in the early nineties, the studio audience was secretly videotaped with a camera hidden in a plant on Phil's desk. At the end of the show, he revealed to an amazed audience footage captured over the last half hour without their knowledge.

With cameras so cheap and easy to use, their use has skyrocketed. At least three million surveillance cameras are being used in America today. No one knows for sure how many cameras there are, or where they are located. CCS International, a company that provides security and monitoring services, calculated in 2002 that the average New Yorker was captured on camera seventy-five times a day, usually without being aware of it.

Even more frightening is the fact that video images are now digital. Until recently, the number of people who could see a videotape of you in a locker room or bathroom was relatively small because the footage was on tape. Sharing the pictures with someone else required making a copy of the tape and sending it to them. But today, captured video can be stored on a hard drive and sent to thousands of people via e-mail with the push of a button. They can also be posted on the Internet to be viewed by millions. There are countless Web sites featuring pictures of innocent people taking their clothes off in a locker room or using the bathroom. You could be next. You might even be there already.

Video surveillance takes place not just in subways and bank lobbies, but in the workplace as well. When the American Management Association polled its members in 2004, they found that 51 percent of employers used surveillance cameras on a routine basis. That number is even higher today. Some of these are legitimate security cameras located in parking garages and stairwells. A person alone in a parking garage late at night is an easy target. But most criminals will think twice about attacking her if they know the incident will be recorded. Many workplace cameras, however, are stationed in places where they do nothing but spy on innocent people.

Video surveillance can also be used to turn jobs into sweatshops. A municipality in New York recently installed what it called security cameras in a building where mechanics service trucks, snowplows, and other equipment. When the mayor was asked what risk he was concerned about, he had no answer. He admitted that he wasn't concerned about someone breaking in and stealing a snowplow. He couldn't have been worried about the mechanics stealing tools, either—the mechanics used their own tools. In fact, nothing had ever been stolen from the building in the entire history of the town.

The workers began to suspect that the cameras were really there to record whether they took too long to go to the bathroom or took a break between crawling out from underneath one broken truck and crawling under the next one. The mayor denied that this was the purpose, but when he was asked to put it in writing, he refused. It doesn't take a neurosurgeon to figure out what was going on there.

Computer Monitoring

Gentlemen do not read each other's mail.

—HENRY L. STIMSON, FORMER SECRETARY OF STATE

Video surveillance is hardly the only form of electronic monitoring people face in America today. Virtually every way we communicate at work is monitored, including e-mail, Internet access, instant messages, the contents of our computers, and even our telephone calls. Some of these methods are well known, such as e-mail monitoring and blocking pornographic Web sites. Every day we hear news of technological breakthroughs such as ID badges that emit a radio signal so your boss will know where you are every minute you're in the office, or GPS-equipped company cell phones that can track you during your private life.

Not so long ago, monitoring was relatively rare. E-mail and the Internet were limited to government agencies and academia. Most workplace communication was written on paper or spoken over the telephone. While it was possible to listen in on telephone calls, few employers did so. Reading employees' mail was virtually unheard-of. An American Management Association survey of its members in 1990 found that only 8 percent maintained any kind of employee monitoring program.

Today the workplace has changed almost beyond recognition. Computers, e-mail, and the Internet have replaced the paper letter and even the telephone call as the primary method of business communication. At least 25 billion business-related e-mails are sent every day. *The Wall Street Journal* reports that employees spend up to four hours per day reading and sending e-mail. As this change occurred, monitoring started to grow. In 1998, the congressional Office of Technology Assessment found that only 8 percent of companies conducted electronic monitoring. Only five years later, *MacWorld* magazine found that 20 percent of companies electronically monitored employees. In a more recent survey by the Bentley School of Business Ethics, at least 92 percent of employers were found to use electronic surveillance. The bottom line is that if you work in corporate America today, you are being watched, whether you know it or not.

This encroachment is especially troubling because of the amount of personal communication that takes place at work. A generation ago, people's work lives and home lives were separate. Work was done at the office and personal matters were taken care of at home. Today home computers, laptops, BlackBerrys, cell phones, and other electronic technologies have made it possible for us to do anything from anywhere. This blessing gives us the flexibility to structure our lives the way we want. If we want to leave work early for a child's school play but can't miss an important telephone call, we can take the call on our cell phone. If we'd like to take a vacation but need to communicate with colleagues about an important project, we can take our laptop and keep up by e-mail.

Maggie Jackson, former workplace correspondent for the Associated Press, estimates that the average professional now deals with over twenty work-related electronic messages at home every week. Sixty percent of executives and professionals take a cell phone, laptop, or pager on vacation in order to stay in touch with the office. Our ability to balance work and family is greater than our parents ever dreamed of.

Employers also gain from this new arrangement. When employees can work at home on evenings and weekends, they spend more time working without costing the employer more money. It's like getting extra employees for free. Some employers abuse this benefit by constantly sending employees questions and assignments when they are home.

This process is a two-way street. When the wall between work and home comes down, not only does work take place at home, but personal matters get handled at the office. An employee who spent much of the evening at home responding to work-related e-mails will think nothing of sending a personal e-mail from the office. And why should she?

Employers have accepted this development. Initially, most employers adopted a policy that company computers were to be used only for business. But this has changed. Employers have come to realize that there is no more harm in a short personal e-mail or a short personal Web visit than there is in a short personal telephone call, which most employers have accepted for years. Employers have also learned that they cannot enforce a rule against all personal use of company computers. The rule was so unreasonable that most employees ignored it. Employers were forced to choose between firing productive employees and creating a more practical rule. According to the most recent study of employer computer policies by the Bentley Center, virtually all employers (92 percent) now officially allow reasonable use of office computers for personal reasons. The remaining few probably tolerate an occasional personal e-mail as an unofficial policy.

Employers have not, however, changed their monitoring policies. In most companies, monitoring practices today are identical to the practices before personal messages were allowed.

Most people know that employers monitor e-mail, but don't suspect that anyone is reading their personal messages. Some employees take comfort in the fact that any particular e-mail message is only a drop in a sea of electronic communication. "The company won't actually read the few sensitive e-mails I send," these people think. "They are mixed in with millions of other messages."

What these people don't know is that most employers don't read e-mails at random. They use special software to identify the messages that use specific terms. Some of these keywords are technical and relate to a company's trade secrets. Employers read these messages to see if anyone is leaking proprietary information to a competitor. Other keywords are sex-related (some people call this the George Carlin system, based on the late comedian's famous routine about the seven words you can't say on television). Employers read messages using these words to look for sexual harassment.

But keyword filtering also catches personal e-mails having nothing to do with sexual harassment. For example, the word "breast" is on many keyword lists. While an e-mail using this word might be sexual harassment, it could just as easily be a message from an employee to her doctor. Some sophisticated keyword systems, such as Red Earth, look at combinations of words. If "breast" is used in the same message as "kiss," the e-mail is flagged for examination, but if used in the same message as "chemotherapy," it would not be.

While this is an improvement, there are still problems. Even if the e-mail really is romantic or sexual in nature, it could be a message from an employee to her husband on their anniversary. It could also be an e-mail between two employees who are romantically involved. The only difference between these messages and sexually harassing ones is in the minds of the parties, not in the words they use. In the end, keyword monitoring, no matter how well intentioned, zeroes in on the most sensitive messages of all.

Some employees try to avoid surveillance by using their personal e-mail accounts instead of the company system. Others use instant messaging instead of e-mail. But these do nothing to protect privacy. Both types of messages pass through the company server, where they can be monitored just like e-mail from your company account. Even encryption doesn't usually help;

your employer can simply order you not to use it. And if your ISP or the party sending you e-mail encrypts the message, the employer simply programs its server to block all encrypted messages.

Many executives and high-level professionals think that only rank-and-file employees (and maybe middle managers) are subject to surveillance. This too is a false assumption. One day Judge Alexander Kozinski, a federal appeals court judge (one step below the Supreme Court) noticed something strange about his computer. When he investigated, he learned that court administrators were secretly monitoring the computers of everyone in the federal court system, including the judges. When they traveled and used their government-issued laptops, this traffic too was monitored. Technically, this was entirely legal; judges are employees just like everyone else. Unlike the rest of us, however, federal judges have a lot of clout. When they demanded the system be removed, they got their way.

It's Not Just Your Employer

Not only is your employer capable of learning everything you've entered into your computer, the information may end up in the hands of others. When corporations are involved in litigation, it is now standard practice for the opposition counsel to demand e-mails from all employees who have any relationship to the dispute. Technically, only business-related messages must be produced, but it doesn't work that way in reality. The company demanding the documents from your employer wants to see everything. It has no incentive to narrow the request to eliminate personal messages.

Your employer could refuse to disclose all your e-mail and produce only those messages that are work-related. But that costs time and money and few, if any, employers are willing to pay to protect your privacy, because it doesn't affect the bottom line. The judge could narrow the e-mail request to what is relevant, but judges are busy and won't take the time to deal with it. In the end, all your e-mail, including your personal messages, will be turned over to the other company and its lawyers.

The government too may be reading your e-mail. Under the Patriot Act, employers are required to turn over any requested e-mails at the FBI's behest. Most of the time this is done without a court order. And employers are prohibited from telling employees that their e-mail has been given to the government. The FBI is supposed to read your e-mail only when they have reason to believe that you are a terrorist, but don't count on it. The FBI refuses to reveal whom it has spied on, even when it has determined that the person is completely innocent. Nor will it reveal how many people it has spied on. Revelations from former FBI agents indicate that as many as fifty thousand people have been spied on, very few of whom had any ties to terrorism. You will never know if you are one of them.

Could My E-mail Get Me Fired?

Monitoring not only invades your privacy, it can cost you your job. Employers frequently fire employees because of what they say in an e-mail or because of the Web sites they visit. According to the Bentley survey, 25 percent of employers have fired employees because of e-mail and 26 percent have fired employees for Internet activity. Dow Chemical, for example, fired fifty people for sending "inappropriate" e-mails. What does "inappropriate" mean to Dow? No one knows; virtually no companies tell employees in advance where the lines are.

It may go without saying that downloading hard-core pornography is inappropriate. But what about sending a risqué joke to a coworker by e-mail? You might consider this acceptable if mild sexual humor is common in your workplace and often engaged in by management. But employers are frequently offended by seeing something in writing that they would have considered innocuous if expressed orally. Repeating a joke by e-mail that no one found offensive in the cafeteria can cost you your job.

Michael Smyth learned about e-mail monitoring the hard way. When his employer, the Pillsbury Company, first set up its e-mail system, Smyth and the other employees were told that the system was confidential; no one would read their messages except for the people to whom they were sent. Employees were instructed in how to set passwords and keep them secret.

Smyth, believing that e-mail was confidential, sent a coworker an angry message about his boss. The boss secretly read the e-mail and fired Smyth after years of good work. When Smyth went to court, his case was dismissed. The court held that Smyth had no right to privacy in his e-mail, even if the company had promised not to monitor it.

Heidi Arace and Norma Yetsko worked at PNC Bank. Jokes, including some that you probably wouldn't tell your children, were common in the office. Employees told them orally and by e-mail, often in the presence of management. But something that Arace and Yetsko sent to coworkers offended their boss and they were fired without warning. "I was frozen," Arace said. "It was like I lost everything in my life."

Even if you don't get fired, electronic surveillance can undermine your health. The University of Wisconsin compared the level of stress experienced by telephone service representatives who knew their supervisor listened in on calls, but never knew when, to that experienced by employees in the same job whose performance was evaluated in other ways. They found that the stress produced by monitoring increased the number of employees with back pain by 21 percent. Heavily monitored employees also had higher rates of anxiety, severe fatigue, and depression. Bell Canada found that the majority of directory assistance operators experienced added stress due to monitoring. Stress is not just unpleasant; it can lead to high blood pressure, heart attacks, and strokes. As monitoring increases, and spreads into our private lives, the effect on our health will grow worse.

Internet Monitoring

Everyone knows that many employers block pornographic Web sites. Making sure that workers aren't frittering away hours surfing the Web to plan their next vacation or check out the latest sports news is easily justified. What is less well known is how sophisticated browser tracking has become. As more people turn to the Internet, so has the capability grown to spy on every click.

When people today look for information, they don't go to the library, they go to the Internet. And when they have a personal problem, they don't write Dear Abby, they search for the answers online. People use the Internet to research subjects they would never discuss on the office telephone, or even discuss in an e-mail. People go to the Internet for information concerning situations they don't want anyone to know about, such as substance dependence, domestic violence, and medical problems. An employer who wanted to build a picture window into employees' personal lives couldn't find a better way than to monitor the Web sites they visit.

That is exactly what most employers do. The majority of employers today (76 percent) monitor the Web sites their employees visit. In most of these companies, managers receive a list of the Web sites visited by each employee. A woman in New Jersey learned she was pregnant. She went to a Web site for expectant mothers while on a break at work. Soon after, her supervisor congratulated her on her pregnancy.

Monitoring and Productivity

Employers often argue that monitoring is necessary to promote productivity. It's no secret that the world of work becomes more competitive every year, or that employers are forced to strive for ever increasing levels of productivity. But it's not at all clear that micromanaging employees by monitoring everything they do improves productivity. "I worked hard every day for the company," said Brad Fair, one of the workers spied on at the Boston Sheraton. "I can't believe they would turn around and treat me like crap." Do you think Brad Fair worked as hard after learning about the spying?

There is also evidence that employees who are closely monitored believe that their employer is more concerned about quantity of work than quality. One study of employees in insurance companies, financial institutions, and government agencies found that employees subjected to monitoring paid less attention to quality. A 1993 Rutgers University study found that people's ability to solve complex problems decreased when they were subjected to video monitoring.

Monitoring can hurt the bottom line in other ways. The employee health problems created by monitoring discussed earlier in this chapter create higher costs for employers through increased cost of employee medical care and higher workers' compensation costs.

Is My Boss Monitoring My Home Computer?

The tentacles of spying now reach out from the workplace to invade your home. If you, like millions of Americans, occasionally work on your home computer, your employer, unannounced, may be pulling up a chair next to you.

Not only is everything you do at work subject to monitoring, but your home computer may be monitored as well. Instead of staying late at work to finish an important report or respond to a final few e-mail messages, we come home in time to have dinner with our families and finish work on our home computer. This benefits both us and our employers. We gain greater flexibility in scheduling our lives to spend more time with our families and friends. Our employers get the benefit of the extra work that we do at home.

What happens to your privacy when you work at home? The most convenient and efficient way to work at home is to log on to the company computer network in order to access your work documents and e-mails. But when you do so, your home computer becomes part of the office network. Any surveillance program your employer has for office computers now monitors your home computer as well, as long as you are logged on. The surveillance software doesn't distinguish between your home computer and any other computer that is part of the network. If you send an e-mail, it passes through the company server, just as if you had sent it from work. Using your AOL or Gmail account won't protect you, since these messages also go through your company server (as long as you're logged on when you send them). Neither will encryption. Your employer can simply order you not to encrypt anything and block all encrypted messages from the outside. If your company monitors the Web sites you visit, the list of Web sites your boss sees will include sites you visited from home.

Even activity on your home computer that doesn't go through the company server may be monitored. If your company uses software that searches hard drive documents for suspicious words, it searches the hard drive of every computer on the company network. If you are logged on to your company computer from home, your home computer is now part of the network and will be searched just like all the others. If you use a sex-related term in a love letter or a message to your doctor, it will be opened and read at work the next day. If your company uses keystroke monitoring, your employer will record everything you write while you're logged on from home.

You may not even have to be logged on at the time the monitoring takes place for your home computer to be monitored. Some 20 million people now telecommute at least part-time, and that number is growing fast. If you're a telecommuter, chances are you don't have a personal computer in addition to your work-issued computer—why would you buy a computer when you already have one? In this case, everything you do is on your office computer and subject to monitoring. Before the company gives you the computer, it simply installs software that records everything you do on the computer.

If you think that your boss isn't interested in learning more about your private life, think again. A survey conducted by the American Bar Association found that most employers are interested in acquiring information from employees' home computers. The cost won't stand in the way; spyware can be purchased over the Internet for as little as fifty bucks. Thousands of employers also read employees' blogs.

Robert Zieminski was a senior executive at TBG Insurance. The company gave him a computer for home use as a perk. While he occasionally did work on it, Zieminski used it primarily for personal purposes, as did his wife and children. The computer contained all of his personal finance records, his tax records, and all of his family's personal correspondence. When the company demanded to see what was stored on the computer, Zieminski went to court. The judge said that because he had signed a form authorizing company personnel to enter the computer "as needed," he had no right to privacy and had to turn it over to his employer.

What happens when your work laptop needs repair, or an update? Your employer's computer technicians now have access to everything in the computer. Harvard professor Ronald Thiemann needed service on his university-issued computer, which he used exclusively in his own house. The service technicians looked at all his personal e-mail and Internet visits. When they found he had visited a sexually oriented site, they reported it. Thiemann was forced to resign his position as dean after thirteen years of outstanding work (fortunately for Thiemann, he had tenure, so he was able to keep his teaching position).

Even easier is for the employer to install monitoring software on the laptop before you get it. You'll never know if this is happening to you; the monitoring software is invisible and your employer has no legal obligation to tell you about it.

Some people argue that you have no one to blame but yourself if your employer reads something you write on a computer owned by the company. But it's not that simple. If your employer allows you to take a company computer home, he virtually never says, "Use this computer only for work." Usually, it's just the opposite. Frequently, employers describe the computer as a company benefit, which means they can spend a little less on other company benefits. Under these circumstances, why would anyone spend the money to buy a second computer? Why should they? Nor do employers level with employees about how their personal information will be treated. Instead they use vague legalese like "the company reserves the right to monitor" and frequently bury it in the fine print.

This argument also misses the real point, which is that it's not who owns the property in question that counts, but whether the employer has any legitimate interest in the information it obtains by monitoring. The fact that your employer owns the company bathroom doesn't mean it should be able to put in a hidden camera. The same rule should apply to computers. If your employer has evidence that you've stolen company trade secrets and put them on your home computer, it should be able to get a court order to search your computer. If your employer has a legitimate concern about something you've done on your company computer, like running an illegal business, it should be able to see the personal information. But an employer should not be able to say, "It's my computer, I can do whatever I want with it."

The Future of Privacy

GPS

As much as surveillance has spread today, the future looks even worse. New technologies are already being deployed that will diminish privacy still further. The Global Positioning System (GPS) is a hot item. Almost half of new cars today are equipped with GPS, and the number is climbing fast. GPS may soon be a standard feature on new cars, just like seat belts.

Employers were quick to see opportunities in GPS. The first to jump on the bandwagon were delivery companies such as UPS. These companies frequently receive calls asking for a package to be picked up immediately. Installing GPS on all trucks allows the company to be more responsive to customer needs.

GPS is also becoming an integral part of our telephone system. In 1999, Congress enacted the Wireless Communications and Public Safety Act, mandating that all new cell phones be equipped with GPS starting in January 2006.

The purpose of this legislation was to improve public safety by helping emergency response teams find injured people faster, particularly motorists. People involved in car accidents frequently don't know exactly where they are or are injured too severely to explain their location. In such situations the GPS system in your cell phone can alert the response team to your exact location. All you have to do is dial 911. Having GPS on your cell phone could save your life.

But GPS also opens the door to a new invasion of privacy. Many employers today issue cell phones to employees to improve communication when they are away from the office. As cell phones become equipped with GPS, employers have the ability not just to call us, but also to know exactly where we are. You can't track your neighbor's phone this way, because you don't have the code to read his signal. But if your employer buys cell phones for employees, it has the information it needs to track you. This may not be so bad during the workday, although it would be nice to take a quick break occasionally without the boss breathing down your neck. But what if your boss says that you must carry your company-issued cell phone on evenings and weekends and that you cannot turn off the GPS system? Your boss would then know where you are every minute of your life.

This may sound like a paranoid fantasy, but it isn't. Complaints about GPS abuse are already beginning to rise. Howard Boyle, president of a fire sprinkler installation company in Woodside, New York, gave all his employees cell phones without telling them the phones were equipped with GPS, and secretly tracked their movements both on the job and at home.

Peter (not his real name) worked for a company in San Francisco. When Peter found out that his boss was tracking him on his cell phone, he thought he could solve the problem by not carrying it away from work or by turning the phone off when he was at home. But his company told him that he had to carry the phone at all times and would be fired if he turned it off. There was nothing special about Peter's job that justified this; his boss was just a dictator who didn't care about the rights of the people who work for him.

Initially, privacy advocates had hoped that the expense of cell phone tracking would limit its use. Once again, however, such hopes proved hollow. Companies such as Loopt and Buddy Beacon provide owners of cell phones with software that allows them to track their phones. The cost is only three dollars a month for each phone whose location is tracked. At this price, GPS could become as popular as computer monitoring. By 2003, a majority of employers (54 percent) were either using GPS or considering its use. In the latest twist, a lingerie company has begun selling bras with tiny hidden GPS transmitters, apparently intended for husbands who suspect their wives are cheating and want to secretly track them.

Biometrics

In the post-9/11 world, employers are very concerned about controlling access to critical facilities. For instance, imagine the consequences if a terrorist were to gain access to the control room of a nuclear power plant. Even less dramatic situations could cause great harm, such as unauthorized access to sensitive areas of a bank or other financial institution.

Traditional methods of controlling access are anything but foolproof. Employees can inadvertently reveal access codes to the wrong person. Magnetic strip cards can be lost or stolen. The information on an access card can even be stolen without taking the card if it is transmitted over a line that is not secure. Employers too can make mistakes. Even if no one makes a mistake, access codes can be stolen from company computers by hackers.

Biometric identifiers offer much greater security. Technology is now available to electronically read fingerprints, palm prints, voices, retinas, irises, and other unique physical features. Unlike pass codes or access cards, biometric identifiers can't be lost.

Employers have been quick to take advantage of this new technology. Access to over twenty thousand computer rooms, bank vaults, research labs, day care centers, blood banks, ATMs, and military installations is now controlled by biometric identification. *MIT Technology Review* calls biometrics one of the "top ten emerging technologies that will change the world." Used properly, biometrics can make workplaces more secure and the world safer.

Used improperly, however, biometrics can undermine privacy and other human rights. Retinal scanning, for example, can reveal whether a person is pregnant or has diabetes, high blood pressure, arteriosclerosis, or AIDS. The blood vessels in the retina are easily visible and reveal much of the same information as other methods of examining blood vessels. Not only is this sensitive medical information none of an employer's business, but knowing that an employee has a potentially expensive medical condition often causes employers to find an excuse for firing them.

Biometrics can also be used to track people. When you enter a location with an electronic handprint or other biometric indicator, the system creates a record. The system "knows" who used it for access and what time they entered. As biometrics spreads, the day may come soon when there will be a record of every commercial and government building you enter. By collecting the data from all these systems, your employer, the government, or someone else could learn a great deal about where you have been.

Identity Theft

Biometrics can also facilitate identify theft. Anyone who has ever experienced identity theft knows what a nightmare it is. It generally takes weeks to get a new driver's license, Social Security card, medical insurance card, new credit cards, and all the other identification we carry around. It can take months to convince everyone to whom "you" owe money that it wasn't really you making those purchases. In the meantime, bill collectors hound you night and day and you worry about losing your house and all your savings.

Currently, however, you can at least replace your identification and cancel the old one so the thief can no longer run up bills at your expense. What happens, though, when a thief steals the digital representation of your fingerprint or iris from a computer? They can transmit this digital representation electronically to anyone who allows remote authorization or even turn it into a replica fingerprint that they can use at your ATM or other locations where biometrics are used to check your identity in person. You can't get new fingerprints. It's almost impossible to stop the damage when the ID that was stolen is one you can't change. The thief would be able to impersonate you only at other locations that use fingerprints (or whatever other biometric the hacked system uses), but that would still be enough to wreck your life. And since the biometric data is stored in your employer's computer, a hacker who gets in can steal everyone's identity.

You might suppose that this could all be prevented by tight computer security. The record of employers avoiding inappropriate disclosure of employee information is anything but encouraging, however. For example, Starbucks lost four laptop computers containing the names and Social Security numbers of sixty thousand employees. They weren't stolen from traveling executives, either—the computers were in the Starbucks corporate offices. No one broke into a locked room or overpowered a security guard. They were just left sitting where anyone could take them, and someone did. Time Warner lost forty computer tapes containing the personal information of about 600,000 employees and customers. These are only two of the fifteen major incidents identified by the Congressional Research Service in which employers lost personal data about employees. Collectively, these lapses affected over 1.5 million employees. Even if the employer does everything right, you're not completely safe. Some hackers are highly skilled computer professionals and have "broken into" a number of highly secure systems.

Biometrics isn't perfect. When biometric systems make mistakes, innocent people suffer. While these systems can be accurate and reliable, they are not perfect. Sometimes the system will not recognize you when you try to enter. Ordinarily, this is only an inconvenience. But what if you are a service engineer rushing to fix a problem at a nuclear power plant? This can happen with traditional systems too, but that doesn't make the consequences any less serious when a biometric system malfunctions. Even worse, a biometric system occasionally thinks you are someone else.

Brandon Mayfield, a lawyer from Oregon, found out what can happen when biometric mistakes are made. His fingerprints were erroneously identified as those of the terrorist who planted bombs in the Madrid subway. (Ironically, the government had Mayfield's fingerprints to compare with those left by the bomber because he was a veteran who had served in the U.S military.) Mayfield had converted to Islam, but had never been linked to terrorism in any way. He wasn't even active in Muslim politics. His only connection was that he had represented in a child custody case a man who had been convicted of terrorism.

Mayfield could prove that he was in the United States when the bombing in Madrid took place. But none of this mattered. Mayfield was publicly arrested and taken away in handcuffs, strip-searched, and thrown into prison. He was held in prison for two weeks before the FBI recognized its mistake and allowed his release, even though the Spanish police were doubtful of the match from the beginning. Without the efforts of the Spanish police, who knows how long Mayfield might have been held? Even when he was released, the damage continued. His arrest had made headlines in newspapers and on television from coast to coast. The news of his exoneration was not nearly as prominent, and many people missed it. Some who heard it probably still wonder. The stigma of terrorism will cling to Mayfield for the rest of his life.

Ironically, it is the accuracy, or the perception of accuracy, that makes biometric mistakes so dangerous. Most people believe that because fingerprints and other forms of biometric identification are scientific, they are foolproof. When the system says your fingerprints are those of a terrorist, people will believe it and treat you like one.

Stealing Your DNA

Your DNA contains more information about you than anything else in the world. Virtually everything about you is to some degree determined or affected by your genes. Sequencing a person's DNA is quite possibly the worst invasion of privacy possible.

Every time you use a hairbrush, a tissue, or a toothbrush, you leave behind a few of your cells. Analyzing this abandoned DNA has become a growth industry, with labs springing up all over the country. Bert Croom, from North Carolina, is only one of many private investigators who provide testing of underwear, bedsheets, and other items to determine whom someone is sleeping with.

And there is no real legal protection against this abuse. Ironically, the workplace may be the one place where you are protected from DNA theft. Under the recently enacted federal law against genetic discrimination, employers are prohibited from acquiring genetic information about employees. Picking up the strands of hair you left in the washroom sink and sending them to a lab would be a violation of the Genetic Information Nondiscrimination Act (GINA), if judges apply it correctly.

Implants

In the ultimate nightmare, some employers are beginning to install silicon chips into employees' bodies as an identification system. These chips, called RFID (radio-frequency identification) transmitters, give off a unique identifying signal. Originally, they were used on pets. But now employers are starting to use them on people. CityWatcher.com, a private video surveillance company, installed chips in the arms of employees with access to a room where it held video footage. The employees probably didn't like having chips implanted in their body, but had to "consent" to keep their jobs. Whether this practice will pass muster with the courts is an open question.

What You Don't Know Can Hurt You

Employees are kept in the dark about surveillance. Most people today know that workplace monitoring occurs. But very few know what actually happens in their own workplace. According to the American Management Association, 12 percent of the companies that monitor do not notify employees. A few, as Pillsbury did, tell employers their communication is confidential, and then monitor anyway.

Most employers claim to notify employees about monitoring. And, in a way, they do. We've all seen the notices when we turn on our office computers. They all say something like, "This computer is company property. The company reserves the right to monitor this computer for any purpose."

What does this notice tell you? It doesn't say whether the company monitors your e-mail, Web access, instant messages, or entire hard drive. It doesn't say whether all messages are monitored or just those messages that suggest that something is wrong. It doesn't even say whether or not the company is actually monitoring. All it says is that the company "reserves the right to monitor." This is called a reservation of rights clause. It was drafted by a company lawyer to give the company the right to do anything it wants to without telling anyone in advance. If the company was trying to keep you in the dark, it couldn't have chosen better language to do so.

Sometimes monitoring is so secret that even company executives are unaware of it. Alana Shoars was the e-mail manager of Epson America. Her job was to make sure the system was working properly and train employees in how to use it. She was told by her superiors that the system was confidential and that the company would not monitor e-mail. When she trained Epson's employees in how to use the e-mail system, she told them that their messages would be confidential and taught them how to create a strong password. According to Shoars, one day she walked into a room and found a team of people secretly monitoring employee e-mail. Shocked, she went to her boss. He told her to forget she'd ever seen the room. When she persisted in arguing that the company should either stop monitoring or tell the employees about it—after all, the employees had been assured their e-mails were confidential— she was fired. "I was stunned," she said. "I had no idea what was going on."

Better Answers

The saddest thing about the loss of privacy at work is that it is unnecessary. Most employers monitor for legitimate business reasons. Let's take the example of e-mail being used as a tool of sexual harassment. Many employers who monitor e-mail do so to identify harassment so that it can be stopped.

Such monitoring may be well intentioned, but it misses the heart of the problem. An employee who is receiving sexually oriented e-mail can always file a complaint with the company. If an employee receives such material and does not file a complaint, she cannot later file a sexual harassment claim in court against her employer.

Employers who monitor argue that some employees receive material they find offensive but do not file a complaint because they are afraid of retaliation. This is undoubtedly true. In such cases, however, the real problem is that the company is run in a way that permits retaliation against those who complain of wrongdoing. Such companies need to change their culture, not allow the infection to continue and attempt to deal with the symptoms by monitoring. Once the company has established a culture where people feel free to raise complaints, it doesn't need to monitor e-mail to identify harassment about which no one has complained.

This does not mean that e-mail and Internet access should never be monitored. When there is a complaint or some other tangible indication that an employee is misusing his company computer, monitoring should be conducted as part of the investigation. Many successful companies operate in this manner. Hewlett-Packard, one of the world's premier computer companies, monitors on what it calls an "event basis." When an event indicating misconduct occurs and the company has reason to believe that an employee's computer contains relevant information, the computer is searched. But the company does not monitor e-mail and Internet access by default.

Nor is it necessary to secretly eavesdrop on the telephone conversations of directory assistance operators and telemarketing employees. If a phone company wants to know how well the operators are treating the public, it can survey the customers. It can also conduct open performance monitoring by having the monitor sit down next to the operator, get on the same line to hear the conversation, and then critique the operator's performance. Or it can do both. There is no need for employees who use the phone at work every day to never know when the boss is listening in.

Employers, as well as employees, would be better off under such a system. Most of the e-mail messages that contain a sexually oriented word have nothing to do with sexual harassment. They are messages between an employee and her spouse or between two employees who have a romantic relationship. Sometimes it has nothing to do with sex at all; it's just the informal use of profanity that is common in modern life. Employers who identify and read every e-mail that contains one of George Carlin's seven dirty words waste a great deal of valuable time. When the e-mail is between employees, the employer must interview both parties to determine whether there is a case of sexual harassment or just a romantic relationship. This requires even more time, and probably offends the employees, who resent the company's probing into their sex life. It is far more efficient, as well as more protective of privacy, to let employees decide for themselves when they are being harassed.

Even if companies believe they need to monitor, they could do so in a far less intrusive manner. For example, most truly sensitive e-mails are sent to only a handful of people, such as the employee's spouse, a few other family members, and (perhaps) their doctor. Companies could allow employees to identify a small number of e-mail addresses (perhaps with verification of identity) that would be exempt from monitoring. At present, however, I don't know of a single employer that gives employees this option.

Employers could also prevent Internet abuse in a less intrusive fashion. Instead of monitoring the Web sites employees visit, employers can prevent abuse by using Web access software. Such software blocks access to sites that are completely off-limits, such as those presenting pornography or hate speech. It also regulates access to sites that are permissible but not work-related, such as sites with information on sports, travel, shopping, and the stock market. For example, if a company wants to allow access to these sites during lunchtime, but not during working hours, it can program the software to automatically enforce this rule. When lunchtime is over, anyone who is on a non-work-related site would be cut off. A company could allow a limited amount of time for personal surfing (perhaps fifteen minutes a day) and have the software cut off access after that limit. Commercially available Web access software can be custom tailored to any employer's Web access policy. Web access software eliminates the need to monitor the Web sites employees visit since it is impossible to visit a site in a manner that violates company policy. Canon, Carnival Cruise Lines, the Robert Mondavi Winery, and many other leading companies prevent Internet abuse this way. The majority of employers, however, still look at every Web site employees visit.

The simplest step employers could take to protect employee privacy is to tell employees involved in the monitoring process not to spy on other employees for fun. IT employees have the ability to see anything on the company computer system they want. It's like being locked in a room with everyone else's diary, and no one will ever know if you look. It's no surprise that such employees often yield to temptation. One IT employee wrote to Dear Abby about how he and his fellow techies entertained themselves by reading personal information about coworkers, including romantic messages and online banking records. "On more than one occasion I knew that someone had bounced a check before he did," this person wrote. He didn't think he was doing anything wrong. His message to Abby was that people should be more careful about what they say online. The idea that he should respect his fellow employees' privacy obviously never crossed his mind.

Why should he think so if his employer never told him not to snoop? One quarter (26 percent) of employers have no policy instructing IT employees not to monitor for personal gratification. Even among those that do, very few take any steps to enforce it, such as reviewing the activity of monitors to verify that their activity has been consistent with company policy. Is it any wonder that IT employees treat our computers as a source of amusement?

But rather than creating policies that meet the company's needs without unduly intruding on employee privacy, most employers are trying to eliminate the very concept of workplace privacy. They post notices on company computer screens stating that not only does the company conduct monitoring, but employees should have no expectation of privacy on company-owned computers. The same notice frequently appears in company policy guides. Leading management consultants encourage employers to take this approach. Nancy Flynn, president of the ePolicy Institute, counsels employers to tell employees that "they should not expect any right to privacy" in their e-mail or anything else involving company computers, even those located in their home. While telling employees they have no privacy is better than secret monitoring, it's not the right answer. The right answer is for employers to develop systems to get the information they need without intruding on employee privacy more than is necessary. We don't have to choose between privacy and productivity.

Legal Protection

Clearly, expecting employers to protect our privacy is not the answer. Employers aren't even trying to protect privacy. Just as with racial discrimination and sexual harassment, we need laws to protect our privacy. Unfortunately, despite the fact that workplace surveillance is widespread and unnecessarily invasive, almost no legal protection for workplace privacy exists. The Constitution applies only to the federal government, not to private corporations. The same is generally true of state constitutions.

Lawmakers could have responded to the lack of constitutional protection by enacting statutes to protect our privacy. When our country decided that racial discrimination by private employers was unacceptable, we enacted new federal and state laws to end it. We could do the same with privacy.

But we haven't. The only significant federal law dealing with workplace privacy is the Electronic Communications Privacy Act (ECPA), a 1986 amendment to federal wiretapping laws. ECPA provides that employers cannot "intercept" electronic communications unless they do so "in the ordinary course of business." Courts have interpreted this to mean that employers can intercept business-related communications, but not personal communications.

This rule works reasonably well for telephone calls, at least in theory. Employers are allowed to listen to work-related calls but are not permitted to eavesdrop on personal calls. An employer is allowed to take disciplinary action over unauthorized personal calls, but may not listen to the call longer than is necessary to determine that it is personal. For example, in the case of *Deal v. Spears*, the employer told the employee not to make personal calls on the office phone. He then secretly monitored her phone. When he heard her talking to her boyfriend, he fired her. The court held that the employer had every right to fire her for not following orders, but violated ECPA by continuing to listen to an employee's telephone calls to her boyfriend after realizing that they were personal. Courts give employers a great deal of latitude on this rule. Employers don't have to hang up the second they realize the call is personal. But if they never hang up they've crossed the line. ECPA also provides decent protection against secretly recording personal conversations at work. Northern Telecom was forced to remove hidden microphones in the company cafeteria when confronted by a lawsuit from the Communications Workers of America, who represented the employees.

Unfortunately, ECPA usually means little in practice. There is no way for an employee to know when her employer is listening to her telephone calls, and ECPA doesn't require employers to tell employees when they are on the line or what calls they listen to. The only employers who are punished for violating ECPA are those who are stupid enough to reveal what they have heard by eavesdropping on the employee or who put the monitoring equipment where employees can see it. The vast majority of violations go unknown, unreported, and unpunished.

Worse, ECPA provides virtually no protection against other forms of surveillance. In monitoring e-mail, Internet access, and other forms of computer-based communication, the employer does not "intercept" the message on its way to the recipient. Instead, the employer retrieves the message after the fact from the server or other part of the computer system. Since there is no interception, there is no violation of ECPA. From a privacy perspective, this distinction is meaningless, and eliminates any privacy protection for e-mail. But the courts consistently make it anyway.

This means that we have no legal protection when it comes to employer surveillance of e-mail, instant messages, Internet access, and hard drives. Even if you could prove that your boss read your personal e-mail for his own amusement, you would not have a case.

It is difficult to blame Congress for this oversight. Few people in 1986 foresaw the revolution in technology that occurred soon after. The laptop computer was a new, relatively unknown device in 1986. E-mail was also new, and the Web had yet to be invented. Congress can't be expected to resolve problems that don't yet exist.

But the loss of privacy due to unregulated employee monitoring has been obvious for many years. As early as 1991, groups such as the American Civil Liberties Union and the Communications Workers of America called on Congress to update federal privacy law to cover new forms of electronic communication. Congress has not acted, however, and shows little interest in the problem.

State legislatures could have filled this void, but they have not. Only California and Rhode Island have passed laws against hidden videos in workplace locker rooms and bathrooms. Connecticut and Delaware enacted laws requiring employers to give notice of monitoring. The other forty-six states have done nothing. Not a single state has passed laws protecting the privacy of e-mail, instant messaging, or Internet access.

The law on privacy of your home computer is just developing, but may be better. It's not going to protect you from monitoring if you log on to your workplace network. But if your employer sends an e-mail with spyware attached to a computer you paid for yourself, you may be protected. The simpleminded legal doctrine that lets the owner make the rules virtually eliminates privacy from company-owned computers, but works to protect your privacy if the computer belongs to you.

There may also be a ray of hope in the growth of handheld communication devices, such as BlackBerrys. E-mail sent from such a device does not pass through the employer's server. One federal court has held that the fact that an employer owns the device doesn't give it the right to monitor messages that are transmitted by an independent system. If other courts rule the same way, we will at least have some privacy when we are away from the office.

In our lifetime, privacy on the job has virtually disappeared. Technology allows employers to monitor every e-mail we send, every telephone call we make, and every Web site we visit. Newer technology, like GPS and biometrics, threatens to make our private lives an open book to our employers. Our judges and legislators could have protected us from these abuses, but they have not. Unless we act, and demand that our lawmakers protect our privacy, our grandchildren may know privacy only by reading about it in history books.

3

Whose Life Is It Anyway?: Employer Control of Personal Lives

> The right to swing my fist ends
> where the other man's nose begins.
>
> —OLIVER WENDELL HOLMES, JR.

Henry Ford had his own private police force. If you worked at Ford, the company police could show up at your door at any time and search your home from top to bottom. If they found anything Henry Ford didn't approve of, you were fired. If you were drinking, you were fired. If you were playing cards for money, you were fired. If there was someone in your bedroom you weren't married to, you were fired.

John B. Stetson, founder of the Stetson hat company, had rules for apprentices that prohibited them from getting married, playing "cards, dice, or any other unlawful game," or going to "ale houses, taverns, or playhouses." Many employers even tried to control employees' religion, refusing to hire Jews or Catholics.

Most employers today would agree that this was wrong. In theory, they would agree that the fact that you write someone's paycheck doesn't give you the right to control his or her private life.

But some employers still act like Henry Ford and John B. Stetson.

Daniel Wynn was fired for having a few beers with some friends on a Friday night. He wasn't an alcoholic. He didn't come to work under the influence, or even suffering from a hangover. The owner of Best Lock, in Indiana, was a teetotaler who believed that drinking was a sin. Somehow he found out about Wynn's having some beer. Wynn's eight years of service with the company meant nothing. The last time I saw Wynn, he was standing outside the factory gate, unemployed, wondering what would happen to him.

Wynn is only one of thousands of people who have lost their jobs, or been denied employment, because of what they do in their private life. You could be next.

The driving force behind this trend is the rising cost of health care. Most employers pay for a significant portion of employees' medical costs. If the cost of health care for a company's employees goes up, it comes out of the employer's pocket, either directly (if the company pays employee medical bills itself) or through higher insurance premiums. These costs have risen sharply in recent years and employers are looking for ways to save money. Efforts to reduce medical costs through HMOs and other forms of managed care have not been successful. So some employers have begun to think, "If we can't reduce the cost of providing health care, let's hire people who won't need as much medical attention."

Smoking

The first target was smokers. Employers not only prohibited smoking in the workplace (to protect nonsmoking employees from secondhand smoke), but some even prohibited employees from smoking in their own homes. According to a survey by the Administrative Management Society, 6 percent of all employers have an official policy of refusing to hire smokers.

Weyco Corporation in Okemos, Michigan, is a typical example. In 2005, company president Howard Weyers ordered all employees to stop using tobacco at any time, including in their own homes. Anita Epolito, who had worked for Weyco for fourteen years, and three other employees who didn't quit, were fired. When she protested that she never smoked on duty and that her smoking at home didn't affect her job, Weyers told her, "You don't like it? Go somewhere else." Epolito says, "How can my boss tell me what to do in my own home? You feel like you have no rights. You're all alone."

Employers defend this policy by stating that smoking employees have higher medical bills than nonsmoking employees, affecting the company's bottom line. This is true. Although solid numbers are not yet available, it is clear that smoking creates health risks and that those risks have financial consequences.

The problem with this argument is that it opens the door to many other forms of employer control of our private lives. Virtually everything you do affects your health. Alcohol isn't all that good for you. Neither is junk food. (Anyone who doubts this should see the film *Supersize Me*.) Eating steak is less healthful than eating broccoli. Too much coffee is bad for you. And if your diet is perfect, how about your hobbies? Skiing, scuba diving, and riding a motorcycle create risks of injury. Riding your bicycle to work is more dangerous than driving a car. Even your sex life affects your medical risks. People with multiple sexual partners have a greater risk of contracting HIV and other STDs than those who are monogamous. If we permit employers to control off-duty behavior when it affects our health, you can kiss your private life good-bye. Everything you do will be subject to your employer's control.

Some employers have already gone to such extremes. Multi-Developers Inc., a real estate firm, refused to hire anyone engaged in high-risk recreational activities. The city of Athens, Georgia, once required cholesterol tests for all job applicants and refused to hire anyone whose score was considered too high.

Kelly Brownell, head of the Rudd Center for Food Policy and Obesity at Yale University, recommends that the government penalize people for unhealthful eating by taxing junk food. He proposes a "fat tax" on unhealthful food so that people will eat less of it. Brownell says we should "regulate food just like we do cigarettes and alcohol." Legislation putting this idea into action has been introduced in California.

You may be wondering how your boss could possibly know what you're doing while off-duty. Janice Bone worked as a bookkeeper for Ford Meter Box in Wabash, Indiana. Ford Meter Box had a policy banning smoking, both on-duty and off. Janice thought she could smoke in the privacy of her own home and no one would know. Janice didn't know that the company had added a nicotine test to its drug testing program. When she tested positive, she was fired. She ended up working for minimum wage in a video rental store. Other companies encourage their employees to turn each other in for off-duty infractions. Your fellow workers don't get a reward for turning you in, but they do earn some brownie points with the boss. Marge Archibold and Michele Kobus lost their jobs at an Omaha hospital when coworkers saw them smoking off-duty, away from hospital property, and told management.

Obesity

The most common form of this type of discrimination is against people who are overweight. According to the most recent government figures, 30 percent of Americans are obese. A few of these people are protected under federal and state disability laws. Most of us, however, are not fat enough to be considered legally disabled. We're just overweight, which means we have no legal protection against job discrimination.

That's too bad, because we need it. While discrimination against people because of their weight is seldom an official corporate policy, it happens every day. Much of the hiring decision is based on subjective factors, including whether you make a positive impression in your interview. And nobody likes fat people. A study conducted by the Mayo Clinic found that prejudice against fat people was more common than prejudice against homosexuals. The majority of fat children report being taunted by their peers. People who would tear their tongues out before putting someone down for their race or religion, or even their sexual orientation, think nothing of making a negative remark about someone's weight. This is the last socially acceptable form of prejudice in America. According to Sally Smith, executive director of the National Association to Advance Fat Acceptance, "job discrimination is a fact of life for our members." A 2009 study by Yale University found that 43 percent of fat people said that their employer stigmatized them. A 2009 survey of two thousand employers found that 93 percent of them would choose an applicant of "normal weight" over an equally qualified applicant who was obese.

Prejudice against fat people is so strong that the stereotypes often trump the facts right in front of employers. Michael Frank was a schoolteacher on

Long Island. He worked for the same school for four years, getting stellar performance reviews. But the school superintendent still fired him because his obesity "was not conducive to learning."

Some people have proposed denying employers the option to hire and fire based on health-related off-duty behavior while allowing them to charge the employee more to participate in the company's medical program. This surcharge would be intended to offset the extra medical costs the employee was likely to incur.

This approach is not inherently unfair. There is nothing wrong with requiring people to accept responsibility for their actions. If smoking or eating junk food creates higher medical bills, there is no reason that employers should be forced to pay them.

But there are problems with this approach. To begin with, not everyone who is fat overeats. Some people are fat no matter how little they eat or how much they exercise. They no more have the ability to be thin than does Shaquille O'Neal. This is also true of many other factors that affect your health, such as cholesterol. Some people live on salad yet have high cholesterol levels. Others live on cheeseburgers but have low cholesterol. Penalizing people for something that isn't under their control is unfair.

There are also serious privacy implications to this policy. Your employer can impose the surcharge only if it knows about the behavior. This isn't a problem with smoking; everyone already knows because they've seen you with a cigarette in your hand. But to impose surcharges based on how much you drink, how much junk food you eat, how much sleep you get, and how often you go to the gym requires that you tell your employer all about your private life. Do you really want to tell your boss how many sexual partners you have and whether you practice safe sex? Turning our private lives into an open book is a high price to pay for employers to save money on health care.

Universal Health Care

Some people have suggested that the answer to this problem is universal health care. According to Frederick Lane, the nationally recognized privacy expert and author of *The Naked Employee*, "Taking employers out of the business of providing health care would eliminate the financial incentive for discrimination based on unhealthy private behavior." Lane makes a good point. If employers aren't paying employees' medical bills, they have no reason to be concerned about who smokes or eats junk food. A few employers might still discriminate against scuba divers and skiers, because of the risk that you might get hurt and not be able to work. Professional athletes frequently have such clauses in their contracts. The team's owner doesn't want to pay an athlete a million dollars (or more) a year just to sit on the bench because they sprained their ankle skiing. But the chances of getting hurt skiing or scuba diving are actually quite low (lower, in fact, than driving a car). With universal health care, the vast majority of employer attempts to control employees' private lives would disappear.

Designing the best health care system is as difficult and complicated a problem as there is. I'm glad I don't have to solve it. (Look what happened to Hillary Clinton's plan.) But some of the objections to universal health care are just plain wrong, if not dishonest. Opponents call it "socialized medicine." Socialism is a dirty word in America, so this is a very damaging accusation. But it just isn't true. Socialism is about having the government own the means of production. But advocates of universal health care aren't suggesting that doctors work for the government. The heart of most universal health care proposals is that doctors would send their bills to the government instead of to an insurance company. The other common charge is that universal health care would take away people's right to choose their own doctor. That's not true either.

Virtually all universal health care proposals would allow all physicians to participate as long as they agreed to the established fee schedule. Everyone would still go to the doctor of their choice, but that doctor might not make as much money as they do today. Perhaps that's why campaigns against universal health care are financed by insurers and doctors. There are a few doctors today who refuse to accept private insurance, but most of the time you can see the doctor you want. If a universal health care system pays doctors the same amount and saves money by reducing the enormous overhead of private insurers, this number wouldn't be affected at all. And as long as the rate of compensation under the universal plan is comparable to what private insurers now pay, the change wouldn't be significant.

Morality

Unfortunately, some employers discriminate for reasons having nothing to do with health. Instead, they attempt to force their own values on their employees.

A Florida teacher was fired when her boss saw a photograph of her lifting up her shirt at an adults-only party. She didn't post the picture on her Web site. She didn't even take the picture. Someone else at the party snapped a picture of her on a digital camera and e-mailed it to the principal. Similarly, Peter Oiler was a truck driver for Winn-Dixie stores. He worked hard for twenty years, showing up on time, getting his work done, and getting along with his boss and the other employees. But Oiler was also a cross-dresser who liked to wear women's clothing. Someone apparently saw him in public and told Oiler's boss. Winn-Dixie fired Oiler. Carol Shaya, a police officer from New York City, was fired for posing nude in *Playboy*.

Isaac Aguero, a forklift driver for CJW Inc. (a Miller beer distributor), was fired for drinking a Bud Light on his day off. The same thing happened to Ross Hopkins, who worked for a Colorado Budweiser distributor and was fired for drinking a Coors in a bar after work.

As discussed previously, Lynne Gobbell lost her job because she had a "Kerry for President" bumper sticker on her car, and Glen Hillier was fired for attempting to ask President Bush a question about the war in Iraq at a political rally.

One employer even fired a woman because she was considering having an abortion. Kimberly Turic worked at a Holiday Inn in Holland, Michigan. When she became pregnant, she talked to other employees about her situation, including that she might have an abortion. When her boss learned that Turic was considering to have an abortion, he fired her. Ironically, Turic later decided to have the baby. But she didn't get her job back.

If You're Gay, Stay Away

One of the obstacles to coming out is the fear that you're going to lose your job.

—BARNEY FRANK

The most common form of discrimination based on an employer's personal values is directed at homosexuals.

Jacinda Meyer was a health insurance agent for a California company that administers employee benefits for its clients. She is a single mom with an eight-year-old daughter. After nine months on the job, she received a glowing performance review and a raise. Her supervisors even gave her handwritten cards thanking her for her good service, teamwork, and positive attitude.

Everything changed when her employer learned that she was a lesbian. The owner of the company approached her and told her to read *The Road Less Traveled*, a book that compares homosexuality to drug addiction and tells gay people how to "cure" their "addiction." When Meyer told the owner that she felt uncomfortable as a result of being given the book, she was fired.

Meyer's experience is familiar to many other gay men and lesbians. A study published in the *American Journal of Public Health* found that 33 percent of gay men and lesbians had experienced employment discrimination. Other studies have found even higher proportions. Some employers even admit they discriminate. A study by the American Psychological Association found that 27 percent of employers would refuse to hire someone if they knew that person was gay, and 18 percent would fire a current employee if they learned he or she was gay. This indicates that such discrimination would be even more widespread if many gay men and lesbians didn't hide their sexual orientation.

Legal Protection

Most people think it's wrong to discriminate based on sexual orientation. In a 2007 Gallup poll, for example, 89 percent of American adults believe that "homosexuals should have equal rights in terms of job opportunities." This represents a dramatic change in public attitudes since Gallup first asked the question in 1977, when only 56 percent supported equal employment opportunity for gay men and lesbians.

Lawmakers have responded to the change in public opinion by enacting new laws. Twenty states now have laws prohibiting employment discrimination based on sexual orientation. In the remaining thirty states, however, your boss can still fire you for being gay.

In an effort to protect gay men and lesbians in these states, a bipartisan coalition of senators and representatives introduced the Employment Non-Discrimination Act (ENDA). In 1996, ENDA came within one vote of passing in the Senate (50–49). But, thirteen years later, it still hasn't passed.

The Dangers of MySpace

The spread of social networking sites increases the odds that you will lose a job because of your private life. Over 90 million Americans now belong to social networking sites such as Facebook and MySpace. Most of these sites make individual profiles visible to anyone. And even the sites that are by invitation only aren't very secure.

Most people don't think twice about what they put on these sites. But they should. Research conducted by About.com's Human Resource Guide found that almost 50 percent of employers check out job applicants on Google and other search engines. And they don't hesitate to drop qualified candidates because of what they find. A survey by Reuters found that a third of companies reported dropping candidates because of information they'd found on social networking sites. The city of Bozeman, Montana, now requires all job applicants to list all the social networking sites they belong to and how to access those that are private.

You don't have to be doing anything related to your job qualifications on your MySpace page to lose a job. You don't even have to be doing anything wrong. Stacy Snyder, from Millersville, Pennsylvania, lost her job as a student teacher after other school staff found a picture of her on her MySpace profile wearing a pirate hat and holding a glass of what appeared to be beer. Snyder was twenty-five years old, well over the required age to drink in Pennsylvania. There was no indication that any minors were around, or even that she was drunk. Still, university officials (most of whom probably have a drink or two on occasion themselves) found her conduct "unprofessional" and fired her.

You might think this represents just a single employer acting irrationally. But it doesn't. I asked the HR professionals in a master's degree course I teach at Rutgers how they would react in a similar situation. Specifically, I asked them what they would do if they were filling an open position, had decided that a particular candidate was best qualified, and sent them an offer letter, and then discovered a picture of them on MySpace dancing on a table with a lampshade on their head.

The majority of these HR professionals said they would rescind the offer of employment. The rest of the group said they would consider rescinding the offer. Not a single HR professional said they weren't concerned.

When I asked them why they felt this way, the situation got even stranger. Every member of the group agreed that the hypothetical employee wasn't doing anything wrong, or even anything all that different from things they themselves had done. But they felt it was "unprofessional" to post the picture on their MySpace page. "But what if they didn't post the picture?" I asked them. "What if someone else took the picture and posted it without the applicant's even knowing about it? On Facebook, you can 'tag' an image with someone else's name and it will be posted on their profile. And what if the applicant asked the person who had posted it to take it down and they refused?" I asked. None of these circumstances had any impact. Even if the applicant wasn't doing anything wrong and hadn't posted the picture themselves, every HR manager in the group held it against them.

The pictures don't even have to be of you to get you in trouble. Daniel Lake, a police officer in North Port, Florida, was suspended for "conduct unbecoming an officer" because his wife posted naked pictures of herself on the Internet. Even when the police commissioner found out that Lake hadn't posted the pictures, and hadn't known that his wife had posted them, it made no difference.

Legal Protection

The vast majority of Americans oppose employer attempts to control off-duty behavior, even when it involves smoking. A poll by the National Consumers League found that 78 percent of respondents opposed job discrimination against smokers.

Lawmakers in many states have responded to these abuses by enacting legislation protecting private lives from employer control. Twenty-nine states and the District of Columbia now have laws in this area. Unfortunately, most of them offer very little protection. New Jersey and nineteen other states protect only the off-duty use of tobacco. All other forms of discrimination based on private lives remain legal. Smokers got protection because tobacco companies are politically influential; they make campaign contributions and have lobbyists. But there is no lobby for the rest of us except the National Workrights Institute.

You wouldn't think anyone would oppose a law telling employers to keep their hands off employees' private lives. But they do. Antismoking organizations fought these laws tooth and nail. These groups, such as the Tobacco Control Legal Consortium and the Tobacco Public Policy Center, oppose laws that restrict employer control of off-duty behavior. They don't oppose just laws to prevent discrimination against off-duty smokers; they oppose laws that protect all legal off-duty conduct, because they include off-duty smoking.

The goal of such organizations is to bring back prohibition, only this time for tobacco. They don't just want to protect those of us who don't smoke from secondhand smoke; they want to force smokers to quit by any means necessary. If taking someone's job away gets them to quit smoking, perhaps that's a good thing. When confronted with the argument that what a person does in her own home is her own business, most of these advocates try to change the subject. But a few are entirely open about their goals. Rob Crane, president of the Preventing Tobacco Addiction Foundation, sees no problem with employers', or the government's, telling people what to do in their own homes. "Tobacco is a dangerous drug," says Crane. "It ought to be banned, just like other addictive drugs." Not only do they want to bring back prohibition, anti-tobacco advocates condemn groups such as the ACLU and NWI for supporting life-style discrimination laws.

Illinois and five other states do a little better. They protect against discrimination based on the use of "lawful products." This protects you from being fired for drinking alcohol on your own time, in addition to smoking. Some have suggested that it protects your recreational choices, since skis and scuba tanks are lawful products. But this argument has never been tested in court.

What the law ought to say is that employers cannot penalize you for your off-duty conduct unless it falls into one of three exceptions:

Conflict of Interest

Employers have a legitimate interest in preventing employees who know trade secrets from working for a competitor. Conflict of interest policies to prevent this should be allowed. Some state laws recognize this exception, such as Colorado's law protecting employees' off-duty conduct.

Values-Based Organizations

Another exception should exist where the employer is a values-based organization, such as a church. A church shouldn't have to hire an atheist as a minister, even if he is the best preacher. Similarly, police (whose business is law enforcement) should be allowed to refuse to hire people with criminal records. This doesn't mean that values-based organizations can discriminate on any basis they want. A church should be able to refuse to hire you because you're an atheist but not because you ride a motorcycle. Police departments should be able to turn you down for having a criminal record, but not for taking off your clothes on the Internet.

North Carolina allows employment decisions based on conduct that "relates to the fundamental objectives of the organization."

Job Qualifications

Finally, your off-duty conduct may affect your qualifications for the job. An employer ought to be able to fire a truck driver who has been convicted of drunk driving while off-duty. New York and several other states contain explicit language covering situations where the conduct relates to "a bona fide occupational qualification."

California, Colorado, North Dakota, and New York have enacted laws that provide comprehensive protection for employees' private lives. If you live in one of these four states, you are relatively safe. Otherwise your private life remains your boss's business.

4

Wrongful Discharge and Employment at Will

No person shall be deprived of life, liberty,
or property without due process of law.

—UNITED STATES CONSTITUTION

Your boss can fire you because he doesn't like the color
of your tie, and there's nothing you can do about it.

—HOWARD LESNICK, UNIVERSITY OF PENNSYLVANIA LAW SCHOOL

Roger Boisjoly worked for Morton Thiokol, the contractor that built the space shuttle *Challenger* for NASA. When Boisjoly learned that NASA was planning to launch on a day when the temperature was below freezing, he immediately called NASA and pleaded for a postponement. The O-rings, rubber seals between the rocket sections that allowed the metal body to expand as it became hot, were not designed for subfreezing temperatures. Boisjoly told NASA that the *Challenger* would explode if they tried to launch the next day. Morton Thiokol's management, however, ignored Boisjoly's concerns, and told NASA they could launch safely. America watched in horror as the shuttle exploded on national television, killing all seven astronauts.

The congressional committee investigating the disaster called on Boisjoly to testify. He told the truth about what happened. Morton Thiokol responded by forcing Boisjoly out of the company. Morton Thiokol was never penalized.

How could Morton Thiokol get away with firing someone for telling the truth and helping to avert future disasters? Because your employer doesn't need a legitimate reason to fire you. Under the doctrine of employment at will, an employer has the legal right to fire an employee for a good reason, a bad reason, or no reason at all.

Under the Constitution, the government cannot punish you without giving you a fair trial. But the Constitution doesn't apply to corporations. Your boss can take away your job, including your health care and your pension, without giving you any opportunity to defend yourself, or even telling you what you supposedly did wrong. Even if you can prove that you were fired for a reason that was completely unfair, you have no legal rights.

Philloria Green was brutally beaten and raped by her estranged husband. Her employer didn't want to deal with a traumatized employee, so he fired her. When she went to court, the judge dismissed her claim under the doctrine of employment at will.

David Shick was injured on the job and went out on workers' compensation. When he returned to work, his boss told him that he was fired for filing a workers' compensation claim. His suit, too, was dismissed.

At least two million employees are fired every year in the United States. Professor Jack Stieber, of Michigan State University, estimates that 150,000 of these people are fired without a legitimate reason.

There are a few exceptions to this rule. Your boss cannot fire you because of your race, gender, religion, or because you have a disability (assuming you can do the job). In a few states, you cannot be fired because of your sexual orientation. This doesn't mean that your boss needs a legitimate reason to fire you if you are black, or a woman. It merely means that you can't be fired because of your race, religion, or gender. Proving that you were fired for an illegal reason can be difficult. I have yet to see an employer sued for discrimination admit to it. But if the company can't back its claim about your job performance and you have evidence of bias on the part of management, a jury may see the truth and give you justice.

The reason you can't be fired on these grounds is because Congress has enacted laws making such firings illegal, starting with the Civil Rights Act of 1964. Before Congress took this action, your employer could admit he fired you because you were black and your case would be dismissed. Most states have done the same. But there is no law saying that your boss can't fire you for other illegitimate reasons.

Exceptions to Employment at Will

In addition to antidiscrimination laws, many states have two exceptions to employment at will.

Contracts

If you have a contract for a definite period, or a contract saying that your employer needs a legitimate reason to fire you, a court will enforce that contract, just like any other contract. This potentially protects a large number of people. Many people have been told by their boss, "We won't fire you if you do a good job." But most of the time, this promise is legally meaningless. Robert Ohanian was told by his boss at Avis that "unless he screwed up badly, there was no way he was going to get fired." Based on this assurance, Ohanian agreed to a transfer to a struggling office to try to turn it around. Despite what his employer agreed was excellent performance, the office continued to struggle. Despite its promises, Avis fired Ohanian. When he went to court, his case was dismissed. A few states are more open to cases like Ohanian's, but in most other states the result would be the same.

Public Policy

The courts in many states have held that employees cannot be fired for reasons that violate public policy. A classic case involved Vickie Nees, who was fired by her employer for reporting for jury duty as ordered. Because Nees had a legal obligation to report for jury duty the court ruled that it was illegal for her employer to fire her. Nees won her case. Again, however, courts construe the exception narrowly. Unless the employer violates a specific statute by the firing, or the employee has an explicit legal right to the action for which they were fired, the employee is generally out of luck. For example, Jerald Schultz was fired by Industrial Coils for writing a letter to the editor of the local paper. The state constitution guarantees every citizen the right to speak and write freely on any subject. The state constitution, unlike the federal constitution, was not limited to government actions. Still, the Wisconsin Court of Appeals upheld the dismissal of his case.

Many people think of judges as being above politics. Conservatives constantly complain about "activist" judges who decide cases on the basis of their own political opinions instead of following the law. But the history of the employment at will doctrine is a stunning example of conservative judges creating law out of whole cloth to suit their politics. While the Constitution doesn't apply to corporations, there is an even older body of law referred to as common law. Judges have been around as long as legislatures, and much of Anglo-American legal history comes from the courts. While legislatures have the ultimate power (except where the Constitution is involved) and can overrule judge-made law, they frequently allow it to stand.

There is good reason for this. In many areas of the law, judges were making decisions for a century or more before legislatures fully matured. Countless judges had gradually created a body of law by considering thousands of individual cases. For the legislature to step in, throw all this out, and create a brand-new set of legal rules would often serve little purpose, and might well make things worse. It's a lot easier to get laws that make sense when you have many years and countless cases to consider rather than trying to create them in a year or two while working in the abstract.

One of the areas that has traditionally been regulated by common law is employment. When this body of law was created, large industrial enterprises didn't exist. Most employees were servants. Courts created rules governing the relationship between masters and servants. Naturally, masters had the upper hand. But servants had rights too. A master who wanted to fire a servant had to give him or her reasonable notice.

In the nineteenth century, the world of work began to change. The ties between employers and employees became less personal and the needs of employers became more fluid. While the master of an estate might be expected to keep a servant on a relatively permanent basis, the owner of a factory or a company building a railroad generally needed workers for shorter periods of time.

The legislatures or the courts could have openly addressed the changes that were taking place and attempted to modify the existing legal rules in a manner more consistent with the new world of work. But they didn't. Instead, the courts radically changed the rules without admitting that they had changed anything.

In 1877, an obscure legal writer from Albany named Horace Wood wrote a treatise summarizing the employment law of the time. Wood stated that, under American law, employment is a relationship "at will" in which an employer could fire a worker at any time, without notice, for any reason, no matter how arbitrary, or for no reason at all. Workers had the supposedly equal right to quit at any time without reason, which reminds many people of Anatole France's comment about how French law in the nineteenth century prohibited rich and poor alike from sleeping under the bridges of Paris.

Wood wasn't much of a scholar. He cited only four cases in support of his claim that employment at will was the law of the land. To make matters worse, in not one of the four cases Wood cites did the court rule that employment was at will. One of the cases wasn't even an employment case. In another, the court held that the employee's termination was illegal and awarded damages. If Wood had produced this work in a decent law school, he probably would have failed. Professor Theodore St. Antoine, of the University of Michigan Law School, describes the employment at will rule as springing "full-blown from Wood's busy and perhaps careless pen."

Despite Wood's shoddy scholarship, courts across the country began citing his treatise in support of rulings that an employer had the legal right to fire an employee at any time without reason. By the turn of the century, Wood's rule had become American law.

Future judicial decisions made the rule even worse. Wood said only that unless the parties had agreed to a different arrangement, an employment relationship was at will. He said nothing to limit the ability of the parties to agree to something else.

This should have opened the door to justice for many employees. The core principle of American contract law is that a court is supposed to find out what the parties intended when they made their agreement. It's not just a matter of what's in the written document. Courts also consider related documents, such as correspondence between the parties, oral statements by the parties regarding their intentions, the manner in which the parties conducted their relationship in practice, and any other evidence that provides insight into the parties' intentions.

Under this principle, many employees would be able to make a decent case that their employment was not at will. Very few employers ever say to employees, "Don't expect any job security here. We will fire you anytime we want, with or without a good reason." And employers frequently say things like "As long as you do a good job, there's a place for you here." Company handbooks frequently contain guidelines for discipline, which virtually never say "We can fire you for no reason at all." Other than the phrase "employment is at will" (which no one but a lawyer understands) buried in the fine print of the employment contract (if there is one), there is little in the communication most employees have with their employer that indicates that employment can be terminated on a whim.

But judges refused to apply this principle to employment law. No matter how clear it was that employment at will was not what the parties intended, unless employees had a written contract specifying other terms, courts consistently held they could be fired for no reason.

A classic case was *Skagerberg v. Blandin Paper Company,* decided by the Minnesota Supreme Court in 1936. Skagerberg had an offer from Purdue University to become an associate professor of engineering. At the same time, he received an offer from Blandin Paper Company. Blandin told Skagerberg that if he would turn down the Purdue offer, it would offer him permanent employment. Skagerberg sent Blandin a letter accepting the job stating, "The essential consideration being, however, that the job will be a permanent one." Meanwhile, he turned down the offer from Purdue. When he was later fired without a legitimate reason and went to court, his case was dismissed. He appealed to the state supreme court and lost again. The court acknowledged that the parties had agreed that Skagerberg's employment would be "permanent," but held that "permanent" means that the employee can be fired at any time, without cause. It's like the caterpillar in *Alice in Wonderland* saying, "When I use a word, it means exactly what I say it means," except that this wasn't fiction.

The Damage Done

The toll taken by arbitrary firings is staggering. The financial losses suffered by employees are only the beginning. Psychologists have found that being fired is the second most traumatic experience a person can have next to losing a loved one. The humiliation and self-doubt that people feel when they are fired, combined with the stress of worrying about how they will take care of themselves and their families, drive many people to mental illness, alcoholism, and even suicide. Dr. Harvey Brenner, of Johns Hopkins University, reports that a significant percentage of these afflictions nationwide are caused by loss of employment.

Even when employees get a new job, the impact can be devastating. Ame Arlt, from Tennessee, lost her job after twenty years of experience as an executive, including several in her last job. When she couldn't find a comparable position, she was forced to take a twelve-dollar-an-hour job as a data entry clerk. Unable to support herself on this income, she has been forced to spend her retirement savings just to make ends meet. "This has been the hardest thing in my life," Arlt says. "It has been harder than my divorce from my husband. It has been even worse than the death of my mother."

What the Law Should Be

The answer to this problem is to change the law to require employers to have just cause before firing someone. This doesn't mean an employer can't fire someone for not doing their job well enough, for breaking the rules, or because their work is no longer needed. It simply means that there must be a legitimate, job-related reason for the termination.

Employers can easily live with such a law. Many employers already do. The Donnelly Corporation, a producer of high-technology glass products in Holland, Michigan, voluntarily gave up the right to fire at will thirty years ago. Donnelly not only allows employees who feel they have been unfairly fired (or passed over for a promotion) to appeal, it gives them a jury trial before other employees. What's more, juries are composed predominantly of rank-and-file employees, not managers.

Most employers would be scared to death of such a system, but Donnelly considers it a big success. Company president John Donnelly told me that not once did he feel that the employees on the jury held for an employee who was in the wrong. "If anything," he said, "fellow employees have been tougher than the managers on the jury. They work hard to do the best job they can and expect their coworkers to do the same." The company went on to become the world leader in its industry. Donnelly credits its employment policy with helping produce this success. "Commitment is a two-way street," he told me. "When we demonstrate that we are committed to treating employees fairly, they increase their commitment to the company."*

Every union contract also requires employers to have just cause for discharge. This does not hurt productivity—unionized companies generally have slightly higher productivity than other employers in their industry. (The reason employers don't like unions is because they have to pay their employees more when they have a union, reducing profits.)

In 1987, Montana changed its law to require just cause for discharge. Montana employers didn't suffer and neither did its economy. In the twenty years since Montana abolished employment at will, the state's economy has more than tripled, growing faster than the economy of the nation as a whole.

In 1991, the Uniform State Law Commissioners tried to do the same thing nationwide. Each state governor appoints members to this little-known but influential group, usually partners in major law firms or prominent academics. The commission is tasked with identifying areas in which conflicting laws in different states cause problems. Having different laws in different states isn't always a bad thing. If one state wants to have a higher income tax than another or a lower drinking age, that's fine. But sometimes having incompatible state laws is a nightmare. If a corporation in Pennsylvania and a corporation in California have a dispute over a contract and the states have different contract laws, it causes a great deal of unnecessary trouble. The commission's first major project was the Uniform Commercial Code, a model statute cover-

* Donnelly is now a division of Magna, Inc.

ing the sale of goods and services. Representatives of all concerned groups provided input and the commissioners tried to write a law that would strike the right balances. They succeeded, and today the Uniform Commercial Code has been adopted by virtually every state.

The commissioners saw the same problem with the law of employment termination. While every state's law was basically at-will employment, there were significant variations in the exceptions. Some states recognized the public policy exception or the contract exception described above, some both, and some neither. For an employer that operates in more than one state, this created significant difficulties.

The commissioners created a committee to study the issue, chaired by Stan Fisher, a prominent management attorney from Cleveland. Fisher's committee, with the advice of Professor St. Antoine, mentioned earlier in this chapter, developed a bold new approach to employment termination. Instead of being able to fire employees for no reason, employers under their proposal—the Model Employment Termination Act, or META—would need to have a legitimate job-related reason for all terminations. Employees who felt they had been fired unfairly would have the right to a hearing before a neutral and independent arbitrator, one whom they would have an equal voice in selecting. If the arbitrator ruled in their favor, they would get their job back plus all the compensation lost while the case was pending.

To make the proposal acceptable to employers, META provided that employees who win in arbitration receive compensation only for their economic losses (primarily lost pay and benefits). They would not be eligible for damages for emotional distress ("pain and suffering") or punitive damages. Under current law, wrongful discharge verdicts under the public policy exception are generally treated as torts, in which the jury can award virtually unlimited damages. When juries believe that an employer has acted in a malicious way, a million-dollar verdict is not uncommon. This can be a financial problem for the company. In addition, employers often believe that these million-dollar verdicts are an excessive penalty based more on emotion than on the facts. Employers constantly complain about "runaway juries." The model act would have solved this "problem" forever.

The first time Fisher presented his committee's proposal to the full body of commissioners, they thought he had lost his mind. A motion was made to dissolve the committee and drop the entire project. It almost passed, but the commissioners ultimately decided to consider the proposal. The more they thought about it, the more the commissioners warmed to the approach. Two years later, the commissioners approved the META proposal by a large majority.

Despite the commissioners' political influence, however, META went nowhere. Employers wanted to get rid of juries in employment cases, but weren't willing to give up the right to fire employees arbitrarily to do so. The lawyers who represent employees, through their professional association, the National Employment Lawyers Association (NELA), also opposed META. They wanted to get rid of employment at will, but weren't willing to give up big jury verdicts. Unions didn't have a dog in this fight, so they didn't get involved. The civil rights community was concerned about the price tag of eliminating employment at will. When the plaintiffs' bar condemned META, civil rights organizations backed off. Virtually the only organization to support META was the ACLU (at a time when I was director of its employment rights office).

One can argue that the price META called for to eliminate employment at will was too high. As discussed above, many people who are fired unfairly lose more than money. To someone so crushed by being fired unfairly that he became an alcoholic and lost his family, getting only his job back and lost wages isn't fair. But maintaining the status quo isn't fair either. Every year approximately 150,000 people lose their jobs unfairly and 98 percent get no relief. On balance, getting some justice for 98 percent of wrongfully fired workers is worth the cost of giving the other 2 percent less relief than they deserve.

The system proposed by the Uniform State Law Commissioners is the system that is used by every union in America. How can a system that is universally chosen by workers themselves when they have a voice be unfair?

Some members of the plaintiffs' bar argued that it was the wrong time to make a deal. Judicial decisions in many states were creating exceptions to employment at will. Many progressives thought that time was on our side and that we would do better letting the courts whittle away at employment at will. This view turned out to be wrong. While there were decisions in many states creating exceptions to employment at will, virtually all of them involved the public policy and implied contract exceptions described above.

But the public policy exception helps very few victims of wrongful discharge. The vast majority of times someone is fired unfairly, the only people hurt are the employee and her family. Being arbitrary and unfair doesn't affect the public. In over twenty years as an employment rights advocate, I've seen literally hundreds of unfair terminations, and I could count on my fingers the ones that truly affected the public.

The implied contract doctrine turned out to be an even bigger disappointment. The first cases held that statements in company handbooks regarding how discipline and terminations would be handled were part of the employment contract. If the company handbook described a progressive discipline policy (such as a warning for the first infraction, probation for the second, and termination for the third), the employer couldn't ignore the policy and fire someone for their first mistake (unless it was extremely serious). Since no employer wants to write a handbook that says "You have no rights here, we'll fire you whenever we want to with or without a reason," these rulings were promising.

But employers found a way to slam the door shut almost overnight. They simply added the words "This handbook is not an employment contract." Courts across the country held that these few words, not always very prominent, trump everything else the handbook says about the rules for termination.

We can and should change the law in the rest of the country. The question is whether we have the political will to do it.

5

No Second Chances:
Background Checks

Kimberly Kelly was a model employee. A single mother, she got herself off welfare and got a job as a pipe insulator with a contractor in an Eli Lilly pharmaceutical plant. Her supervisor and fellow workers were pleased with the way she did her job. But Kelly was fired anyway, for the offense of bouncing a sixty-dollar check. While going through a divorce, Kelly had moved to a new town and closed out her bank account, unaware that one of her checks hadn't yet cleared. Instead of looking for her and requesting another form of payment, the company to which she had written the check pressed charges. The local magistrate held the hearing without notifying her, and in her absence Kelly was found guilty and fined $179. She never even knew it had happened until she was fired.

Many other people lost their jobs when Eli Lilly decided to run a criminal records check on all their employees and contractors. Paul Gibson lost his job as an electrician because of a misdemeanor conviction he received for breaking up a fight between his girlfriend and another woman. Worse, the event had happened nine years earlier, long before he started working for the company.

Eli Lilly is far from the only company checking criminal records. According to the congressional Office of Technology Assessment (OTA), the majority of employers today (52 percent) check criminal records. Large employers are even more likely to test; almost 80 percent of major employers check criminal records. The FBI receives five million requests for criminal records from employers every year. These requests (plus those from landlords) exceed the requests from law enforcement agencies. Other employers get criminal records from private information brokers.

If you haven't had to go through a criminal record check on the job yet, you probably will. The number of employers conducting such checks is growing rapidly, especially since 9/11. Automatic Data Processing's orders for employment criminal record checks grew 30 percent in 2002 alone, according to Mike McGrorey, marketing director for ADP's Screening and Selection Services division.

The logic behind this trend is hard to follow. Few, if any, of the 9/11 terrorists had criminal records. Nor did they use their jobs to further their conspiracy. Even if every company in America, including those of the hijackers, had conducted criminal records checks, nothing about 9/11 would have changed. Crime in America has generally declined in recent years and with it the risk to employers. But employers' fear of crime has increased and it is the emotion, not the reality, that drives employers' behavior.

The increased use of criminal records isn't necessarily a bad thing. There are times when a criminal conviction ought to be a job disqualification. No one wants a person convicted of drunk driving to operate a school bus, or another convicted of stealing money to work in a bank. But refusing to hire anyone who has a criminal record is going too far. Unfortunately, this is exactly what many employers do. The OTA report found that 19 percent of employers will not consider hiring anyone who has ever been convicted of anything at any time in their life. It doesn't matter how minor the offense, whether it's related to the job, or how old the conviction is—if you've ever been convicted of anything, "you can't work here." If you were arrested for shoplifting or underage drinking as a teenager, you can't work for these companies for the rest of your life. If every employer adopted this policy the way they've adopted drug testing, you'd never get a job. Even if the company doesn't have an official policy not to hire people with criminal records, there's a good chance that having a criminal record will keep you from being hired.

Sometimes it's not the employer that's responsible for people losing job opportunities because of a criminal record. There are laws in virtually every state that make it illegal for employers to hire people with criminal records for certain jobs.

Some of these laws make good sense. A person who has been convicted of child abuse should not work in a day care center. Employers shouldn't even have the option to make such an irresponsible decision. But other times the prohibitions make little sense, or are overly broad. There are now at least 350 different jobs for which you may need a state license. In my home state of New Jersey, for example, there are sixty-eight jobs for which you need a state license. This includes not only doctors and lawyers, but beauticians, manicurists, athletic trainers, and barbers. The grounds for denying a license are very broad. The American Bar Association, in a survey of two thousand state licensing provisions, found that 90 percent included the requirement that an applicant have "good moral character." Conviction of any crime, at any time in your life, generally leads state licensing boards to rule against you for all types of licenses.

Consequences of Zero Tolerance

If every company refused to hire anyone with a criminal record, chaos would ensue. At least 46 million people in America have criminal records. Some are hardened criminals, but most are ordinary people who made a mistake, from shoplifting to getting caught with marijuana. If no one with a criminal record could get a job, all 46 million people (and their families) would be forced to go on welfare.

Zero tolerance policies also make crime rates go up. When someone breaks the law, the most important step toward rehabilitation is having a job. People without a job hang around on street corners and get into trouble. If people can't make an honest living, they turn to crime to support themselves. Agencies that help ex-offenders straighten out their lives consistently say that employment discrimination is one of their greatest problems. Employers that won't give someone with a criminal record a second chance (at an appropriate job) are working overtime to increase the crime rate. This isn't just the view of bleeding-heart liberals. Senator Sam Brownback of Kansas, one of the most hard-core conservatives in Congress, is a leading advocate for removing employment barriers to people with criminal records.

Blame the Courts:
The Doctrine of Negligent Hiring

When challenged on these overly broad policies, some employers blame the courts and the recent development of the law of negligent hiring. A number of courts have ruled that an employer can be liable to the victim who is hurt because an employer hired someone with a criminal record for the wrong job. For example, America's Best Carpet Care, in Oakland, California, hired Jerrol Woods, a man with seven armed robbery convictions, as a cleaner, sending him into customers' homes. When Woods fatally stabbed a customer's daughter, a court found the company negligent and awarded the parents $9 million. The company went out of business.

America's Best Carpet Care deserved what it got. What could be more irresponsible than to send someone with a lifetime of violence into people's homes? If management had conducted a records check, Woods's victim would still be alive (assuming the company would have had enough sense not to hire him for this job once it knew about his record).

But if America's Best Carpet Care had hired Woods for a different job, one that didn't put him in a situation where people are particularly vulnerable, they wouldn't have been liable. American Hawaii Cruises hired a cook who had been convicted of sexual assault for one of its ships. The man later assaulted another employee on the ship. The court dismissed the victim's suit against the cruise line because it had not put the man in a position that gave him any special opportunity to hurt someone else.

The bottom line is that the doctrine of negligent hiring simply requires an employer to refrain from hiring people with criminal records for jobs where the nature of their past behavior creates a special risk of harm, which is something all employers should do anyway. It's no reason to refuse to hire anyone with a record.

You Don't Have to Break the Law to Lose a Job

Sometimes, even people who have never committed a crime are denied employment. Many employers will refuse to hire you if you've ever been arrested, even if you were found not guilty.

Sandy Snodgrass had never been arrested in his life, but he still lost his job. The company performing criminal-record checks for his employer (Johnson Controls, in Milwaukee) confused him with a relative with a similar name and erroneously reported that he had been convicted of theft. After fifty-six years of obeying the law, and eighteen years on the job, he was fired because the record checking company was careless. Fortunately, his boss questioned the report, the error was discovered, and Snodgrass saved his job. Most people aren't so lucky. Their bosses just accept the report and fire them.

That's too bad, because criminal records are often wrong. The United States Attorney General's office admits that 50 percent of the FBI's criminal records are inaccurate or incomplete. One common error occurs when someone who is arrested gives a false name. Giving a false name makes it harder for the police to track someone down if they don't show up for their trial. Judges give longer jail sentences to people with prior offenses, so criminals can spend less time locked up when they're convicted if they give a false name. Since there are no penalties for getting caught giving a false name, it happens all the time. SEARCH, a highly respected think tank that conducts research for the United States Department of Justice, estimates that 400,000 people every year give the police someone else's name when they are arrested.

Worse yet, if you lose a job because of an inaccurate criminal record, you'll probably never know. The law doesn't require the FBI to give you a copy of your record when it gives one to your employer. Under the Fair Credit Reporting Act (FCRA), an employer is supposed to tell you if you are turned down for a job because of something it learned in a background check. The definition of background check is very broad and covers criminal records. Many employers, however, don't understand this and turn people down because of their records without telling them why.

There is little legal protection in this area. Several states have passed laws requiring a connection between the nature of the job and the nature of the offense before you can be turned down for a job because of a criminal record. Under New York law, for example, you can be denied a job because of a criminal record only if the conviction is related to the job. But in practice, these laws usually don't mean much. A New York court held that failing to pay taxes is related to being a pilot. Meanwhile, in most states, there is nothing you can do.

There isn't even much you can do if you've never broken the law but lose your job because of an erroneous record. There is no right to sue the FBI for making a mistake. You can sue a credit reporting agency for negligence. But if the credit agency accurately reported incorrect records it received from the government, you have no case. Even when it was the credit agency's mistake, successful lawsuits are rare.

False Hope from the Federal Government

At one time, it looked as though the federal government was going to address this problem. Under federal antidiscrimination law, it is illegal to have a job requirement that screens out minority applicants unless the requirement is job-related. This legal development (called "disparate impact") began in 1971, when the Supreme Court ruled that the Duke Power Company could not require a high school diploma for manual laborers when one wasn't necessary to do the job and when this requirement (especially in 1971 North Carolina) had the effect of eliminating a disproportionate share of the black applicants.

The Equal Employment Opportunity Commission (the federal agency responsible for enforcing antidiscrimination law) takes the position that it is permissible to turn someone down for a job because of a criminal conviction if the conviction is job-related, but that an across-the-board ban on hiring anyone with any conviction for any job is illegal.

Just as a requirement of being a high school graduate eliminated a disproportionate number of black applicants, so does having a criminal record. This doesn't mean employers can't disqualify people with theft convictions from working as bank tellers, but it does mean, according to the EEOC, that you can't automatically disqualify everyone with a record from every job.

Initially, the courts backed the EEOC. In *Green v. Missouri Pacific Railroad*, the federal court of appeals from the Eighth Circuit held that it was illegal for the railroad to refuse to hire anyone with a criminal conviction other than a traffic offense. Green had been turned down for a clerical job because he had been convicted of refusing military induction three years before. Other federal courts reached similar decisions. Then came the Reagan and Bush administrations, which filled the federal courts with judges who were unsympathetic to employment claims and to civil rights claims in general. It also brought new EEOC commissioners like Clarence Thomas, who went on to become a Supreme Court justice. Thomas wanted to cut back on the scope of civil rights claims, not expand them.

By the time the Democrats regained control of the White House, the character of the judiciary was changed. When the EEOC sued the Carolina Freight Carriers Corporation over its policy of refusing to hire anyone who had been convicted and incarcerated for any felony or any crime involving theft, the court sided with the employer. It said that an employer has a right to hire only honest employees for any job and could refuse to hire anyone who had ever been convicted of stealing. Faced with such decisions, President Clinton's new appointments to the EEOC did not issue complaints against employers for blanket policies against hiring people with criminal records. When pressed by civil rights advocates, the new commissioners privately admitted that they were concerned that cases like *Green* would be overturned if new cases were brought.

Today, the EEOC's position against blanket hiring bans on people with criminal records still exists, but only on paper.

Prospects for the Future

In many areas, employment law is getting better, although very slowly. But the law regarding the use of criminal records by employers may be getting worse. Many bills have been introduced into Congress in recent years making it even harder for people with criminal records to get a job. Usually, the titles of these bills are very misleading. For example, the proposed Private Security Enhancement Act was presented as a way of preventing dangerous felons from getting jobs as security guards. Who would oppose this? Nobody wants a convicted rapist or armed robber acting as a security guard. There was no evidence that employers were hiring inappropriate people as security guards, but why take a chance?

In reality, the bill applied to anyone who had been convicted of a crime involving "force" or "dishonesty." This covers almost every crime in the book. Paul Gibson's conviction of simple assault for breaking up the fight between his girlfriend and another woman involved force. Kimberly Kelly's bounced check involved dishonesty (at least to the magistrate who convicted her without hearing her side of the story). The net cast by this proposed law would have swept up everyone from teenage shoplifters to people who cheat on their taxes.

Perhaps this wouldn't have been so bad if it applied only to real security guard jobs. But the definition of "security guard" covered anyone who has responsibility for another person's property. This means virtually everyone. The sales clerk in a shoe store has custody of the stock. Even the janitor has control of the broom (which is the employer's property).

Worse yet, the bill would actually have made it illegal for an employer to hire someone who fell within these sweeping definitions. Even if Eli Lilly had decided that Kimberly Kelly was someone they could trust and wanted to hire her, giving her a job would have been a violation of federal law. The manager who hired her could have been sent to prison for two years.

Fortunately, the so-called Private Security Enhancement Act didn't pass. But members of Congress who want to look tough on crime keep introducing similar bills. Sooner or later, some of them will probably pass. This won't make our country any safer, but it will keep you (or your children) from getting a job if you do anything illegal, no matter how minor.

Credit Checks

A criminal record isn't the only thing that can cost you your job. Just having bad credit is often enough. *The Wall Street Journal* reports that over a million credit checks are performed by employers every year. If an employer doesn't like what it finds, you won't get hired, regardless of your qualifications. A Louisiana woman was turned down for six jobs as a nurse and drugstore clerk because she was slow in paying off her college loans.

Sometimes it makes sense to deny someone a job because of bad credit. A bad credit report might indicate that you don't handle money responsibly. In such a case, it might make sense to hire someone else for a position as a bookkeeper. But it's hard to find the logic behind refusing to give someone a job in a nursing home because she paid off her college loans too slowly.

This could have happened to you without your knowledge. Under the federal Fair Credit Reporting Act, employers are supposed to tell you if you are rejected because of information from a credit check. Many employers, however, are unaware of this requirement or deliberately don't follow it. And even if the employer notifies you, nothing in the law restricts an employer's ability to deny you a job because of your credit under any circumstances. Even if you can prove the report is wrong, the company doesn't have to hire you.

Even if you've always paid your bills on time, you can still lose your job because of a credit report. You might think that companies providing credit checks to employers would be very careful because the consequences of a mistake are frequently serious. But you'd be wrong. Credit bureaus simply compile and report the information they receive from banks and other creditors. They make no effort to verify the accuracy of the information. When the U.S. PIRG Education Fund examined credit reports, they found that 79 percent contained errors. The Federal Reserve Board of Governors found that 70 percent of consumer reports had at least one item with incomplete information. Sometimes the mistakes are massive. In 1991, the credit bureau TRW (now Experian) incorrectly reported that every citizen in Norwich, Vermont, hadn't paid taxes.

One of the most common ways to get a bad credit report, even if you've done nothing wrong, is identity theft. Identity theft is a large and growing problem; thieves obtain your Social Security number or other personal data and use it to charge items to your credit card, or even get a credit card in your name. It's not that hard to do. A dishonest store clerk can steal your credit card number when ringing up a sale. You could be tricked into revealing personal information by an e-mail that purports to be from your bank or another reputable institution. Identity thieves even go Dumpster diving looking for credit card receipts or other scraps of paper with personal information. The Federal Trade Commission found that over eight million people were victims of identity theft in 2005 alone.

You might think this would be easy to clear up, but it's not. It can take months, or even years, to get all of the credit bureaus in the country to correct their records. In the meantime, your bad credit report can prevent you from getting a bank loan or a mortgage for your new home. It can also cost you a job with the many companies that do pre-employment credit screening.

Sometimes creditors issue incorrect reports on purpose. If your bank provides inaccurate information about you to credit bureaus and your credit rating goes down you will have a hard time getting loans from anyone else. In congressional testimony in 2003, Capital One admitted that it routinely withholds credit limits, which has the effect of reducing credit scores.

Hope on the Horizon?

Recently, state governments have begun enacting laws that would give much more protection to employees. Five states, the most recent of which is Washington, have enacted laws that allow employers to acquire and use credit reports in making employment decisions only when they are relevant to the job. But for most jobs, credit reports will be off-limits. Several other states are now considering similar laws. These laws will not improve the quality of credit reports, but will dramatically reduce the number of jobs lost unfairly because of them.

Helping Yourself

One small thing you can do to protect yourself is to get a copy of your credit report and check to see if it is accurate. Getting your credit report is easy; and it's free. But don't use one of the "free" credit checks that probably pop up on your computer. Many of these companies slip in charges. A somewhat better way is to contact one of the three major credit agencies. The best way to get your credit report is to go to www.annualcreditreport.com, the Web site that the three major credit reporting agencies use to comply with federal law.

If you see something incorrect in your credit report, report it to all three major credit bureaus (Equifax, Experian, and TransUnion). Do it immediately. Don't wait until you apply for a job or a mortgage. The major credit agencies have a procedure to fix errors in reports. This isn't benevolence, or even enlightened self-interest; having such a procedure is required by federal law. Generally, they get it right. That's the good news. The bad news is that it's a cumbersome process that is never quick. If you wait until you need to apply for a job or a loan, by the time the bureau gets the mistake fixed, it will be too late.

I almost learned this the hard way. When I was applying for a home mortgage several years ago, the bank that held the mortgage on my existing home mistakenly reported to the credit bureau that I had often been late making my payments. The credit bureau forwarded this information to the new bank, which would have torpedoed my new mortgage and left me and my family unable to close on our new home with no place to live. Soon afterward, my old bank realized their mistake and sent the credit bureau a letter informing them that I had actually made all my payments on time.

I thought the problem was solved. ChoicePoint, the credit bureau, realizing that their initial report was wrong, would send a correction and my mortgage would be approved. But, just to be sure, I called ChoicePoint to confirm that they had issued a correction. I was stunned to learn that they had not. I asked them to send such a letter right away, since they knew their initial report was wrong. I was even more amazed when they refused.

In a scene straight out of Kafka, ChoicePoint told me I would have to start by requesting a copy of my credit report. I explained to them that I didn't need a copy, I already knew what the mistake was and so did they. They said it didn't matter, I had to start by getting a report to tell me what I already knew. I reluctantly agreed and said I wanted to place an order for my credit report, only to be told that the order had to be sent to them in writing, by mail (e-mail was not acceptable). Once I got the record, I had to write them a letter to tell them what they already knew. Phone calls and e-mails were unacceptable. I explained to them that by the time all these letters went back and forth, my mortgage would be denied. They said, in essence, "We don't care if we issued an incorrect report about you. We don't care if our system for fixing errors is irrational and slow and causes you to lose your home mortgage. Unless you follow our cumbersome procedure, we will keep issuing a report on you that we know is wrong."

By pleading with the bank and the seller for a few more days and doing everything by overnight express mail, I managed to save my mortgage, but only by the skin of my teeth. It seems cynical to think that credit reporting agencies deliberately make it difficult to correct records so that most people won't make them do it. But I can't think of any other explanation.

6

A Penny for Your Thoughts: Psychological Testing by Employers

Do you love your mother and your father?

Do you think your sex life is normal?

Are you troubled by constipation?

—FROM THE MMPI, A PSYCHOLOGICAL TEST

USED BY MANY EMPLOYERS

Sibi Soroka was shocked. He had applied for a job as a security guard at the local Target to provide some steady income while he pursued his career as an actor. At the end of the process, he was required to take the Minnesota Multiphasic Personality Inventory, a psychological test used by many employers. The tests included questions about his sex life, religious beliefs, intimate feelings about family members, and even his bathroom habits.

"I couldn't believe anyone would ask me such personal questions," Soroka said. "These are questions you wouldn't even answer for your own mother, let alone some personnel director at a company." The more he thought about it, the more upset he became. When the company called him to offer him the job, he told them to find somebody else; he didn't want to work for a company that treated people this way.

Soroka is not alone. An estimated 15 million Americans are required to take the MMPI every year, including two million people who are required to take it as part of applying for a job. Applicants who are forced to take the test range from doctors and priests to retail sales clerks. The test has been translated into

115 different languages, including Hmong, Turkish, and even sign language. The MMPI is only one of many psychological tests used by employers. According to the American Management Association, over 40 percent of employers nationwide use psychological tests, including eighty-nine of the *Fortune* 100.

History of Personality Testing

How did so many employers come to use such an invasive test? Like so many other peculiarities of corporate life, it is more of a historical accident than a deliberate policy. Large-scale personality testing began during World War I, when the Army turned to Columbia University professor Robert Woodworth to help identify recruits who would be unable to withstand the stress and trauma of battle. Woodworth's test was crude; he used questions like "Does the sight of blood make you sick or dizzy?" It was limited to the single psychological dimension that Woodworth called neuroticism, which he thought would predict those who would develop shell shock (today called post-traumatic stress disorder, PTSD) if put into combat. But the idea of a written test that would reveal the mysteries of human personality caught the attention of other psychologists.

One of them was Starke Hathaway. Hathaway worked in a state mental hospital in Minnesota and wanted a more systematic way of diagnosing the problems of the inmates than the subjective observations of his staff. After years of effort, he created the MMPI in 1942. Because he was trying to gain insight into deep-seated and serious mental conditions and dealing with inmates in a mental institution, he gave little or no thought to the intrusiveness of his questions.

World War II was the largest employment project in American history. Millions of people had to be selected, evaluated, assigned to specific positions, and trained. The sheer numbers involved forced the military to develop systems for these purposes. After the war, employers faced with the challenge of bringing millions of veterans back into the civilian economy adopted many of these practices. When they looked for a test to help evaluate people's personalities and the jobs they might be best suited for, the MMPI was the only game in town. It quickly became an industry standard. It also became an industry of its own. Test publishers and psychologists started making a living (sometimes a handsome one) around the MMPI and acquired a strong financial interest in protecting it.

Defending the Tests

Faced with challenges about the intrusiveness of the MMPI, its defenders argue that your privacy isn't really compromised because your employer will never see your answers to the questions, only the ultimate evaluation. This is probably true. The test is designed in this way and psychologists would consider it inappropriate to reveal the raw questions and answers, even if the employer were to ask.

But that doesn't mean that your privacy hasn't been invaded. You have still been forced to answer sensitive personal questions from a stranger, who has stored the information where it may be viewed by other strangers. If it's stored in a computer, there's also the chance that a hacker may get hold of it. Experience has shown that virtually any computer system can be hacked and that hackers are tempted by "sexy" information even when it has no commercial value. Revealing your innermost feelings on a psychological test may not be as bad as revealing the information to someone you know and work for, but it's still an invasion of privacy.

Tyranny of the Normal

Behind the invasion of privacy, there is a deeper and more subtle problem with most psychological tests. Your personality isn't something tangible that can be directly observed, like a pulse. Tests like the MMPI analyze your personality by comparing your answers to the answers of a control group that is supposed to be "normal." When the MMPI says that you are too attached to your parents or distrustful of people in authority, what it really means is that you are more like this than the people in the control group.

Who made up the original control group? People Starke Hathaway had access to: patients at the hospital where he worked. They were all from Minnesota. They were all white. Almost all were married. The majority were rural. On average, they had an eighth-grade education. They are about as unrepresentative of America at large today as it is possible to be. But if your thoughts, attitudes, or feelings were different from those of these rural white Minnesotans, the MMPI said you were abnormal. For example, only 9 percent of the control group agreed with the statement "I am an important person." Answering "yes" to this question was interpreted as evidence of narcissism and could cost you your job. Today, many people would consider this answer to be a healthy sign of self-esteem. But it still counted against you on the MMPI. Countless people were denied jobs simply because they were different from the "Minnesota normals."

Over the years, the publishers of the MMPI have tried to make the control group more of a true cross section of America. But even if the control group is completely representative, it doesn't solve the problem. You still fail the test just because you're different. The MMPI has become a nationwide system to punish nonconformists. This may not be what employers intended, but that's what it is. Annie Murphy Paul, former senior editor at *Psychology Today* and the author of *The Cult of Personality*, calls it "the petty tyranny of the average."

The Response from Employers

When employers are challenged about asking such invasive questions, they generally defend their conduct by arguing that your personality is relevant to your ability to do the job. This may well be true in many cases. An extroverted person might do better in a sales job than someone who is quiet and shy. But some outgoing people aren't very good at sales, and some quiet people have been known to succeed through sincerity and trustworthiness. One of the most successful salesmen I've ever known was a complete nerd. He dropped out of MIT to get married and no one would hire him as a scientist. He got a job selling chemicals. Ray's chemicals were the same as everyone else's, but if you had a problem using his product he used his MIT training to solve it at no extra charge. Guess whom the customers preferred?

If a prospective employer wants to know how well you perform at sales, why doesn't he just ask your boss from your last sales job? That would be far more reliable than a psychological test.

Employers claim they can't ask your former employers about your job performance, but that's not really true. Certainly, it's not as easy as it used to be to conduct a reference check. There have been a few cases in which employers have been found liable for defamation because of something they said about a former employee in the course of a reference check. There have been very few of these cases, only about ten a year nationally. And employers win most of them. In order to win, the ex-employee has to prove not only that what the former employer said was untrue, but that they said it with malice. Saying you were fired for excessive lateness isn't illegal, even if you weren't late more often than anyone else. Courts find malice only when the former employer accuses the ex-employee of doing something that reflects negatively on their character. In addition, it has to be untrue.

For example, the owner of a lumber company told a prospective future employer that his ex-employee had made improper sexual advances toward his coworkers, mooning one of them. Not only was this untrue, but the employer had absolutely no evidence to support the allegations. All an employer needs to do to stay out of trouble is limit their comments to their former employee's work and avoid gratuitous cheap shots.

This hasn't stopped corporate attorneys from crying wolf. Virtually all corporate legal departments tell management not to provide any information about former employees other than to confirm that they worked there and to verify their period of employment and job title (often referred to as the "name, rank, and serial number" policy). Most human resources departments dutifully issue official policies to implement this advice.

But competent recruiters know how to evade these policies. They ignore the HR department and go straight to the applicant's former boss. After all, who knows more about what kind of job someone did, the HR department or the person he or she actually worked for? Before they make the call, good recruiters tell the applicants. The applicants then call their former bosses and ask them to speak candidly to the recruiters. If the applicants were good employees, their former bosses want to help them, not torpedo their chances of getting a good job. I ran an HR department for ten years in my corporate life and never once had a former supervisor refuse to speak to me about an applicant. Edward Andler, a professional reference checker whom *The New York Times* calls "the acknowledged dean" of reference checking, says the idea that you can't get former employers to talk about an applicant is a myth and reports that 95 percent of the people he calls for references are cooperative.

But what if you're applying for a job you've never done before? In this case, an employer might want to consider indirect information, like a personality test. But he doesn't have to follow you into the bedroom to do it. There are many personality tests that do not ask invasive questions. One of the most popular is the Myers-Briggs Type Indicator. Myers-Briggs asks questions about whether you are often late for appointments and whether you prefer to read or go to a party. About the most probing question on Myers-Briggs is whether you find it difficult to talk about your feelings. I've taken the Myers-Briggs test myself and never once felt that my privacy was being invaded.

But despite the existence of less intrusive tests, the MMPI remains the most popular with employers. This is probably because employers who want to use personality tests generally look to see what other employers are using. So the MMPI stays popular even though no sensible employer would choose it over the other options that are currently available, if they bothered to compare them.

Legal Protection

If you live in California or Rhode Island, your employer can't force you to take the MMPI or other invasive psychological tests. Sibi Soroka sued Target, and the California Supreme Court ruled that the test had violated his right to privacy under the state constitution. In Rhode Island, the ACLU and National Workrights Institute filed a complaint with the state antidiscrimination agency, claiming that the MMPI discriminates on the basis of religion. The MMPI doesn't discriminate against Catholics, Jews, or any other specific faith.

But it does discriminate against those who are too zealous in their faith. On this basis Rhode Island banned the use of the MMPI.

Senator Sam Ervin, who later became famous for chairing the Senate hearings on Watergate, tried to ban intrusive psychological testing by the government in 1966. "The government should not send out an investigator to peer through an employee's bedroom window," Ervin said. "Nor should the government ask, through subtle psychological questioning, what a person does and thinks after he draws the curtain." Ervin introduced a bill that would have almost eliminated psychological testing by the government and persuaded thirty-five other senators to be cosponsors. But he failed to secure majority support and the bill died. Since then, no other senator or representative has taken up the issue.

Phony Reform

In response to these legal actions and an ongoing stream of negative publicity, the publisher of the MMPI decided to revise it. In 1989, it issued the MMPI II, which used a different group of people as its standard, one the publisher claims is truly representative. No independent researcher has ever tested this claim, however, because no one outside the company is allowed to see the data. From a privacy perspective, the MMPI II is a complete failure. While a handful of extremely personal questions were eliminated, overall it is still by far the most invasive of popular personality tests.

The reality today is that in forty-eight states employers are allowed to use any psychological test they choose and frequently choose the most invasive test available. Your only option if you don't want to bare your soul is to find another job.

Honesty Tests

People have longed for a way to tell who is honest and who isn't since Diogenes roamed the earth with a lantern looking for an honest man.

Some psychological tests claim to be able to tell who is honest and who is not. Many employers, especially those who have entry-level positions involving access to cash, require all applicants to take an honesty test. The journal *American Psychologist* reports that at least five thousand companies use so-called honesty tests and that as many as five million people are forced to take them every year.

The good news about honesty tests is that they are not intrusive. The bad news is that they are unreliable. The Congressional Office of Technology Assessment (Congress's private think tank, which it called upon for unbiased research until its funding was cut off as part of the Republican "Contract with America" in 1995) reviewed the results of the five major studies in which everyone a retail establishment intended to hire was given a written honesty test but hired regardless of the results. These tests collectively identified over half (55 percent) of the new employees as dishonest. But only about 5 percent of the employees the tests said were dishonest ever did anything dishonest at work. The other 95 percent of the so-called dishonest employees never did anything wrong. Admittedly, not everyone who does something dishonest at work gets caught. Anonymous surveys of employees report that about 25 percent of employees admit to doing something dishonest at work. But these surveys call it theft if a nurse takes home a scrub shirt or an office worker takes home a Bic pen. If you define dishonesty as taking something of value, the incidence of theft drops to no more than 10 percent. Either way, the vast majority of times written honesty tests said someone was dishonest, they were wrong. OTA concluded that the tests were completely unreliable.

Testing the Tests

Honesty-test publishers often claim that their tests have been proven reliable and valid. But these claims are based on a definition of reliability that is straight from *Alice in Wonderland*. When test publishers talk about reliability, they mean that a person who takes the test several times will get roughly the same score each time. Their definition of validity, called "construct validity," means that the results of an honesty test are consistent with the results of other honesty tests.

What a real honesty test needs is called "predictive validity." Whether honesty tests have predictive validity depends on your point of view.

On the one hand, some tests have been shown to correctly identify most of the truly dishonest people in a group of applicants. Consider a company that has one hundred job applicants to sort through. Ten of these people will be dishonest in a manner that would be of concern to an employer. An honesty test will detect about eight of them, greatly reducing the chances that the employer will hire the wrong person. But to do so, the test has to reject fifty of the applicants as dishonest, including forty-two honest people. Using a test that's wrong 80 percent of the time* may work for employers, at least if they have more applicants than they need, but it isn't fair to the many honest people who are denied the opportunity to work.

Why Honesty Tests Are Unreliable

Worse yet, if you fail one test, you will probably fail all the others. Honesty tests ask for your reaction to hypothetical situations involving dishonesty. If your response is not sufficiently punitive, the test concludes that you are being soft on the thief because you are one too.

There is some basis for this assumption. Research shows that criminals have different standards for judging behavior than other people. But you might also be "too soft" because you are a kind person who doesn't like to punish others. This may have been the case with Sister Teresa, a nun who applied for a job in a B. Dalton bookstore in Minneapolis. Not only did she fail the test, but the person who scored it said she had the worst score he had ever seen. Since all honesty tests have the same basic methodology, if one test mistakes your compassion for dishonesty, so will all the others. This will prevent you from getting any job in certain fields, such as retail sales.

You can also fail an honesty test by being too honest. Many tests ask for

* The forty-two honest applicants who were rejected represent 84 percent of the fifty rejected applicants.

your perception of the extent to which other people are honest. If you believe that most people are not honest, the test assumes you are rationalizing your own dishonest behavior. Sometimes this is true. But it can also mean that your standards of honesty are very high. For example, do you believe that "most people steal from their employer"? Most people would say no. But what about a Bic pen an employee takes home from work? Technically, that pen is the employer's property.

Most would wave off a pilfered pen, but if your standards of honesty are extremely high, you might call something like this theft. Being this honest may make you the ideal employee, but you'll never get hired. S. E. Nichols department stores once had difficulty filling vacancies in the Bible Belt because the applicants were so honest they admitted to misdeeds in the honesty test that most people would consider too trivial to mention. For example, they would answer "yes" to the question "Have you ever stolen from your employer?" because they once took home a pen.

No Room for Judgment

The harm done by unreliable honesty tests is especially great because employers treat them as infallible. This is partly due to testing's scientific aura. Honesty tests are developed by trained psychologists, many of whom are doctors or university professors. The tests are complex and scored by computers. It all seems so scientific that the average person, including the average employer, assumes that it must be reliable.

Test results are also treated as infallible because of the personal incentives of the HR employees who make the hiring decisions. Consider the position of the HR executive who had to make a decision about Sister Teresa. Considering the fact that she was a nun, he probably suspected the test was wrong, and may well have thought she was the best possible candidate. But what would happen if he hired her, ignoring the test result? If anything went wrong with Sister Teresa, he would look like an idiot. Even if he wasn't fired, his superiors would never have the same confidence in his judgment. But if he hired someone who passed the honesty test, no one would blame him if that employee turned out to be a bad apple. To protect their own jobs, HR employees have to follow the test results, even when they think they are wrong.

Test publishers claim it's not their fault that employers treat honesty tests as infallible. Most test publishers' instructions tell employers that test results should be only one factor in the hiring decision. But tests are constructed in a manner that makes it difficult, if not impossible, to follow this advice.

The result of an honesty test isn't just a score. If this were the case, the person making the hiring decision could conclude that one applicant's lower score on the honesty test was outweighed by other factors, such as more experience and better references. But that's not how the tests work. Instead, most test publishers establish a "cutting score" and tell the employer whether an applicant's score falls above or below this point. In effect, the test publisher tells the employer that one candidate is honest and another is dishonest. Professor Stephen Guastello of Marquette University has spent many years studying psychological testing. "If publishers were trying to find a way to get employers to blindly follow honesty test results," he explained, "they couldn't have found a better way than cutting scores."

Ironically, many employers started using written honesty tests only when they were forbidden to use polygraphs. In 1988 Congress passed the Polygraph Protection Act, which essentially bans the use of polygraphs by private employers because they are notoriously inaccurate. Rather than turn to better ways of making employment decisions, most polygraph users turned to honesty tests, which may be even less reliable.

Legal Protection

You might think that the government would require test publishers to prove that their products are reliable. After all, countless other products are regulated to protect the public. You can't sell any kind of medicine, even cough syrup, without proving to the Food and Drug Administration that it is "safe and effective." In many states, you can't even cut hair without a license. We regulate air conditioners, hammocks, and even coffee mugs in the interest of public safety. But there is no law saying honesty tests have to be reliable, even though people's jobs are at stake.* Their inaccuracy is legally irrelevant. There is no law that says employers have to be fair in their hiring practices, or even rational. A company can flip a coin or use a Ouija board to decide whom to hire if it wants to.

At one point, employee rights lawyers thought they might be able to attack honesty tests through state polygraph statutes. Prior to the enactment of the federal Polygraph Protection Act, many states passed similar laws. Unlike the federal law, many of these state laws are not specifically limited to polygraphs. But when the Minnesota Supreme Court considered this issue in the *Century Camera* case in 1981, it held that the statutory language applied only to mechanical devices, not to paper-and-pencil tests. Subsequent cases reached the same decision.

Only one state, Massachusetts, has a law prohibiting the use of honesty tests. Rhode Island's law prohibits employers from using them as "the primary basis of an employment decision." If you lose your job in any other state because you fail a written honesty test, all you can do is pick yourself up and look for another job.

---

* Psychological tests, like all other employment screening devices, are subject to antidiscrimination laws. Employers are not allowed to use a test that disqualifies people of one race or religion more than others.

7

Drug Testing

Watch out for that poppy seed bagel. It could cost you your job.

—PROFESSOR JOHN MORGAN, TOXICOLOGY DEPARTMENT,
CITY UNIVERSITY OF NEW YORK

Becky Thompson didn't use drugs. She was a small-town girl from Tennessee who had never been in trouble with the law and who taught Sunday school every week. But she lost her job because of a drug test.

Thousands of other people have suffered the same fate. As concerns about drug use proliferated in the 1980s, the majority of employers began drug testing. By 1990, the American Management Association reported that 80 percent of its members had drug testing programs in place.

Unfortunately, many of these programs were badly flawed. Drug testing was a booming business and many unqualified laboratories rushed to sell their services to employers. The error rates were staggering. A study by the Centers for Disease Control found that more than 37 percent of all drug test results were wrong.

As staggering as this error rate is, it is misleadingly low. Testing accuracy is usually expressed as the percentage of all tests obtaining a correct result. For example, if one hundred drug tests were administered and the right result was reported for ninety of them, the accuracy is 90 percent. But the critical number isn't "How many of the total tests were accurate?" but "How many of the positives were truly positive?" In other words, how many of the people who lost their jobs because of a drug test had actually used drugs?

This can lead to a very different rate of error. In a typical batch of urine samples from one hundred employees, only about eight will contain drugs. We know this because the federal Department of Health and Human Services conducts a study of the extent of drug use by Americans that is the most reliable source of this information. If the test identifies five of the eight correctly and reports a total of twelve samples as positive, the overall accuracy of the test is reported as 93 percent—three false negatives and four false positives. But when you look at the percentage of positive tests that were wrong, it is almost 60 percent (seven of twelve positive samples were actually negative). That means that the majority of people who lose jobs because they fail a drug test probably don't use drugs at all.

Firing Innocent People to Save Money

Employers share in the blame. A properly conducted drug test consists of two stages: a screening test (which identifies a large group that contains almost all of the samples containing drugs plus many that do not) and a confirmation test (which determines which samples from the large group are actually positive). Screening tests are usually very inexpensive. Confirmation tests cost much more. Many companies, in order to save money, make decisions based on screening tests alone, especially where job applicants are concerned. Thousands (perhaps millions) of people have been turned down because the screening test could not distinguish between over-the-counter medications such as Advil, Sudafed, or NyQuil and illegal drugs. Minute traces of actual drugs are also found in legal substances such as poppy seeds (which contain trace amounts of opium). These, too, can cause you to fail a test.

The federal government responded by creating a certification program for drug testing laboratories. In order to receive federal certification, a lab must achieve near-perfect performance on blind samples. The Department of Health and Human Services issued regulations requiring all labs participating in government-funded drug testing to be certified. While the federal government has made many mistakes regarding drug testing, it deserves credit for the certification program. The federal scientists who designed it did a good job. Shoddy labs can't pass HHS's demanding quality standards.

While the HHS certification program greatly reduced errors in government-sponsored testing, problems remain in private industry. While many employers, anxious to avoid mistakes, choose to work only with certified labs, others, caring more about cost than accuracy, continue to use uncertified labs. Because use of certified labs by private corporations is entirely voluntary, people who lost their jobs in these companies have nowhere to turn.

Strip-Search Testing

Worse yet, drug testing is often carried out under strip-search conditions. Most employer programs involve urine testing. As testing spread, so did efforts to cheat. Employees learned to "spike" urine samples with common substances such as bleach to make a positive specimen test negative. Others tried to carry samples of clean urine to the testing center to submit as their own.

Good lab work can spot these tactics by testing urine's temperature (if less than 98.6 degrees, it probably came from someone's pocket), pH level (if the acidity is wrong, the sample is probably adulterated), and other methods.

Again, however, some employers cared more about saving money than about doing the right thing. Rather than pay for the extra lab work, they instructed lab employees to watch the person urinate, often at close range. Rachel Adams, an employee subjected to this procedure, described it like this: "I waited for the attendant to turn her back before pulling down my pants, but she told me she had to watch everything I did. I am a forty-year-old mother of three: nothing I have ever done in my life equals the humiliation, degradation, and mortification I felt."

Legal Protection

Despite all this abuse, there are very few laws protecting us in this area. A handful of states (Connecticut, Iowa, Maine, Minnesota, Montana, Rhode Island, and Vermont) have passed laws regulating drug testing. Vermont, for example, prohibits random testing of employees. Employers may require employees to take a drug test, but only if there is reason to believe that the person is under the influence of drugs at work. The courts in California and New Jersey provide some protection under their state constitutions. For example, New Jersey and West Virginia allow random testing only in safety-sensitive jobs such as driving a truck. In all other states, employers can do anything they want. Even strip-search drug tests are often permitted. A federal court in Philadelphia ruled that it was not an invasion of privacy to watch job applicants while they gave urine samples.

Testing Doesn't Help

None of this harm is necessary. No employer wants people on the job under the influence of drugs. But urine testing doesn't tell an employer whether someone is under the influence of drugs. A positive urine test, even if accurate, indicates only whether the person has ingested an unknown quantity of drugs at some point in the last several days. The drug test doesn't tell the employer when the employee ingested the drug, how much he or she used, or how often it was used. The vast majority of people who lose their jobs because of accurate drug tests are Saturday night marijuana smokers who are no more impaired on the job than a coworker who had a few beers over the weekend. When the National Academy of Sciences studied drug testing, they found that it did nothing to increase workplace safety and did not improve productivity.

If random drug testing doesn't increase safety or productivity, why do so many employers use it? Sometimes it's because the government forces them to. For example, federal law requires employers to test truck drivers and other employees in the transportation industry. An employer who doesn't test is breaking the law. In other cases, it's a matter of business necessity. Any company that is bidding on a government contract needs to have a drug testing program—it's not legally required, but any executive who thinks his company is going to get a government contract without a drug testing program must be using drugs himself.

In some companies, the decision to conduct drug testing is political in another way. I once asked the president of a *Fortune* 1000 company why he had a drug testing program. "I know drug testing is a waste of money," he told me. "But we have a stockholders' meeting every year and someone always asks me what the company is doing to fight drug abuse. I tell them we have a drug testing program and everyone is satisfied. To a company of our size, it's worth one or two million dollars a year to avoid the controversy."

In most companies, employers test because they have been misled. The federal government, especially under the Reagan and first Bush administrations, proclaimed that drug abuse was a cancer that was destroying our society. These reports were dutifully discussed on the news and in high-profile stories in virtually every major newspaper and magazine in the country. The government spent millions on television ads such as the famous one comparing a frying egg to "your brain on drugs." This campaign was meant to scare people, and it worked. Employers became scared that they were at risk of hiring drug abusers who would ruin their company. When drug testing industry salesmen showed up promising an inexpensive solution to the crisis, many employers decided to play it safe and start testing.

Paying Employers to Test

Drug testing salesmen, however, were more successful with large companies than with smaller ones. Smaller companies are less likely to be federal contractors, so they don't need to test to get federal contracts. They are also less likely to be public, so they don't have to worry about a little old lady in tennis shoes showing up at the stockholders' meeting and demanding to know what the company is doing about drugs.

For small companies, drug testing is more a matter of dollars and cents. When the testing industry was unable to demonstrate that making employees pee in a bottle improved safety and productivity, many small employers decided against the practice. The testing industry responded by lobbying state governments to create new incentives for employers to test. New Jersey, for example, changed its unemployment compensation law to deny compensation to anyone who was fired for testing positive for drugs. Since the amount of money employers have to pay into the state unemployment compensation system is based on how many former workers of that company collect benefits, employers with a testing program end up paying less.

This change conflicted with the basic principles of New Jersey's unemployment compensation law. For years, the law said that employees who lost their job were entitled to unemployment compensation unless they had committed a serious act of workplace misconduct. Even if you did your job poorly and your boss was right to fire you, you still got compensation unless you had behaved so badly on the job that the company had no real choice but to fire you.

Showing up for work drunk or stoned might well be grounds to deny someone compensation, but smoking a joint on Saturday night and showing up sober on Monday morning doesn't cut it. In essence, the New Jersey government decided that everyone gets unemployment compensation if they are fired for anything other than workplace misconduct, except for people who use drugs.

Alabama took a different approach to bribing employers into testing. Workers' compensation insurance companies charged employers the same amount for coverage whether or not they had a drug testing program. The reason was simple. Insurers give lower rates only to a person or a company that is less likely to file a claim. Health insurers charge lower premiums to nonsmokers because they are less likely to get sick and file a claim. Insurance companies have small armies of actuaries (a specialized type of statistician) whose entire career is spent measuring risk. Workers' compensation insurers didn't offer lower rates to companies with drug testing programs because the data showed that companies with testing programs had just as many accidents as companies that don't test.

So the state changed the rules. Alabama passed a new law requiring workers' compensation insurers in the state to charge lower rates to companies with drug testing programs, whether they had lower accident rates or not.

In all, ten states passed new laws giving economic incentives to employers to conduct drug tests that are unsupported by any economic benefit. They are purely political programs that pay employers to test whether testing helps the company or not.

Phony Studies

Like many ad campaigns, the War on Drugs was long on hype and short on substance. The "studies" that provided the information for the campaign were hopelessly inept. For example, the claim that employers lost $33 billion of productivity to drug use among employees was based on a study by the Research Triangle Institute. RTI, however, never looked at any productivity data, even though it is widely available. Instead, it looked at the income of people who use drugs and compared it to the income of people who don't.

This wouldn't be completely unreasonable if the people in question had the same jobs. If plumbers who smoke marijuana make less money than those who don't, then the reason might be drug use. But RTI didn't look at people in the same job; they assumed that if a plumber who smokes marijuana makes less than a heart surgeon who doesn't, then the surgeon's higher income is due to not using drugs. RTI didn't even look at individual income; it looked at family income. If a plumber who smokes marijuana makes more than one who doesn't but the nonsmoker is married to a heart surgeon, RTI assumed the higher income of the second family was because the second plumber abstains.

In some cases, the antidrug campaign was a complete fraud. Many of the claims made about the relationship between drug use and absenteeism and safety came from the Firestone Study. As it turns out, there is no Firestone Study. The Firestone Company never conducted a study of any kind about drugs. In 1972, a speaker at a luncheon of Firestone executives made numerous claims about drugs and the workplace. No one knows where the speaker got these numbers. Even the speaker's identity is unknown at this point. All we know for sure is that Firestone never conducted a study of any kind.

How then did the "Firestone Study" get quoted so many times? In 1983, Sidney Cohen, editor of the widely read *Drug Abuse and Alcoholism Newsletter*, reproduced the statistics from the unknown speaker, implying that they had come from a systematic scientific study. From there, the bogus statistics spread like wildfire. The government cited the nonexistent report in many of its publications. The Partnership for a Drug-Free America featured them in its ads. Soon journalists were reporting them as facts.

Phony Crisis

People paid attention to these bogus "studies" because the government had convinced everyone (or at least most people) that America had a drug crisis. President Reagan said that drugs, whose effects were "terrifying," were a "scourge" that had "overwhelmed our nation." His wife, Nancy, declared that every casual recreational drug user was an "accomplice to murder." Carlton Turner, President Reagan's drug czar, called for the death penalty not only for all drug sellers but for all drug users (including young people caught smoking marijuana). The federal government created an ad claiming that snorting cocaine was the equivalent of putting a revolver up one's nose and pulling the trigger.

This campaign had the desired effect. Before 1984, drug abuse did not appear at all in the results of Gallup polls discussing the greatest problems facing the United States. By 1985, about 4 percent of Americans considered drugs our greatest problem. In 1986, it had risen to 8 percent, making it the fourth most serious problem in American minds. By 1989, a *New York Times/* CBS poll showed that the majority of Americans (64 percent) considered drug abuse the nation's biggest problem, more than crime, national security, the economy, and all other issues combined.

But it was all hype. Drugs are a problem, but they have never been a crisis. Almost 400,000 Americans die from tobacco use every year. That's a crisis. Another 100,000 die from the effects of alcohol every year. That's a crisis. Motor vehicle accidents claim the lives of 40,000 Americans every year. That, too, is a crisis. Deaths from drug abuse don't even make the top ten. The number of people who die annually from drug overdoses is only about 3,000. More people die by drowning than from drugs. Even the number of deaths from slipping and falling in your own home is greater than the number of deaths from drugs. Does this make falling in the bathtub a national crisis? To be sure, drug abuse is a problem that has ruined many lives (in addition to lives it has taken). But the claim that drug abuse is a national crisis simply isn't true.

No one knows for sure why the Reagan and Bush administrations made drugs into a national priority. Some people think the decline of the Soviet Union created a need for some other source of fear to avoid close scrutiny of the administrations' records. Some think it was a way to avoid the charge that Republicans didn't care about the poor. By fighting to save inner-city residents from the scourge of drugs, Reagan and Bush could claim to be helping the poor without spending money on education or health care.

Whatever led these politicians to turn drugs into a national crisis, it wasn't the facts.

Real Solutions

The fact that the government and the drug testing industry have lied so often about drugs in the workplace doesn't mean that drug abuse isn't a real problem for employers. Most of us know someone whose drug use damaged his or her life. No employer wants a stoned employee operating heavy machinery or even doing the filing.

What the National Academy study and other legitimate studies show is that most people who use drugs are recreational pot smokers whose job performance isn't any different from that of people who drink beer or martinis on their own time, and that the probability of someone who uses drugs becoming an addict is no greater than the probability of someone who drinks becoming an alcoholic.

What employers need to do is focus on the real issue, which is job performance. If an employee's performance is slipping, their supervisor should confront them with the facts and let them know they need to do better to keep their job. The supervisor should also say that if the employee has a personal problem that is affecting their performance, they should use the company's employee assistance plan (EAP).

In an EAP, employees can speak in confidence to someone about their problem and get a referral to a professional who can help them. In most cases, the employer helps by paying part of the cost. In the end, the employee's job performance either improves, in which case the problem is solved, or it does not, in which case the employee is terminated. The employer never pries into the employee's private life. Study after study has shown that EAPs are by far the most effective way to prevent drug abuse (or any of the many other personal problems people have) from hurting company performance.

Drug testing can actually make safety worse. Every dollar an employer spends on one program is a dollar it can't spend on something else. While EAPs are effective, they are expensive. Not all employers have them, and most of those that do place limits on the program because of these costs. Some employers, for example, will pay only for outpatient drug treatment. This is all some workers with substance abuse problems need. But when the problem is serious, sometimes inpatient treatment is needed. When this isn't covered, workers don't get the help they need. Sometimes the company can't pay 100 percent of the cost. This, too, sometimes means the difference between a worker's getting the help he or she needs or not. Drug testing doesn't create these resource limitation problems, but it makes them worse by wasting money that could be used on EAPs.

My former employer, Drexelbrook Controls, is in the most safety-sensitive business imaginable. We designed, manufactured, and installed control systems on toxic chemical tanks for companies like DuPont and Dow Chemical. Because our systems used proprietary technology that was the best in the world, we got the most difficult and dangerous applications. Union Carbide, for example, has plants in the United States that have tanks full of methyl isocyanate, the same chemical that overflowed in Bhopal, India, killing an estimated eight thousand people. Unlike the tanks in India, the ones in the United States have Drexelbrook control systems to keep them from overflowing. If those systems were to fail, it would be like 9/11 all over again, only worse.

You might think that Drexelbrook would have been among the first companies to adopt drug testing. But we weren't. In fact, we never had a drug testing program. It wasn't an oversight. It wasn't because we didn't have the money. We didn't have a drug testing program because it would have made our customers less safe.

Drexelbrook had a quality control system unlike anything I've ever seen. Before an order even went to the factory, a team of engineers studied the intended application—if they weren't certain the system would do what the customer needed, the order stopped cold and didn't go to the factory. There was no appeal. This team reported to the vice president of engineering, but even he had no authority to overrule their decision. The order went forward only once modified to the engineers' satisfaction.

Before leaving the factory, the system was checked for flaws again, and the supervisor in charge had to sign a form stating that everything in the system was right. Then the system went to the quality assurance department, where it was inspected again. If the QA inspector found anything that didn't look right to him, the order didn't ship until the issue was corrected. The system could have passed every test and met every point on the inspection checklist, but if the QA inspector wasn't completely confident that everything was right, the order stopped cold. No one could overrule the QA inspector except the CEO, who never once did it.

Anytime an order, no matter how small, didn't pass QA, a report was immediately sent to the CEO's office. Very soon, the vice president of manufacturing was called in to explain why his department had passed on an imperfect system. I sat in on a few of these meetings. They weren't pleasant. Michael Cesaro, Drexelbrook's vice president of manufacturing, once told me, "I'd rather have root canal surgery than a meeting with the boss about a quality problem." I never saw the subsequent meetings between the VP of manufacturing and the supervisor who erroneously signed off, but I have no doubt they were most unpleasant as well.

The result was a corporate culture where everyone was obsessed with quality, from the CEO to the factory workers. And it was phenomenally successful. Drexelbrook operated for over forty years before being sold. It installed thousands of control systems for managing the deadliest chemicals known to man all over the world. And not one person ever died, or was even injured, because one of its systems failed.

The effort to maintain that system was expensive, not just in terms of money, but in terms of mental energy. As ingenious as it was, it worked perfectly only because we focused on it every single day. Anything that took even a small amount of money or attention away from the system, including drug testing, would have put our customers in jeopardy.

Drexelbrook's management is not alone in opposing drug testing. Tom Peters, whose *In Search of Excellence* is one of the most successful and influential management books of all time, calls drug testing "a solution in search of a problem" that "will cause much more harm than good."

Employers as Police

Some proponents of drug testing say that employers should test even if testing doesn't help the company. They say employers should test to be good citizens and help law enforcement win the War on Drugs.

But the legal system isn't asking for employers' help. In the chorus of voices calling for drug testing, the voice of judges is conspicuous in its absence. That's because judges don't want drug users to lose their jobs. Judges know that having a job is the foundation of avoiding crime and that when someone loses their job, he or she is much more likely to get in trouble with the law. It's not hard to see why. If you were trying to find a way to get someone in trouble, you couldn't come up with anything better than making them hang out on street corners all day.

Judges bend over backward to help people keep their jobs, even when they've been convicted of a crime. Judges put people on probation with the condition that they go to work every day; if they don't, they go to jail. Judges allow some people convicted of a crime to serve their sentence on weekends so they can keep working. Even convicts serving time in the penitentiary are often given work release if they aren't a danger to the community. Former Philadelphia criminal court judge Marvin Halbert once told me that he wished employers would stick to their work and let him handle drug enforcement.

Having employers play policeman is a scary idea. If employers are going to help enforce drug laws, it follows that they should help enforce other laws too. Do you want your boss to tell you to bring in your income tax returns every April so the company accountants can make sure you aren't cheating on your taxes? This may sound ridiculous (and it is), but it's no different from making employees pee in a jar to help enforce drug laws. Turning every employer in America into an unofficial police department would cause far more harm than good.

Hair Testing

As bad as urine testing is, there are other forms of drug testing that are even worse. Hair testing has recently gained in popularity. Virtually every substance you ingest eventually enters your bloodstream, leading to microscopic traces in your hair. By cutting a small amount of your hair and analyzing it, a laboratory can learn a great deal about what has entered your body.

Yet qualified experts agree that it is unreliable. The Department of Health and Human Services, which is responsible for the federal certification program, considers hair testing so unreliable that employers are prohibited from using it in federally funded testing programs.

The problem with hair testing is that it cannot distinguish between drug by-products inside the hair, which come from ingestion, and drugs on the surface of the hair, which may be entirely innocent. Merely being in a room where someone has recently smoked marijuana leaves enough residue on your hair to make you fail the test. J. Michael Walsh, who designed and ran the federal drug testing program under President Reagan and is widely known for his tough stance on drug use, calls hair testing "an unreliable technology that costs innocent people their jobs."

Patrick Forte was an exceptionally diligent New York City police officer. Not satisfied with patrolling the grounds around city housing projects, Forte walked project stairwells and hallways at night, a dangerous practice that many officers avoided. Forte's devotion to duty got him fired. Walking around in areas where people had smoked crack left residue on his hair and caused him to test positive for cocaine. Forte had taken multiple urine tests and passed them all with flying colors. No one doubted that failing the hair test was due to being exposed to crack fumes on the job. His sergeant called Forte one of his best officers and said the test was wrong. But it did no good; the police commissioner's office ordered that Forte be fired anyway. His record followed him wherever he went. Forte never worked in law enforcement again.

What About Pilots?

It's true that an airline, let alone the FAA, can't wait for a pilot to make a mistake to learn that he has a problem. But drug testing isn't the answer. It's impossible to test every pilot every day. And, even if you could, it wouldn't help. Urine tests don't provide any information about a person's current condition. Not until the substance has been metabolized will the test be positive. If pilots snorted ten lines of cocaine and then took a urine test, they would pass. They'd be unfit to fly. They might well kill a planeload of people. But they would pass the urine test. If the same pilots took the urine test two days later, when they were sober and able to fly safely, they would fail the drug test.

What kind of a safety test gives pilots the green light to fly when they're stoned out of their minds and fails people who are sober and can fly safely? It would be funny if it weren't so serious. And even if a urine test could reveal a pilot's current condition (which it can't), it still wouldn't help. It takes hours, or days, to take the urine sample to the laboratory and get the results. If a pilot climbs into the cockpit of a 747 under the influence of drugs, we would see the tragic results on the evening news long before the test results came back.

The right answer is to test pilots for what really counts: their ability to fly a plane safely. The reason stoned pilots are dangerous is that their vision, reflexes, coordination, and judgment are impaired. Systems are available that will test whether someone is impaired in this way in a matter of minutes. The technology for these systems was originally developed by NASA for testing astronauts. Taking the test is a lot like playing a video game. You take the test a few times to establish a baseline. Every time you take the test later, the system compares your score to the baseline. If your score is significantly lower than the baseline, the system reports that you are impaired.

Being impaired doesn't mean that you're under the influence of drugs. The list of things that could make you impaired is almost endless. You could have a hangover. You could be sleep-deprived from being up all night with a sick child. You could be ill. You could be going through a divorce or other traumatic experience. No matter what the reason, an impairment system will determine that something is wrong before you hurt yourself or someone else.

Because it detects that someone is unsafe from any source, and does it immediately, impairment testing provides real safety protection.

Impairment testing systems have been around for almost twenty years. They have been used in a wide variety of safety-sensitive jobs, including firefighting, construction, transportation, manufacturing, police, and emergency medical response. A detailed study of impairment testing found that every employer who used it considered it a success. For 82 percent of these companies, safety improved after the introduction of impairment testing and 87 percent found it superior to urine testing.

Despite its impressive results, impairment testing is still used by relatively few employers. The companies marketing impairment testing bear some of the responsibility. These companies believed the old adage that "if you build a better mousetrap, the world will beat a path to your door." Many firms thought that because their product was so much better at increasing safety than urine testing, employers would embrace it right away. When sales didn't materialize as quickly as planned, they didn't have the financial reserves to keep going.

But almost everyone involved shares the responsibility. Line supervisors frequently objected to impairment testing because they didn't want a machine taking over one of their job functions. Workers sometimes objected because they were afraid of failing the test when they came in with a hangover or were exhausted from being up with a sick child. Or they didn't want to change the bad habits that affected their performance. Nor did they trust their employers to handle the results fairly—they were afraid they would be disciplined if they came to work impaired through no fault of their own.

The most fundamental problem of all is that employers and the public don't know what to do with the information impairment testing provides. In reality, millions of Americans show up for work every day at least slightly impaired. A few are stoned or drunk or have hangovers. Far more are simply ill, most often from a cold or the flu. Some of these people are also drowsy from the medication they have taken. Others are fatigued, due to everything from insomnia to working a second job to make ends meet. Still others are going through an emotional trauma, such as a divorce or the death of a loved one.

Employers wouldn't know what to do if they had to acknowledge that so many employees were impaired. There aren't enough desk jobs to accommodate them all. Sending so many people home with full pay would be a financial burden. And sending them home without pay would cause a rebellion, since most of the people penalized have done nothing wrong.

Employers could compensate by calibrating their impairment testing systems so that it takes a higher degree of impairment to fail. But this scares the company lawyers. If a bus driver had an accident and it turned out that he was impaired and was allowed to drive only because the testing system had been changed, a jury might well find the company negligent and award a huge penalty to the people who were injured.

So, in the end, most employers in safety-sensitive jobs decided to keep making employees pee in a bottle, knowing they were ignoring the real safety problems.

Employers Turn Away from Testing

Fortunately, this is one problem that is diminishing in scope. The number of employers with a drug testing program increased steadily from 1987 (21 percent) to 1996 (81 percent). But then the tide turned. Drug testing began to decrease, and by 2004 only 62 percent of employers tested. Moreover, many employers that still tested cut back on their programs because they found that the promised increases in safety and productivity never materialized. Random testing dropped dramatically. Most employers today conduct only pre-employment tests. But this is little comfort to the people whose privacy is invaded and lose their jobs because of laboratory mistakes in the thousands of companies that still conduct random testing.

8

Brave New Workplace: Genetic Discrimination

> **Progress is a storekeeper. You can have anything you like, but you have to pay the price. You can have the airplane, but the birds will lose their wonder and the clouds will smell of gasoline.**
>
> —CLARENCE DARROW IN *INHERIT THE WIND*

Terri Sergeant lost her job because of her genes. Sergeant worked as an office manager for an insurance broker in South Carolina. Because her family had a history of alpha-1 antitrypsin deficiency, a rare genetic disease, Sergeant had herself tested to see if she carried the gene. She tested positive. When she began a program to help prevent the disease, her boss fired her, despite outstanding performance reviews.

A Georgetown University survey of people with genes linked to diseases such as breast cancer and Alzheimer's found that 13 percent had been fired when their employer learned that they carried the gene.

This would have been hard to imagine not long ago. Humanity has known about the existence of genes only since the nineteenth century, when Austrian scientist Gregor Mendel proved through experiments with plants that certain traits were inherited from generation to generation. But neither Mendel nor anyone else knew anything about how this worked for another hundred years. It wasn't until 1953 that Francis Crick, James Watson, and Maurice Wilkins deduced the double helix structure of the DNA molecule, for which they won the Nobel Prize. Fifty years later, in 2003, the Human Genome Project (a $3 billion federal research program) had mapped all 25,000 human genes.

One of the things we learned along the way is that certain genes are linked to specific diseases. In extreme cases, your fate is genetically predetermined. For example, if you carry the gene linked to Huntington's disease, you are certain to get the disease and you will die from it. There is no prevention, no cure, and no escape. In most cases, the connection is more complex and the outcome less certain. Most women who carry one of the two genes linked to breast cancer will not develop the disease, and most women who develop breast cancer do not carry either gene. In every case but Huntington's, whether a person contracts a disease linked to genetics depends on many factors, including the substances to which the individual is exposed. Carrying the gene only increases the probability of getting the disease. In some cases, the increase in risk is low. In others, it is much higher. Women who carry the genes linked to breast cancer are almost twice as likely to develop the disease as those who do not.

Scientists have also identified the specific genes that are linked to Alzheimer's, ALS (Lou Gehrig's disease), cystic fibrosis, hemophilia, sickle-cell anemia, Tay-Sachs, and dozens of other conditions. Technology has been developed that can determine the presence or absence of many of these genes in particular individuals.

In the long run, this knowledge could be a blessing. The first step to finding a cure for any disease is learning about how it is contracted. These genetic breakthroughs could represent first steps toward finding cures for breast cancer, Alzheimer's, and other diseases. Bill Frist, who in addition to being the former Republican Senate majority leader is a physician, says that "research involving the human genome may open doors to new methods of medical diagnoses and treatment—to a new practice of medicine involving drugs designed for specific genes, genetically engineered organs for use in transplants, or even the ability for preventative care based in large part on genetic testing."

I watched my mother die of Alzheimer's four years ago. It was one of the most horrible things I've ever seen. Every year millions of women die of breast cancer, slowly and painfully. Many are younger women who are still raising children. If genetic technology can help save future generations from this suffering, it will be one of the greatest developments in human history. But the immediate implications of these genetic breakthroughs are anything but benevolent.

In most industrial countries, medical care is publicly financed. In the United States, the elderly get access to doctors and hospitals through Medicare. Poor people get health care (of a lower quality) through Medicaid or the SCHIP program that provides health insurance for children of low-income families. But most of us get our medical insurance through our employers.

This creates a problem. Since our employers are paying for much of our medical care, they have a financial incentive to keep the costs down. In recent years, the cost of medical care has soared. The cost of medical care in the United States has increased 800 percent since 1980. We now spend $2.4 *trillion* a year on health care. This cost consumes almost a fifth (17 percent) of our gross domestic product. We spend over four times as much money on medical care as we spend on national defense. And it's getting worse. Health care costs are increasing twice as fast as inflation. Over the next ten years, medical costs are projected to reach $4.3 trillion.

Employers have been hit hard by these escalating costs. Over the last ten years, the annual premium that a health insurer charges an employer has more than doubled. It now costs an employer $12,700 a year to provide health insurance for an employee with a family and $4,700 for a single employee. And, just as the total cost of medical care is rising twice as fast as inflation, so is the cost to employers. Employers sometimes cry wolf about costs (such as the cost of improving environmental protection or workplace safety). But the unending increase in medical costs is a real problem.

Employers have tried everything they can think of to reduce these costs. They put employees into HMOs and other managed care plans. Health care experts had high hopes for these different approaches. But costs kept going up. Employers increased co-payments (the amount the employee must pay to participate in the medical plan). The average co-pay is now $3,400 a year, up 12 percent in a single year. This has imposed hardship on many families. A Harvard University study found that 50 percent of all bankruptcy filings were the result of medical debt. But it didn't solve employers' problems; medical costs are simply too high to shift any more to employees.

Some employers began to think, "If we can't hold down the cost of health care, let's hire people who will need less of it." One result of this new idea was the attempt to control employees' private lives, as we've seen earlier—penalizing employees for smoking or drinking off-duty or for being fat. Another was medical discrimination. Employers can save money by finding out which applicants are likely to have high medical costs and not hiring them (even if they are the best qualified).

This wasn't hard to do. Many companies were already conducting pre-employment medical evaluations. One goal of such programs was to determine whether an employee was capable of performing the job for which he or she had been tentatively selected. Many people have medical conditions or limitations that are invisible or that they don't know about. For example, many people's backs are incapable of accepting the strain of a job that involves heavy lifting. If one of these people is hired for the wrong job, they could be seriously injured and the employer would get stuck with a workers' compensation claim for both their medical bills and their lost wages while they were out of work.

The other primary goal of pre-employment physicals is to avoid paying for medical care for "pre-existing conditions." Many health insurance plans cover only injuries and illnesses that occur after you become insured. If you have the condition before you get the insurance, it isn't covered. In practice, however, it can be difficult to determine when a person acquired a disease that was diagnosed in the present. If you had the condition when you were hired, but the employer can't prove it, they have to pay. By conducting a pre-employment medical examination, the company can determine which medical conditions you had the day you started work. Today, the majority of companies (68 percent) have a pre-employment medical evaluation program.

The same medical exam that can meet these two goals can also tell an employer whether you have a medical condition that could lead to high medical bills. The list of conditions that might cost you a job is almost endless: diabetes, heart trouble, psychiatric conditions, even pregnancy (the Washington, D.C., police department was caught conducting secret pregnancy tests of all female applicants and rejecting those who tested positive). With the breakthroughs in genetic technology, finding out whether you carry a gene linked to an expensive disease can be added to the list. The American Management Association surveyed its members and found that 6 percent conducted some form of genetic testing. This indicates that about eight thousand employers were prying into employees' and applicants' genes. (The AMA later reported that these numbers may have been too high because some employers didn't understand what constituted a genetic test.)

Secret Testing

You'd never know if your employer (or prospective employer) was conducting genetic tests. The same blood sample that is taken for other purposes can also be used to conduct genetic tests. Lawrence Berkeley National Laboratory, a division of the University of California, secretly tested job applicants for the gene linked to sickle-cell anemia and refused to hire anyone who tested positive.

Employers can acquire genetic information about you even without conducting tests. Many people today whose family history includes genetically linked illnesses choose to be tested privately for purposes such as family planning. The results of these tests become part of a person's permanent medical record in their physician's office (and often with their insurer and in other places as well). When employers conduct pre-employment physicals, a company doctor reviews the applicant's medical file. This review is not limited to information that is job-related; the entire medical file is reviewed. This unlimited review alone is an invasion of privacy. A prospective employer has every right to know if you are medically capable of doing the job. But why should your prospective employer know about your psychiatric history, gynecological problem, or STDs?

Worse yet, this unlimited medical review could cost you the job. If you have tested positive for a gene linked to disease, you may not be hired. You won't know why, either; employers are not required to inform applicants why they aren't hired, and virtually none do.

Family history is also part of most medical records. Even if you've never had a genetic test, your family medical history can reveal a lot about your probable genetics. For example, if you are a woman whose grandmother and mother both died of breast cancer, there is a good chance that you carry the gene too. While it's only a probability, that's often all it takes to lose a job, especially when you're only one of many applicants.

In theory, you could avoid this problem by asking your doctor to leave out any genetic information when she sends your file to a prospective employer. But in practice it's very difficult. Your doctor (or at least a nurse) would have to go through your entire file, page by page, and take out the few that contained genetic information. This would be very time-consuming. If the records are computerized, the problem is even more difficult. Medical records software isn't currently designed to include or exclude parts of a file. Your doctor would have to hire a computer technician to leave something out of the record. You have nothing to lose by asking your doctor to do this, but don't expect her to comply.

Sometimes employers get genetic information without collecting any medical information. Christine DeMark, a sales representative with an exemplary record, was fired when her employer found out that she was at risk for Huntington's disease. She was never tested for the Huntington's gene. She didn't know herself whether she had it. But a relative came down with Huntington's (something her employer knew nothing about). DeMark was concerned she might have the gene too and was considering being tested.

A positive test result for the Huntington's disease gene is a death sentence. It's a great relief to those who test negative to learn they are safe. But it is traumatic for those who test positive. Many develop serious depression and other psychological problems. Before you can be tested for the Huntington's gene, you are required to have counseling to make sure you are emotionally prepared. DeMark mentioned to a coworker that she had begun the counseling. Her "friend" then told their employer, who immediately fired her.

In the near future, genetic testing might become much more frequent. Few employers test today because the cost is high. But as the cost of testing drops, genetic testing may become standard practice in corporate America, just like drug testing.

Betting Your Life

The harm is more than economic. Many people who know they are at risk of carrying a disease-linked gene decide not to be tested because they are afraid employers will find out and discriminate against them. Not getting tested may eliminate this risk, but it creates others. With some diseases, if you know you are at increased risk because of your genes, there are steps you can take to reduce that risk.

For example, women who carry BRCA1 or BRCA2 (the genes linked to breast cancer) can have mammograms more often, or even have a mastectomy if they want to be completely safe at any price. When people decide not to be tested to avoid discrimination, they generally don't take these defensive measures. And who can blame them? It's hard enough to undergo a double mastectomy when you know you are at risk of breast cancer. Why would any woman do it without knowing for certain that she is at risk? Even the expense of having mammograms more often might be too much for many people when they don't know for sure that it's necessary.

Not taking precautions because you don't know whether you are at risk is dangerous. Detecting breast cancer early greatly increases your chances of survival. Many people are dead today because they didn't take precautions. If they had been able to be tested without fear of discrimination, many of them would be alive today.

Ironically, no money is really saved by genetic testing. It's all just passing the buck. The people who were going to develop breast cancer or Alzheimer's still get sick, they still need medical care, and the care still needs to be paid for. The only change is that the employee loses the chance to have a career while they are still healthy and our society loses the benefit of the contribution they could have made. Even employers may not save money. If the people who contract genetic diseases don't have medical insurance, the government will ultimately have to pay for their care. This means that taxes go up for everyone, including employers.

Good Genetic Testing

Some genetic testing helps employees. One example is genetic monitoring. The tests described so far are screening tests. Their purpose is to keep people who might have high medical costs off the employer's payroll. Genetic monitoring is different. Instead of keeping people out of the workplace, it's designed to help keep people in the workplace healthy. Some jobs create the risk of harmful genetic mutations.

For example, exposure to X-rays can cause genetic mutations in sperm cells that make men unable to have children. In most cases, the harm is either invisible or there are no symptoms until it's too late. Employers in this situation often conduct regular genetic tests of workers in order to detect these mutations quickly so the employee can be moved to a different job before he is irreparably harmed.

The other type of potentially helpful genetic monitoring involves people who are at elevated risk of harm in specific jobs. When an employer refuses to hire someone because they carry the gene linked to cancer or other disease, no one is any safer. The applicant isn't any less likely to get sick because the employer didn't hire them; they are no more likely to get cancer if they work in an office than if they work in a grocery store. The employer just shifted the cost of their care to someone else.

But there is at least one case in which people with a particular gene are at higher risk in some jobs than in others. Exposure to beryllium (a rare mineral used in the aerospace industry) is hazardous to everyone. Breathing the dust that is created when beryllium is machined can cause chronic beryllium disease (CBD), a serious lung disease that disables and often kills its victims. But there are a handful of people who carry a gene that puts them at much greater risk of getting CBD if they breathe the dust than others. These people are much safer working in any other job. Testing potential employees for this gene before placing them in a beryllium factory can save lives.

Who Decides?

What happens when a genetic test shows that an employee will be safer by not taking a particular job? It may sound like a simple question, but it isn't. Everyone would choose to be safer if it were free, but it almost never is. There are almost always trade-offs. What if the employer doesn't have another job to offer an employee who is beginning to test positively for genetic mutations? Or, what if the employer does have another job, but it doesn't pay as well?

What if the alternative to working in a beryllium plant is flipping hamburgers for minimum wage, and you have children?

These are agonizing choices. In a perfect world, no one would have to make them. But in our world people do. The least an employer can do in such cases is let employees decide for themselves whether to take the risk. The beryllium industry testing program works this way. The testing is conducted by the University of Pennsylvania Medical School; the employer is not involved. Test results are given directly to the employee, who then decides whether to take the job or not. The employer never learns the results.

Some employers, however, automatically keep people at increased risk out of the job in question. These employers probably mean well, but their paternalism is misplaced. If the employee needs the job badly enough to take the risk, keeping them out of the job only makes their difficult situation even worse. Competent adults should be able to decide for themselves which risks to take.

Employers argue that the employee isn't taking all the risk. If the employee takes (or keeps) the risky job and becomes ill, the employer will have to pay his or her workers' compensation claim. Under workers' comp, employers must pay the medical expenses and lost wages (up to a cap) of anyone who is injured or becomes sick on the job. The employer doesn't even have to be negligent—the accident can even be the employee's fault. The rule is simple: if the employee is hurt on the job, the employer pays.

This isn't unfair to employers. While employees automatically get compensation when they're hurt on the job, they receive compensation only for their medical expenses and lost pay (and sometimes an additional payment for a permanent injury such as loss of a limb). But workers can't sue their employer. Even if the employee can prove that her employer was negligent, she can't sue for emotional distress. The legal bargain is that, in exchange for giving all injured employees some compensation, employees who were hurt by their employer's negligence give up most of their claim.

In the genetic testing context, this means that if a worker stays on the job after she knows she is at risk, the employer will have to pay workers' compensation if she gets sick. Employers argue, "It's not fair to make us pay when we didn't want the employee to take the risk. If the employee wants the advantages of the risky job, she should bear the loss if things go wrong." There is something to this argument. In principle, the person who wants to take the risk should be the one who accepts the consequences (good or bad).

Here, both the employer and employee lose if the employee gets sick because of her job. But the employee loses much more. She loses her health, or even her life. The employer's risk is much lower. In a situation like this, the fairest course is to let the person who has the most to lose make the decision.

Legal Protection

Amazingly, genetic discrimination has been legal for many years. The primary defense against discrimination based on medical conditions is the Americans with Disabilities Act, a federal law passed in 1990. The ADA protects people with disabilities from job discrimination. If your disability keeps you from being able to do a job, an employer can turn you down. But if your disability doesn't interfere with your job performance, employers can't consider it when deciding whether to hire you.

In some areas, the ADA goes quite far. Employers are prohibited from asking applicants about their medical condition and how it might affect their ability to do the job until they make a "conditional job offer." This means that the applicant has the job as long as the pre-employment medical evaluation doesn't turn up something that interferes with her ability to do the job. This prohibition is absolute. If an employer is hiring people to build a skyscraper, which requires walking down steel girders twelve inches wide while one hundred feet in the air and an applicant shows up for his interview in a wheelchair, the employer is not allowed to ask, "How can you do this job in a wheelchair?" It has to go through the entire hiring process and can address the issue only in the pre-employment medical evaluation.

The ADA's Limitations

To be protected by the ADA, you must qualify as "disabled." To be disabled, you must be "significantly limited in a major life activity." People who carry a gene linked to a disease, but have not been diagnosed with the disease itself, are not limited in any way. They are at increased risk of becoming disabled in the future, but they aren't disabled now. Since they aren't disabled, they aren't protected.

There is another provision in the ADA that many people had hoped would help. The law protects people who are "perceived to be disabled." Without that clause, it would be illegal to refuse to hire someone because they had diabetes, but legal for an employer to turn someone down erroneously thought to have diabetes.

Disability rights advocates argued that the "perceived disability" clause in the ADA should prevent genetic discrimination. Some felt so strongly about this that they wouldn't support legislation specifically banning genetic discrimination because such bills implied that the ADA didn't apply. Others, including NWI, argued that this was a false hope. An employer who won't hire a person with a genetic marker doesn't "perceive" them to be disabled today. The employer knows perfectly well that their abilities aren't limited in any way. The employer doesn't want to hire them because they are likely to cost the company more for medical care in the future.

This debate became contentious. Finally, the Supreme Court settled it. The Court didn't rule on the coverage of genetics under the ADA. It issued a series of other decisions that construed the act very narrowly. For example, in the *Sutton* case, the Court held that employees who were legally blind weren't disabled because they could see when they wore glasses. The writing was now on the wall. A Court that would say a blind person wasn't disabled would never accept our "perceived disability" theory. Clearly, new laws were needed.

The Road to Reform

The road to reform started in 1990. Several members of Congress asked the congressional Office of Technology Assessment (OTA) to consider the legal and social implications of the emerging breakthroughs in genetics. (OTA was a remarkable institution, a think tank working for Congress that did not depend on private funders for support. Their only incentive was to tell Congress what they really thought. Unfortunately, when the Republicans gained control of Congress in 1994, part of their "Contract with America" was to eliminate "unnecessary" government agencies. Congress refused to provide future funding for OTA and it closed in 1995.)

OTA assembled a diverse group of experts to tackle the issue, including Mark Rothstein (now head of the Institute for Bioethics, Health Policy, and Law at the University of Louisville), a nationally recognized leader in this field; Thomas Murray, the esteemed bioethicist from the Hastings Center; and Bruce Karrh, the head of occupational safety and health at DuPont. I had the privilege of being part of this group as the representative of the ACLU, to provide a civil rights perspective.

Even at this early stage, anyone with vision could see the potential consequences for genetic discrimination and the need for new legal protection. The OTA report called on Congress to take action to prevent these problems. Unfortunately, Congress ignored the findings. As elected representatives of the citizens of their state or congressional district, members of Congress spend most of their time (when they're not campaigning or fund-raising) working on the problems that currently concern their constituents. It's hard for a congressman to spend much time working on a problem that doesn't exist yet and that his or her constituents don't know or care about.

States Take the Lead

Some states acted to fill this void. Twenty-nine states enacted laws to prevent genetic discrimination by employers. Many of these laws, however, are seriously flawed. For example, Florida's statute applies only to genetic information acquired through laboratory testing; it does not cover genetic information obtained through review of medical records. Florida employers can acquire genetic information from applicants' medical files and use it against them without violating the law. Other states, such as Texas, ban genetic discrimination, but do not prevent employers from acquiring genetic information. Such laws are of very little use. Given the amount of money an employer might save by refusing to hire someone who carries the "wrong" gene, many will discriminate where they have genetic information even if it is technically illegal. Rothstein explains that employers who function as health insurers will act like conventional health insurers and exclude people who are medical risks because of the cost.

As more and more states began to enact laws, Congress began to pay attention. This is a common pattern in employment law. Many other federal statutes, such as the Polygraph Protection Act (which generally outlaws polygraphs in the private sector), have started in the states. Trickle-up politics, unlike trickle-down economics, is frequently effective.

In 1995, the Genetic Information Nondiscrimination Act (GINA) was introduced into Congress. GINA's prohibitions against employer use of genetic information were very broad. Not only were employers not allowed to make decisions on the basis of genetic information, they were not even allowed to acquire it. We knew that it would be impossible for employers to have the information and not use it. Employers couldn't even get genetic information voluntarily. The word "voluntary" has a tortured history in employment law. Courts frequently hold that an employee who "agrees" to something as a condition of staying employed has done so voluntarily. We were determined to avoid this problem with GINA.

GINA also improved upon many state laws with its definition of genetic information. Most state laws, such as those in New Jersey and New York, prohibit only genetic *testing*. This protects employees only if the employer gets genetic information through a medical test. If the employer sees an employee's medical records and finds that he tested positive for a genetic mutation, or learns that the employee is at risk from his family history, there is no protection. Florida's law specifically states that it covers only DNA testing. In Florida your employer can even learn about your genes by administering a medical test itself, as long as it isn't a DNA test. For example, some forms of heart disease are genetically linked. If an employer finds out about your predisposition to heart disease by testing your cholesterol level, you have no protection. GINA solves this problem by providing that employers cannot acquire genetic *information*. To be doubly safe, GINA specifically includes family history in its definition of genetic information.

Insurance

GINA also prohibits genetic discrimination by health insurers. Insurers' incentives to discriminate against people with genes that put them at increased risk are even stronger than those of employers. If an employer finds that the most qualified applicant for an open job has a disease-linked gene, the money it saves by hiring someone else is offset by the cost of losing the best employee and taking someone not quite as qualified. For at least some employees, the employer would find the risk of hiring the person worth taking.

For health insurers, on the other hand, there is no benefit to insuring someone at increased risk—it's pure loss. Insurance companies have armies of actuaries whose job it is to measure the risk of providing insurance in a wide variety of situations so that the company can avoid issuing policies where it will lose money. Asking a health insurance company not to deny coverage to people who are at elevated risk is like asking a bird not to sing. To address this problem, GINA included a provision prohibiting discrimination by health insurers.

Health insurers argued that this would be a hardship because they would be forced to provide insurance at rates that leave them in the red. This isn't correct. If a single insurance company started to provide policies to people whose genes put them at elevated risk, it would lose money. If it tried to avoid the loss by raising premiums, its customers would go somewhere else. But if all insurers are forced to take this step together, they could increase rates enough to cover the increased costs without losing business. This is exactly what would happen with GINA enacted.

Life Insurance

A person who knows she has the gene linked to breast cancer or Alzheimer's can't use this knowledge to take advantage of her health insurance company. She can't decide to get sick, just to get the health insurance payment. And why would anyone want to? All health insurance does is pay your medical bills. You can't make a profit. You can't decide to make health care cost more. You can't, in the jargon of insurance, "game the system."

This isn't true of life insurance. Life insurance payments are not based on how much money you need, they're based on how big a policy you buy. If you buy a $1 million life insurance policy and then die, your family gets a million dollars, even if you weren't working and your death represents no financial loss to your family.

This means that if you know that you're at increased risk, you can (and logically should) buy a larger policy. If I were a forty-five-year-old man who had just learned I had the Huntington's gene, I'd take out a second mortgage on my home and buy a $10 million life insurance policy, knowing I'll be dead in five years and my family will be wealthy. This truly would be an unfair burden on insurance companies, which is why GINA doesn't cover life insurance.

But people at risk of an early death because of their genetics still need life insurance. In fact, they are the people who need it the most. Just because they shouldn't be able to buy a multimillion-dollar policy at standard rates doesn't mean they should be barred from buying life insurance altogether. Nor should they be essentially forced not to have children because they can't buy insurance to give them financial security.

One approach that might work is to handle life insurance for people at genetic risk the same way we handle car insurance for drivers with bad records. It's important for everyone that all drivers are insured. If not, people hurt because an uninsured driver made a mistake would have no way to get compensation. But insurance companies don't want to issue policies to people who have speeding tickets and accidents on their record, or, if they are willing to write a policy, offer it at a price no one can afford.

We generally handle this dilemma by creating risk pools (groups of drivers that no one wants to insure) and requiring each insurance company to write policies on some of them. The drivers in the risk pool pay a higher premium than other drivers, but not as high as the insurance company would like to charge. Insurers generally lose money on these policies, but no insurer is hurt badly because they have to take only a limited number of bad drivers and because they are allowed to charge a slightly higher premium.

The same approach might work with genetics. People who need life insurance (which isn't everyone) would be allowed to buy a basic policy for a slightly higher, but still affordable, premium. Each insurance company would be required to issue its share of these policies.

Employer Reaction

The employers' community vigorously opposed GINA and testified against it in a series of congressional hearings that began in 1998 and continued until 2005. As usual, they didn't oppose GINA in theory; saying that genetic discrimination is a legitimate practice would have made them look like ogres in the eyes of Congress and the public. Instead, they said they supported GINA in principle but then followed with a series of alleged defects in the bill.

Some of their arguments were legitimate. For example, the Americans with Disabilities Act (ADA) is enforced through a set of procedures that begins with a complaint to the Equal Employment Opportunity Commission (the federal agency that enforces antidiscrimination laws). There are prescribed maximum penalties, which vary with the size of the employer. The maximum penalty for the largest employers is $300,000. GINA, however, allowed employees to skip the EEOC and go directly to court, where a jury could award virtually unlimited damages. Employers argued that GINA's enforcement system and penalties should be consistent with other disability discrimination. NWI agreed that the employers had a point and eventually convinced GINA's other supporters to change the bill.

Another legitimate employer argument was that they could be penalized because an employee gave them information they hadn't asked for. As discussed earlier in this chapter, GINA provides that employers are prohibited not just from using genetic information but from even acquiring genetic information. Harold Coxson, a spokesperson for the business community, brought up the situation in which an employer notices that his secretary looks like something is bothering her and asks, "Is anything wrong?" and she replies, "My mother was just diagnosed with breast cancer." Although the employer hasn't done anything wrong, he has acquired genetic information, which is a violation. In response, we inserted a provision in GINA that said employers were not liable for accidental acquisition.

Other employer objections, however, were nonsense. The one we heard most often was "There aren't very many cases of genetic discrimination. We don't need a law against it." To begin with, this was factually incorrect. While most employers didn't practice genetic discrimination, the ones that did affected a significant number of people. The surveys discussed earlier in this chapter, including those conducted by the employer community's own organization (the American Management Association), consistently showed that thousands of people had already been the victims of genetic discrimination.

Even had employers been right on the facts, they would still have been wrong to oppose GINA. Their approach would require Congress to sit around doing nothing until the problem became so severe that legislation was essential. Congress is frequently slow to recognize and act on problems. The privacy problems of employer surveillance and attempts to control employees' private lives have been with us for twenty years now and Congress still hasn't acted. They should be praised, not criticized, on the rare occasions when they react quickly.

Getting Through Congress

Genius is one percent inspiration and ninety-nine percent perspiration.

—THOMAS EDISON

GINA didn't pass the first time it was introduced, or the second. In fact, it took thirteen years before Congress finally passed GINA in May of 2008. Some of the delay resulted from the need to educate members of Congress about the issue. Some of it came from Congress's need to deal with other issues, some of which were truly more pressing. But most of the delay came from the resistance of the employer and insurance lobbies, which spent a small fortune fighting GINA.

There was no magic moment at which GINA won Congress's support. The Coalition for Genetic Fairness, a group of 250 organizations working together to support GINA, just kept working. (NWI's legal director, Jeremy Gruber, was the driving force in organizing the Coalition.) GINA's sponsors, led by Ted Kennedy in the Senate and Louise Slaughter in the House, also continued chipping away at the issue. Every session of Congress, the Coalition picked up a few more supporters. By 2003, GINA had unanimous support in the Senate and passed ninety-five to zero.

But the House of Representatives wouldn't go along. The House majority leader during this time was the infamous Tom "The Hammer" DeLay, a right-wing extremist from Texas who opposed teaching evolution in public schools and blamed it for causing the Columbine massacre. The Coalition kept working, convincing one representative at a time that genetic discrimination was wrong. Eventually, enough Republicans supported GINA that it passed the House in 2008. A great deal of credit for this belongs to Congresswoman Judith Biggert, a Republican who became a cosponsor in 2005 and convinced many of her Republican colleagues to join her. It also helped that Congressman DeLay's campaign against immorality came to an abrupt end in 2006 when he was forced to leave office after having been indicted for violating campaign finance laws.

But just when it seemed as though we had won, we were blindsided. Because the House passed GINA in a different session of Congress than the Senate had, the bill had to go back to the Senate. Everyone involved thought this was a formality, since the Senate had now passed GINA twice, the second time by one hundred to zero. But then Senator Tom Coburn, a Republican from Oklahoma, put a hold on the bill. This was a complete surprise. Coburn had never voiced any objection to GINA in all the years it had been in the Senate; he had even voted for it initially. But Coburn has a well-earned reputation as an obstructionist. His Senate nickname is "Dr. No." He has put holds on more bills than any other senator.

We thought at first that Coburn might be sincerely concerned about some provision of GINA. It isn't rare for a member of Congress to pay little attention to a bill until it comes close to passing and then find a problem that hadn't previously been noticed. Kennedy and other sponsors met with Coburn to ask about his concern. It turned out he didn't have any; he was just being an obstructionist. Coburn doesn't like any bill that protects civil rights and uses holds to try to kill them, even when he has no specific objection to the bill.

This put Senate majority leader Harry Reid in a difficult position. He could bring the bill up for a vote. GINA would pass, but only after Coburn used every trick in the book to stall, starting with a filibuster. Under Senate rules, any senator can speak on a bill as long as he or she wants; there is literally no time limit. The only way to stop a filibuster is with a cloture motion that requires sixty votes to pass. Since there weren't that many Democrats in the Senate at that time, Coburn could have spoken until he literally passed out from exhaustion. Time is a precious commodity in Congress; an extra week spent on GINA would mean that the Senate would lose the opportunity to deal with at least one other important issue. No one wanted this. Even Coburn's Republican colleagues pleaded with him to remove the hold.

Eventually, the pressure on Coburn became too great and he had to throw in the towel. In order to avoid admitting that he had just been acting as a spoiler, he asked for a meaningless change in the bill in exchange. Reid and Kennedy agreed to change the bill so that employers could be sued only in their capacity as employers, not as insurers. Many employers act as their own insurers, at least in part. They self-insure the cost of employee health care up to a point and get a policy from an insurance company for any amount over the limit. If an employer discriminates against an employee when it is acting as an insurer, it should be liable, just like any other insurer. In practice, however, this means little or nothing. There will be few, if any, cases where an employer discriminates against an employee only as an insurer; they will also be liable as an employer. Because of this, Reid and Kennedy agreed to the change to get GINA passed.

On April 24, 2008, GINA passed the Senate without dissent. On May 21, President Bush signed it into law.

Why Bush signed GINA is something of a mystery. As president, he had never been a champion of civil rights, to put it mildly. He issued a Statement of Administrative Support for GINA while it was pending but never lifted a finger to help get it enacted. Perhaps he realized that if he vetoed GINA, the Senate would override his veto, adding one more embarrassment to his final days in office. Or perhaps he believed that genetic discrimination was wrong.

Unsolved Problems

It ain't over 'til it's over.

—YOGI BERRA

You might think that with the passage of GINA, the threat of genetic discrimination is over, but it isn't. Federal laws have regulations explaining in more detail, and in plainer English, what the law says to provide guidance to those who are affected. The Equal Employment Opportunity Commission is now writing the regulations implementing GINA. This represents one more opportunity for GINA's opponents to take away your rights. Interested parties are allowed to provide the EEOC with suggested language interpreting a statute. The business lobby submitted suggested language that waters down the protection against discrimination. NWI and other GINA supporters submitted stronger language that captures what Congress really intended.

For example, employers are lobbying the EEOC to define the unintended acquisition of genetic information described earlier as including any question where the answer is not specifically genetic. This would allow employers to ask general medical questions, knowing that the answer might well contain genetic information, without violating the law. For example, an employer could continue to ask for a prospective employee's entire medical record during the pre-employment medical evaluation. Since the question isn't specifically asking for genetic information, it would be legal under this interpretation. This could virtually eliminate GINA's rule against employer acquisition of genetic information.

Both sides will lobby the EEOC staff, trying to persuade them that their suggested language is the best. The recent change in administrations helps this situation, since the new president gets to appoint the next commissioner of the EEOC. But we still have to fight to keep from losing what it took so long to win.

There are also problems concerning how employers will comply with the new law. When employers conduct pre-employment medical evaluations, a standard part of the process is reviewing the file from your personal physician.

Because medical records are confidential, you have to sign a consent form giving your physician permission to give the file to your prospective employer. (Technically, you don't have to sign the consent form, but you won't get the job if you don't.) Today, employers use a "blanket" waiver form that authorizes the doctor to turn over the entire file.

Under GINA, employers are not allowed to acquire genetic information, even with the employee's consent. If the regulations are written properly, employers will be required to modify their consent forms to exclude genetic information. The form should now say in effect, "Give us the entire medical record except for any information that is related to the applicant's genes."

But what's going to happen in real doctors' offices when they start receiving these new forms? There is no section in your current medical file called "genetic information." Your family medical history, DNA test results, and other genetic information are in one big file in no particular order. To comply with the new consent form, your doctor (or nurse) is going to have to go through the file one page at a time to find the pages that can't be disclosed. It is hard to imagine a busy physician's office taking the time for this labor-intensive process every time a routine medical information request comes in from an employer.

The obvious answer is to make medical records electronic. This is something doctors are already beginning to do to make their practices more efficient. Software could be developed that would allow doctors to quickly isolate specific types of information from a patient's complete medical record. One benefit of such software would be that it could identify genetic information and delete it from the record that is sent to an employer.

Unfortunately, such software does not yet exist, but this could change. The federal Department of Health and Human Services has a proposal to provide funding for the development of this kind of software. The proposal went nowhere under the Bush administration. Perhaps the Obama administration will give it a higher priority.

There is also the possibility that a market for such software will drive its development. Once GINA goes into effect, employers should begin to instruct physicians not to include genetic information in the medical files they send. If physicians follow this instruction, they will spend a great deal of expensive time sorting out the records. If they don't follow it, and send an entire file that includes genetic information, they will have violated their legal obligation to keep medical information confidential and will be liable. If a patient loses a job because her physician disclosed genetic information to the employer without consent, it might very well result in damages being paid. So physicians have an economic incentive to purchase appropriate medical record software—and that demand could lead to its development.

The Ones Left Behind

Even if GINA provides perfect protection for people who carry disease-linked genes, there is still work to be done. The law should be that no one can be denied a job because of a medical condition that does not interfere with his or her ability to perform that job. Even with both GINA and the ADA, our laws fall short.

To qualify for protection under the ADA, you must be "disabled." You don't have to be in a wheelchair to be considered disabled, but your condition must "substantially limit your ability to perform a major life activity." There are many medical conditions that might lead an employer not to hire you that are not serious enough to qualify as disabilities under the ADA. Among the conditions that courts have found not to be disabilities are hypertension, strabismus (crossed eyes), psoriasis, and poor eyesight. The biggest gap in the law concerns weight.

Under the ADA, being too heavy is a disability if you are "morbidly obese." Essentially, this means that you are so fat that you can't move around like other people. If you're just twenty pounds overweight, you aren't considered disabled. An employer can legally refuse to hire you because he thinks you're too fat. The only requirement is that the employer can't make weight-based hiring decisions in a discriminatory way. The airlines got in trouble by creating weight requirements for flight attendants (who were almost exclusively female at the time) but not for the other crew members. But discriminating against people the airline considered overweight would be legal if applied to the entire flight crew.

This happens all the time. To begin with, many of us don't like to be around fat people because we think they're ugly and don't want to look at them. In addition, employers are concerned about the cost of medical care for people who are overweight. According to the federal government's Centers for Disease Control, 30 percent of Americans are obese and are at increased risk of heart disease and many other medical conditions. The CDC also reports that obesity is rapidly overtaking smoking as the most expensive health care problem in America. With employers as concerned about health care costs as they are, these 59 million people are prime targets for employment discrimination.

The situation improved somewhat last year when Congress enacted the ADA Amendments Act to correct mistakes the courts had made in applying the original ADA. The biggest change was to overrule the *Sutton* case and require that the determination of whether a person is disabled "shall be made without regard to ameliorative effects of mitigating measures." In other words, if someone is disabled without medical aid (such as glasses or a hearing aid), the fact that he is able to function normally with help doesn't change his legal status. The new act also tries to broaden the standard of disability to include more people. While these are both improvements, the fundamental flaws of the ADA still remain.

To achieve real equal opportunity in America, your health should affect your ability to get a job only if it interferes with your ability to do it. We have a long way to go to reach this goal.

Future Issues

Employers and insurers are not the only organizations with a financial stake in your long-term health. Banks might want to know about your genetics before giving you a thirty-year mortgage loan. And there are other uses of genetic information on the horizon that are positively frightening. Scientists are beginning to discover genes that are linked to behavior (rather than any physical or mental condition). We are just beginning to see the implications of this new field of behavioral genetics.

One area where behavioral genetics is likely to play a part is the criminal justice system. Studies have discovered a link between the gene known as MAOA and violent behavior. While most people who carry MAOA are no more violent than anyone else, men who carry this gene and have been abused as children are almost four times as likely to be convicted of a violent crime as the population in general.

While I doubt that we'll ever see a world like the one in *Minority Report,* a film where people are imprisoned for crimes they have not yet committed, I would not be the least surprised to see people who are convicted of crimes that carry MAOA receive harsher punishment than other people who commit the same offense.

Judges have a great deal of discretion in sentencing a person who has been convicted of a crime. For virtually all crimes, the law gives judges the option of imposing a jail term. This is true even of minor offenses, such as disorderly conduct. For felonies such as robbery or assault, most states allow the judge to impose a sentence of up to twenty years.

Judges are not supposed to impose the maximum sentence in each case. They are supposed to look at all the relevant circumstances and decide what the appropriate penalty is. When a person is convicted of a crime of any significance, the judge usually orders a pre-sentence investigation. An investigator prepares a report telling the judge everything that might be relevant, including whether the person has committed prior offenses, whether he has a job, what his family situation is like, and a great deal more.

There are two questions foremost in the judge's mind when deciding on a sentence. The first is "How serious was this offense?" All robberies are serious, but some are more serious than others. A person who robs a bank with a loaded gun probably deserves more jail time than a person who punched someone and took their wallet.

The other key question is "How likely is this person to commit another offense in the future?" If the person convicted has never broken the law before, has a steady job, and supports a spouse and children, the judge will probably conclude that there is little risk that he will break the law again and will give him a light sentence, maybe even probation.

But if the person has several prior offenses, doesn't have a job, and spends most of his time hanging out in bars, the judge will probably conclude that this person is highly likely to commit another offense. In this case, the judge wants to get him off the street for as long as possible to protect the community.

If the initial findings about MAOA are substantiated by additional evidence and become generally accepted in the scientific community, carrying the MAOA gene (combined with childhood abuse) could be one of the strongest predictors of the likelihood of future offenses available to judges. Under these circumstances, it would be very surprising if they did not use it in sentencing.

They Can't Put You in Jail for What You're Thinking—Can They?

In an extreme case, carrying MAOA could turn into a life sentence. Many states today evaluate sexual offenders who have completed their prison sentences. If the evaluation concludes that the person has not changed, that whatever kink in his soul caused him to commit a sexual offense is still there, the offender stays locked up, even though he has served every day of his sentence. Since whatever is wrong with him may never be cured, he will be locked up for the rest of his life, not for what he did, but for what he is likely to do in the future. The United States Supreme Court has upheld this practice.

With this precedent, what is to stop the government from not only giving someone with MAOA the longest possible sentence, but, if the offense was serious, keeping him in jail forever because his genetics makes him likely to commit crimes in the future?

9

Plant Closings

Honesty is the best policy.

—BENJAMIN FRANKLIN

Employees are like mushrooms.
Keep them in the dark and feed them bullshit.

—ANONYMOUS

Sam Vaughn went to work on May 23, 2008, just as he had every day for the previous fifteen years. Vaughn drove a truck for Jevic Corporation, in Delanco, New Jersey. While he was driving his route that day, his wife called to tell him a letter had just arrived from the company telling him he was fired. The other 1,200 employees at Jevic had received the same letter.

The terminations were effective immediately. As of five o'clock that day, Jevic was going out of business and the employees were out of work.

Not only did Vaughn and his coworkers lose their paychecks, they lost their medical benefits as well. As of midnight that day, all medical benefits were canceled. Vaughn suffered from bladder cancer and was in the middle of a course of chemotherapy. But there was no exception for illnesses the workers had contracted prior to the shutdown, or even for treatments that had already begun. As of that day, Jevic would no longer pay a single medical bill.

Vaughn was stunned. He knew that the company had been hurt by rising fuel costs, but no one had told him they were even thinking of going out of business. "Why didn't they tell me?" Vaughn asked. "If they had just let me know what was happening, I would have started looking for another job. Now

I don't know how I'm going to keep my home or if I'll be able to continue my cancer treatment." The last time I tried to contact Vaughn, his wife, Libby, told me he was dead.

No one knows when Jevic made the decision to close the plant. But management clearly knew before they told the employees. Just the process of writing the letter, producing 1,200 copies, and mailing one to each employee took several days. Planning the shutdown, contacting their lawyers, and drawing up the papers for bankruptcy court took even longer. Jevic's management planned and carried out the shutdown while deliberately keeping employees in the dark.

Jevic is far from the only company that pulled the rug out from under its employees this way. Nationwide, nearly two million people lose their jobs every year due to plant closings and mass layoffs. Sometimes this is unavoidable. Companies don't last forever. Typewriter companies have gone out of business because of the development of personal computers. Some types of jobs disappear thanks to technological advancements—the number of jobs answering business telephones has plummeted with the rise of voice mail. Change can't be prevented, even though it is often painful for the individuals affected.

But that's no reason for employers not to be honest. There is no excuse for keeping employees in the dark when the company is in trouble and thinking about shutting down. Actually making the decision, and still withholding that information from employees, is even worse.

Yet that's what many employers do. Studies by the General Accounting Office consistently show that the majority of employers provide employees with little or no advance notice when closing a plant or conducting a layoff.

Some employers do more than just keep employees in the dark about bad news; they lie to employees about the company's situation. Dave Gorman, Jevic's CEO, visited the facility in Illinois where Chris Kowalski worked and told employees that the recent shutdowns of some of the company's other terminals had solved its financial problem and that Jevic would be "open for a long time to come." Six weeks later it shut down completely.

Not being honest with employees is more than morally wrong—it has practical consequences. If you know you're going to lose your job in the near future, you can start looking for a new job now. With advance notice, other family members can start looking for a job too. People can avoid major expenditures, like buying a new car or taking a vacation, if they know hard times are coming. Or they can just cut back on small expenses, like going out to dinner. With advance notice, losing your job is a hardship, but it's manageable.

Without advance notice, losing your job is a catastrophe. Millions of us live from paycheck to paycheck. If we don't get paid, we can't pay our bills. Employees who lose their jobs without warning frequently go bankrupt. They lose their homes, their cars, and their medical care. Tasha Blocker, one of Vaughn's coworkers in New Jersey and a single mother with two young children, couldn't pay her rent when her paycheck disappeared overnight. She and her children became homeless. Some families are literally destroyed; the stress and conflict causes many workers and their spouses to divorce, with permanent harm to the children.

It isn't just the employees and their families who suffer when a plant closes without warning. Often the entire community suffers. Quaker Fabric was one of the largest employers in Fall River, Massachusetts. Quaker shut its doors without notice on July 2, 2007, while the employees were on their July 4th holiday, throwing nine hundred people out of work. The city's income plummeted when ex-Quaker employees couldn't pay their real estate taxes. Local businesses closed because most of their customers couldn't afford to buy anything. But while revenue went down, the city's expenses went up because nine hundred families suddenly needed more government assistance. "It's a nightmare," said Mayor Edward Lambert. "This would have been a blow to the city under the best of circumstances. But to have it happen overnight, with no chance to prepare, is a catastrophe."

Employers inflict all this harm to make money. If the company tells employees that it is shutting down in two months, those employees will start looking for other jobs. As employees find new jobs, the employer will begin to have difficulty getting all the work done and will make less money (or lose more money than it's already losing). In order to reduce the company's financial difficulties, management deliberately keeps employees in the dark, knowing that it will destroy many of their lives.

Reform

In 1988, Congress responded to this problem by passing the Worker Adjustment and Retraining Notification Act (WARN). WARN requires employers to give employees sixty days' notice when they intend to close a plant or conduct a mass layoff. It also requires employers to notify local government. Getting the bill passed wasn't easy. The first time WARN passed (as part of a trade bill), President Reagan vetoed it. But Senator Howard Metzenbaum reintroduced WARN as a stand-alone bill and crusaded for it. Congress passed WARN again, this time by a veto-proof majority that included Senate majority leader Robert Dole. This time Reagan saw the writing on the wall and allowed it to become law (without his signature).

The creation of WARN was considered a great achievement. Advocates of employment rights hailed the act, saying that it would ease the hardship on employees when plants are closed. The business community took a more negative view, saying that the new law would hurt American competitiveness by making it harder for employers to adapt to changing markets. President Reagan called it "a ticking time bomb." But all agreed that WARN was a historic development.

Before long, however, questions began to arise about WARN's effectiveness. These questions prompted the U.S. General Accounting Office to conduct a study. The GAO examined the practices of every employer that conducted a plant closing or mass layoff in 2001. Its findings were astounding. Despite the existence of the federal law, the vast majority of employees who lost their jobs in plant closings or mass layoffs were not receiving notice. In fact, only 9 percent of the employees WARN was intended to help were being told about layoffs and closings in advance. Not only was WARN a failure, but it wasn't clear that it had even made a difference. The number of employers providing notice of shutdowns and layoffs wasn't significantly higher than it was before WARN was passed.

How WARN Failed

How could such a well-intentioned law have such little impact? Part of the answer lies in the fine print. Many employment laws contain an exception for small businesses, largely because of the sense that "mom and pop" businesses shouldn't be regulated by the government and would have trouble complying with the regulations and forms involved. The WARN Act followed this pattern. But instead of setting the minimum number of employees at fifteen (as in most antidiscrimination laws), or even twenty-five (as in the Americans with Disabilities Act), the minimum number of employees a company must have to be covered by WARN is one hundred. A company with fewer than one hundred employees has no legal obligations under the act.

This threshold means that for most employers, WARN doesn't exist. The vast majority of employers (over 98 percent) have fewer than 100 employees. From the perspective of the total number of employees covered, the situation is slightly better. Only about two-thirds (64 percent) of all employees work for these small companies. But for this 64 percent of all working Americans, the WARN Act offers no protection at all.

Even if the company is large enough to be covered, a plant closing or layoff it conducts may not be covered. To fall under WARN, at least 33 percent of the employees at a facility must lose their jobs.* If only 32 percent are fired, WARN does not apply. In addition, at least fifty people total must be fired. If only forty-nine people are let go, WARN does not apply, even if this is more than 33 percent of the workforce. This takes another huge bite out of the act. Of the 8,350 plant closings and layoffs studied by the GAO, only 24 percent were covered by the act. Three-quarters (76 percent) of the people who lost their jobs had no rights under the act.

To make matters worse, most employers that are covered simply violate the law. GAO found that a large majority of employers (64 percent) that were required to issue WARN notices to employees failed to do so. This leaves only 9 percent of employers giving notice.

* If five hundred or more people are fired, WARN applies, even if this is less than 33 percent of the workforce.

And even when employees get the required notice, it often isn't enough. The average length of unemployment in the United States is about four months. This means that only about half of employees who receive the sixty days' notice under WARN are able to find another job before their paychecks run out. The rest still have to find a way to support themselves and their family with no income.

No Justice in Court

Few of the employees whose rights under WARN had been violated got any justice in court. To begin with, very few of them filed a case. The GAO found that only sixty-eight reported decisions under the WARN Act over a five-year period. One reason so few employees went to court is because they can't afford to. Litigation has become an expensive process and WARN Act cases are more complicated and difficult than most. But an employee who wins her case gets only two months' back pay. Even if the employee gave the entire recovery to her lawyer, it wouldn't begin to cover the legal fees.

The only way employees can afford to bring cases under the WARN Act is with a class action suit. In a class action, a large number of people with identical claims file a single lawsuit. Because only a small fraction of the legal fees come from each individual plaintiff, smaller claims can be brought.

But not all lawyers know how to handle a class action or have a large enough staff to handle all the paperwork. And not all law firms big enough to handle a class action understand the WARN Act. There are only a handful of firms in the entire country that bring WARN Act class actions. Unless the employees who were fired without notice are lucky enough to find one of these firms, they will probably never see the inside of a courtroom.

And even if they find one of these lawyers, the employees may still be out of luck. Class actions are enormously time-consuming. The lawyers who bring them work for at least a year and spend hundreds of hours on each case. Unless the number of employees is large enough, even a class action may be financially impossible. According to Jack Raisner, a WARN Act litigator at Outten & Golden, the leading employees' rights law firm in the country,

"Unless there are at least a hundred employees in the group, we can't afford to bring the case. We'd like to help everyone, but it just isn't possible."

In theory, this problem is addressed by allowing the employees' lawyer to be awarded legal fees at the end of the case. But this isn't mandatory; it's up to the discretion of the judge. Many judges find reasons not to award attorney's fees or to reduce them. Even if the judge wants to do the right thing, the company's assets may not be worth enough to pay the lawyers. And if the plaintiffs' lawyer doesn't win the case, she gets nothing. The combined effect of these limitations is that lawyers can't afford to take small WARN Act cases.

Even the few employees who find a law firm capable of handling their case usually get shortchanged. Employers don't usually shut plants that are making money. Many of the companies that conduct shutdowns without giving notice are bankrupt. A federal bankruptcy judge determines how to divide the remaining assets among the many to whom the company owes money. There's never enough to go around, so employees get less than the sixty days' pay to which they're entitled. They don't even come first. There is a complicated series of rules regarding who gets highest priority when a bankrupt company's assets are divided.

You might think that employees would come first, because they need the money most. But that's not the way it works. With most loans, the party borrowing the money simply promises to pay it back. If they don't, the party who lent the money has to sue them for breach of contract. Then, if they win, they have to send a local government employee (usually from the sheriff's office) to find an asset that belongs to the debtor that they can take.

Some lenders, however, want more than this. In exchange for the loan, they want the debtor to agree that they can seize a particular asset without going to court first. The classic example is a home mortgage. The borrower has to sign not only a written promise to repay the loan (called a promissory note) but also an agreement that if the loan isn't repaid, the bank can automatically seize the house. If the borrower goes bankrupt, the bank gets the house before the remaining assets are divided up among all the creditors. Sometimes banks require employers to sign such an agreement when making a loan. This makes it a "secured creditor" who gets precedence over other creditors, including employees to whom the company owes money.

No Help from the Government

Traditionally, people whose cases are too small to litigate get help from the government. For example, if your employer treated you unfairly because of your race or gender but your losses aren't large enough to go to court, the Equal Employment Opportunity Commission (EEOC) can help you. The EEOC is a federal agency whose mission is to help people who have been discriminated against on the job. Because its funding comes from Congress, not from the people it represents, the EEOC can and does take cases that are too small for a private lawyer. Other agencies, both federal and state, exist to help people whose rights under other employment laws have been violated.

But there is no agency to help people with small claims under the WARN Act. When Congress wrote WARN, the only enforcement mechanism it provided was a private lawsuit. People with small claims were left out in the cold.

Reform

Because the WARN Act has been so ineffective, concerned members of Congress are trying to strengthen it. Senator Sherrod Brown of Ohio introduced legislation to strengthen the WARN Act. This bill, called FOREWARN, would reduce the total number of employees required for a company to be covered from one hundred to fifty. It would also reduce the minimum number of employees laid off for WARN to apply from fifty to twenty-five. These changes would bring the majority of employers (and the majority of layoffs) under the law for the first time.

FOREWARN also increases the penalties for violating the law. Under WARN, the only penalty for an employer that doesn't give employees sixty days' notice is to give them sixty days' pay. An employer that decides to close a plant knows that it probably won't get sued if it breaks the law and that the only cost if it gets caught is the compensation it would have had to give the employees anyway during the sixty-day notice period. An employer that obeys the law gets the benefit of the work that gets done during this period by the employees who don't find other jobs before the closing. But an employer that breaks the law doesn't lose production by having employees quit before the closing.

In addition, employers who break the law generally don't have to pay employees everything they owe them because there won't be enough money to go around after the company closes and files for bankruptcy. Overall, there is little or no penalty for breaking the law today. FOREWARN raises the penalties to two days' pay for each day of notice employees don't receive. This gives employers a financial incentive to obey the law.

Finally, FOREWARN increases the amount of notice employers must give to ninety days. This gives workers whose employers obey the law an extra month to find another job.

The combined effect of raising the required notice to ninety days and doubling the penalty to two days' pay for each day of notice not given makes the damages that a court can award three times higher than today. This would make it financially possible for attorneys to file many cases they must turn down today, increasing the number of people whose rights are violated who will receive justice in court.

Currently, political support for FOREWARN is modest, even among Democrats. This is understandable; there are many workplace injustices that have been ignored for too long and Congress can't deal with all of them at once. But it's also a mistake. The number of people who lose their job in a plant closing or layoff is over one million per year. Many workplace injustices don't affect this many people. The harm done by failure to give notice is also huge, more than in most other situations. This may not make WARN Act reform the most important workplace issue facing Congress, but it surely deserves a higher priority than it is currently receiving. Much more support will be needed for it to pass. Until then, millions of Americans will be kept in the dark about plant closings and layoffs.

10

There's Strength in Numbers: The Right to Organize

> Employers are prohibited from interfering with the right to organize and strike.
>
> —NATIONAL LABOR RELATIONS ACT

> Any competent management attorney can keep most companies from becoming unionized.
>
> —PETER SAUCIER, MANAGEMENT ATTORNEY

Most of the time, there isn't much you can do when your boss violates your human rights. There is no law to protect you, and you have no bargaining position. If you don't like your company's policy, it can easily replace you with someone who does (or at least won't object).

Employees who belong to unions do much better. In the classic work *What Do Unions Do?*, Harvard economists Richard Freeman and James Medoff found that workers who belong to unions consistently make more money than comparable workers in nonunion companies. While it varies from industry to industry and company to company, workers in unions make about 20 percent more. They also get better benefits. Most union members (79 percent) have access to company-paid health care. Only 52 percent of nonunion workers receive this benefit. Union members are also almost twice as likely to have pension plans (86 percent) as nonunion workers (51 percent). Low-income, women, and minority workers gain the most from union membership. In fact, union membership does more than any other single factor to lift people out of poverty.

Not only do they get higher pay and benefits, but union members' rights are often protected. For example, virtually every union contract in the country includes a provision requiring the company to have "just cause" to terminate an employee. This allows the company to fire you for doing your job badly, or breaking company rules. But your boss can't fire you because he doesn't like your politics or because you smoke or drink off the job. It also means your boss can't fire you because of a personality conflict. If the issue is job performance, the employer has to show that your job performance really is deficient and that you have been given notice of your shortcomings and an opportunity to fix them.

The "just cause" provision can also protect you from other abuses. For example, if the company attempted to require all employees to turn in DNA samples (something the military is already doing), you could probably refuse without losing your job. Refusing to participate in such an unreasonable program isn't "just cause" for termination. Several arbitrators have forced employers to rehire employees who refused to participate in unfair drug testing programs.

Union contracts (called collective bargaining agreements) are enforced through arbitration. If you (and your union) believe the company has violated your rights under the agreement, an arbitrator selected by both the company and the union will resolve the dispute. The union provides you with a representative and pays all the costs.

Arbitrators are generally fair to both the employee and the company. Those who consistently favor one side stop getting cases. Studies indicate that employees win about 50 percent of arbitrations.

Employers don't agree to these provisions because they like them. They agree because they have to. If management is unwilling to negotiate a contract that is acceptable to the majority of employees, the employees have the right to strike. The company can easily replace you, but it can't easily replace its entire workforce. This is the leverage that makes collective bargaining successful.

Union Criticisms

Many criticisms have been directed at unions, mostly by employer groups pretending to be neutral public interest organizations. Among the most common is that the higher wages and benefits received by union members drive up the prices the public must pay. This is only partly true. There are many ways employers can pay more money to their workers. One is to pay slightly less inflated compensation to management. The average CEO at one of America's five hundred largest companies made $14.2 million in 2007, more than three hundred times as much as the average employee. Some make a great deal more. Steve Jobs, president of Apple Inc., made more than $600 million in a single year.

Defenders of this system say that such astronomical pay is necessary to attract top-performing CEOs, and that a good one is worth a multimillion-dollar salary. There is something to this. If the CEO of the smallest company in the *Fortune* 1000 (Helmerich & Payne, with $1.6 billion a year in sales) could increase profits as a percentage of sales by 2 percent (say from 7 percent to 9 percent), she would have added $32 million to the bottom line. If I were a shareholder in this company, I'd gladly pay her several million dollars a year. But you have to wonder if Steve Jobs would quit and go to work somewhere else if he were paid only $100 million a year. What's more, executive compensation isn't determined by corporate performance. When Harvard economics professor Lucian Bebchuk and Berkeley law professor Jesse Fried compared the compensation of top executives with the bottom line of the companies they ran, they found that executive compensation had little or nothing to do with company performance. Numerous other studies have reached the same conclusion. In 2008, the American economy was in the worst nosedive since the Great Depression of 1929. Corporate profits were down. But a study reported on CNN found that the majority of companies (61 percent) are planning to give their executives raises in 2009.

You can even get rich by running a company into the ground. Lehman Brothers CEO Richard Fuld was paid $27 million a year before the company went bankrupt. Citigroup CEO Charles Prince received a $25 million paycheck while the company's value fell over 90 percent. Bear Stearns CEO James Cayne got $34 million for managing the company out of existence.

American executive compensation is also out of step with the rest of the world. American CEOs make at least twice what the heads of comparable companies in Europe and Asia receive. The presidents of Honda and Toyota, which have gone from nowhere to the world's leading automotive companies in a generation, are paid less than the presidents of General Motors and Ford, who were last heard from when flying to Washington in their private jets to beg for a government handout.

Why Do Executives Get Paid So Much?

One reason this happens is that corporate boards of directors have little incentive to avoid overpaying the CEO. Corporate directors are usually paid a flat fee for each year of service, sometimes with additional compensation for attending board meetings. (Being a corporate director is the only job I know of where you can not show up for work and still get paid.) The fees are usually substantial, especially at large companies. According to the Corporate Library, a watchdog group, half of the directors at publicly held companies make more than $100,000 per year. Even for those at the top of the corporate food chain, this is good pay for a few days' work.

You don't make any more money as a director by going over the reports closely and asking hard questions. All it does is make the board meeting longer and make you less likely to be invited to stay on the board the next year. In theory, directors work for the shareholders, who elect the board periodically. The reality is that most shareholders have no idea who the members of the board of directors are or what kind of a job they are doing. The real decisions are made by the nominating committee of the board. If you make everyone's life easy, you get renominated. If you make things difficult by asking hard questions, you probably won't get nominated again and you lose $100,000. In many companies, the CEO has a great deal of input on who is nominated. Questioning the CEO's big raise in these companies is like submitting your resignation from the board. What's more, if you're dropped from one board for being a "troublemaker," there's a good chance it will keep you off other boards. It's a small world at the top of corporate America, and the people there talk to each other.

I have served on a few corporate boards and seen this dynamic in action. In one company, the head of the compensation committee walked into a board of directors meeting and said we should raise the CEO's pay to a certain amount because traditionally the company had paid its CEO at the seventy-fifth percentile (halfway between the middle and the top) of a list of CEOs at comparable companies. We received no written materials. Neither I nor the other directors knew what the other companies were and how comparable they were. In addition, the company had been doing poorly. Sales were flat and profits almost nonexistent. When I spoke up and said that we might need to spend a little time going over this, the head of the compensation committee gave me a glare that would have melted the polar icecap. The other directors either looked out the window or glanced at me as if I were slightly daft. I said nothing more and the CEO got his raise. It took less time than ordering dinner in a restaurant.

You don't have to be a card-carrying Naderite to be angry about executive compensation. Warren Buffett, the chief executive of Berkshire Hathaway and the most prominent investor in the country, says the game is rigged. Buffett is especially hard on compensation consultants who recommend big raises for CEOs. If they don't, they're not likely to be rehired. Buffett calls these consultants "Ratchet, Ratchet, and Bingo." Countrywide, one of the country's largest mortgage companies (and a major promoter of subprime mortgages), hired compensation consultant Ross Zimmerman for advice on the compensation package of its CEO, Angelo Mozilo. Considering that Mozilo was being paid almost $40 million a year, this seemed like a good idea. Zimmerman concluded that the performance targets in the contract that affected the size of Mozilo's bonus were too easy to meet. Instead of following Zimmerman's advice, Countrywide hired another consultant, Towers Perrin, to give it the answer it wanted. Ultimately, Countrywide nearly went bankrupt and was taken over by Bank of America. Mozilo was charged with securities fraud by the SEC.

So if paying rank-and-file workers more means a few million less for the CEO, maybe that's not so bad.

Improving Efficiency

Another way for workers to get better pay and benefits without raising prices is to help make the company more productive. People often think that unions decrease efficiency, but the opposite is more often the case. One way unions make employers more productive is to reduce the number of unnecessary terminations. Most people who get fired probably have it coming. But sometimes individual supervisors make arbitrary decisions and fire workers when they shouldn't.

This hurts the company as well as the employee. Until someone new is hired to fill the position, the company (or at least the department) is short-handed and less work gets done. Then there is the expense of hiring someone new. The company needs to run advertisements about the job opening. Then the staff in HR needs to read all the résumés that come in. Next come the interviews, followed by reference checks.

Even when the new employee starts working there are costs. Depending upon the nature of the job, it will take the new employee anywhere from a couple of weeks to several months before he is completely up to speed. While some job skills are portable, like how to run a turret lathe or how to take out an appendix, every organization has its own way of doing things. Until the new employee learns the system and becomes completely integrated into the organization, he is not fully productive. Finally there is the cost of paying other employees to train the new one. Often these invisible costs are the highest of all. When I ran an HR department in my previous career, we estimated it cost us $15,000 (in today's dollars) to fill a rank-and-file position.

Finally, there is the cost of unemployment compensation. While UC law varies from state to state, the core concept is that everyone who loses her job receives temporary compensation to help pay the bills while she looks for a new one. It doesn't matter that the employer had legal grounds to fire you or even that you weren't doing a very good job, you still collect.

There are only two situations in which you are not entitled to compensation. The first is if you quit. The program is designed to help people who wanted to work but had their job taken away, not for people who decide to stop working. The other exception is if you are fired for what is commonly called "willful misconduct." This doesn't mean being five minutes late or forgetting to call in one time when you were sick. Willful misconduct means conduct that was so severe that the company had no real choice but to fire you, like assaulting a coworker or stealing company property. In such cases, you essentially fired yourself by your misconduct.

While the unemployment compensation check comes from the state government, the money generally comes from the employer. Every employer makes payments to the state UC fund. These payments are separate and in addition to other state taxes. The amount of money an employer pays is determined by its history. The more former employees of the company collect unemployment compensation, the more the employer has to pay.

In unionized companies, the employer needs a legitimate reason to fire an employee. If the employee thinks she's been fired unfairly, she can appeal to an arbitrator. When the termination was a mistake and the arbitrator gives the employee her job back, the company avoids the cost of hiring someone new. It also avoids the cost of unemployment compensation.

The corporation where I used to work changed the rules for terminations while I was there. Line managers no longer had the last word. If an employee thought he had been fired unfairly, he could appeal his boss's decision to the head of human resources and the general counsel (me). Unless both of us agreed that the termination was fair, the employee got his job back.

In the first year of the new system, the HR manager and I reversed 30 percent of the decisions to terminate. It was almost never because the employee hadn't done anything wrong. What happened was that the employee did something wrong, like coming to work late. His supervisor was unhappy, but didn't say anything about it, either because he was too busy or because he was uncomfortable with confrontations. Since the supervisor didn't say anything, the employee started to develop a pattern of coming in late. One day the employee came in late one too many times. It was the straw that broke the camel's back. The supervisor said, "I'm sick and tired of you being late. You're fired."

This wasn't the way discipline was supposed to be handled. Like many companies, we had a progressive discipline policy. The first time you did something wrong, you got an informal oral warning. The second time, it was a formal warning in writing. The third time, you were put on probation. If it happened again, you were fired. (If the offense was bad enough, the process could be accelerated by skipping steps.) The idea was that an employee should know that her performance is unacceptable and have a chance to improve it before she is fired. About half the time, when the HR manager and I rejected a termination, the manager went back to the employee and told him what he needed to do to keep his job, and the employee got the message. This saved the employee's job, saved the company money, and improved morale by showing all the employees that they would be treated fairly. After the first year, supervisors understood the rules and followed them. The HR manager and I almost never had to review a termination decision.

Unions can also improve productivity by giving workers a voice. This gives them more opportunity to make suggestions on how to do things better. It also gives workers more ability to complain about things that bother them and sometimes get changes. This improves morale and makes workers less likely to quit.

Union-Management Cooperation

One dramatic example of a union and management working together for everyone's benefit is the remarkable partnership between Parsons Engineering and the Service Employees' International Union (SEIU). Several years ago, a division of Parsons took over performing motor vehicle inspections for the state of New Jersey. The inspection operation had been hemorrhaging red ink for years and Parsons was under intense pressure to cut costs. The six hundred workers expected the worst: layoffs, salary cuts, and reduced benefits. But that's not what happened. Instead, the manager of the division, Jim Nobles, told the union that if they could work together to increase efficiency, everyone could keep their jobs and no one's pay or benefits would be cut. The union leaders were skeptical, but decided they had little to lose by giving it a try.

The results were spectacular. Before Parsons got involved, inspecting motor vehicles was one of the most dangerous jobs in the state. Just as the transition was beginning, a car in the middle of being inspected went out of control and pinned a worker against the wall, tearing off his leg. Management asked the workers what they thought should be done to make the job safer. The answer to this particular problem was simple. All they had to do was install rubber-coated concrete poles about three feet high in the right locations, and a runaway car would be stopped before it hurt anyone. This and other changes suggested primarily by the workers (who, after all, were most familiar with the job) completely eliminated workplace injuries. It has literally been years since a vehicle inspector has been hurt on the job. The company saved so much money on medical care, workers' compensation claims, and lost work time that it was able to keep every employee, with no pay cuts, and still make a profit. When NWI gave Parsons an award in 2007 for being a good employer, Maurice DeCandia, from SEIU, joined in the presentation.

Of course, there are cases where the higher pay that unions negotiate for workers has some effect on prices. But is this really so terrible? Millions of Americans pay a little more for products from corporations that do a good job of protecting the environment. We willingly pay a little more for coffee for which the pickers get better than starvation wages, or for sneakers we know weren't made by child labor in a sweatshop. What's so wrong with occasionally paying a little bit more for a product so that American workers receive fair wages and benefits?

Strikes, Violence, and Corruption

Some people dislike unions because they think unions conduct strikes that are at best disruptive and often violent or because they think union officials are corrupt. But the facts don't support these stereotypes. The number of strikes in the United States is very low. According to federal government figures, there were only twenty-one significant work-stoppages (involving at least one thousand employees) in 2007. The number decreased to fifteen in 2008. The majority of these strikes (60 percent) were over in ten days or less. Some of these stoppages weren't strikes, but lockouts (where the employer shuts the plant down and "locks out" the employees without pay, to put pressure on them to accept its position in contract negotiations).* The effect on the economy is almost too small to measure.

Union critics claim that strikes are violent. The Center for Union Facts claims to have a list of over nine thousand violent acts carried out by strikers

---

*Federal statistics do not distinguish between strikes and lockouts.

over the last thirty years. But they don't publish it. I wrote to the president of the organization and asked for a copy of the list, but I never got it. But among the ten crimes they list on their Web site is one where a striker threatened to hurt the dog of a nonstriker (a threat that was never carried out). If this makes their top ten list, I can only imagine what was involved in the ones they didn't publish. This doesn't mean that striking workers never commit violent acts. But the claim that workers on strike are more violent than other people just isn't true.

If their numbers don't seem to add up, perhaps it's because of where they're coming from. The Center for Union Facts presents itself as a broad coalition. On its Web site, under the FAQ entitled "So who are you guys, really?," the Center says that it is supported by "foundations, businesses, union members, and the general public." The truth is that the Center is funded and run by the business community, with a handful of workers and members of the public who don't like unions. The business community has as much right as everyone else to advocate for its point of view, but the least they can do is to be honest about it. Unions don't create phony organizations that claim to speak for employers. Employers shouldn't create phony organizations that claim to speak for workers or the public.

A study by the National Institute for Labor Relations found that there were only 238 criminal convictions stemming from labor disputes in the entire country over a twenty-five-year period. That equals fewer than ten convictions in the entire country over a year's time. You're at more risk of a violent assault walking down the tree-lined streets of Princeton, New Jersey (where I live), than of being hurt in a labor dispute.

The real figures on corruption are no more impressive. The United States Department of Labor listed six cases of labor racketeering in its semiannual report to Congress in 2006. Of the six cases, four involved misconduct by employer executives, not by union officials, such as Peter Wong (who controlled Pacific Group Medical Association) pleading guilty to insurance fraud and money laundering charges. Only two of the cases involved misconduct by union officials. Both were serious matters, but two cases is not exactly a crime wave.

If you're looking for real corruption, look in the executive suite. Enron, led by former president George W. Bush's good friend Kenneth ("Kenny Boy")

Lay, perpetrated the largest act of theft in human history (at least until Bernie Madoff came along), defrauding employees and investors out of at least $40 billion. And Madoff was part of the business community, not a union official. Even a company of Enron's size couldn't pull off something this big alone. It got help from Merrill Lynch, Bank of America, and Arthur Andersen, among others. A list of the companies found to have violated criminal laws in the 1990s reads like a Who's Who of American business, including:

Hoffman–La Roche: $500 million fine for violating federal antitrust laws

Exxon: $125 million fine for violating environmental safety laws

Pfizer: $20 million fine for violating antitrust laws

Warner-Lambert: $10 million fine for violating food and drug laws

Georgia-Pacific: $5 million fine for tax evasion

Blue Cross Blue Shield of Illinois: $4 million fine for fraud

The scale of corporate wrongdoing dwarfs the wrongdoing done by unions. The simple truth is that unions are made up of people, just like every other organization in America. And, just like every other type of organization, unions have made some mistakes. But on the whole their record is no worse than any other organization, and considerably better than that of employers.

Employer Resistance

Employers have always hated unions. When employees first tried to organize in the nineteenth century, employers got courts to say that unions were criminal conspiracies and had the leaders thrown into jail. If that didn't work, employers hired private armies to attack workers who went on strike. Sometimes, the federal government sent the U.S. Army to break a strike.

In 1894, the workers at the Pullman Company, the country's largest manufacturer of railroad cars, went on strike after management cut wages by 28 percent. The union tried to talk to the owner, but he refused to speak to them. The company's owners went to the attorney general of the United States, Richard Olney, a former railroad official. Olney went to court and the judge, without holding a hearing, issued an injunction ordering the employees back to work. When they didn't comply, President Grover Cleveland sent U.S. troops into Chicago to break the strike, even though the governor of Illinois asked him not to. The troops fired into the striking workers, killing at least twenty-four of them.

The only legal action taken was against Eugene Debs, president of the union, who was convicted of contempt of court (for not calling off the strike). Debs served six months in a federal penitentiary.

When confronted with violence, striking employees often fought back. Bloody battles were fought in which over seven hundred people died, mostly strikers and members of their families. In the twentieth century, employers gradually turned to less violent, but equally successful, methods to keep employees from forming unions. Many employers required all employees to sign "yellow dog" contracts in which they promised, as a condition of employment, not to join a union. If that failed, employers shared lists of the names of all their employees who belonged to a union (or had tried to join one). Employers refused to hire anyone whose name appeared on the blacklist.

Employees responded by striking. In 1919 alone, four million workers representing 20 percent of the workforce went on strike. In 1921, the Boston police department went on strike. Looting swept the city, and stores like Filene's had to station armed guards to protect their property. Eight people were killed and seventy-one more were injured before the National Guard restored order.

Many were alarmed by the continuing industrial conflict. Some were concerned that the lower classes might rise up and seize power as had happened in Russia. It appeared that the United States was, in the words of historian Nell Painter, "standing at Armageddon." A growing consensus emerged that labor-management conflict needed to be regulated to protect the public interest. In 1935, the National Labor Relations Act was passed, giving employees the right to organize and strike through a process regulated by a new federal agency, the National Labor Relations Board.

Legal Protection

The right to join a union ought to be protected by the Constitution, as part of our right to freedom of association. But this right, like all other constitutional rights, applies only to the government. There is no right to freedom of association in the private sector.

The right to organize a union is protected by the National Labor Relations Act. Section 7 of the NLRA explicitly protects the right of employees to organize a union or engage in other "concerted activities" (i.e., working with other employees on issues of common concern).

In practice, however, the right to organize means very little, primarily because the penalties for violating the NLRA are so trivial. Unlike many other laws, the NLRA does not create a "private right of action." If your company fires you for trying to join a union, you cannot sue your employer in court and have your damages determined by a jury. Your remedy is to file a complaint with the National Labor Relations Board, a federal agency whose job is to enforce the NLRA. All the NLRB is authorized to do is offer you back your job and require the company to pay you the difference between what you managed to earn and what your old job would have paid during the time the case was pending. In practice, the average NLRB award is only about $5,000.

Ernest Duval worked in the King David nursing home in West Palm Beach, Florida. Despite an excellent work record, he was fired immediately after he started talking to other workers about forming a union. Management denied that he was fired for organizing, but the National Labor Relations Board, after conducting an investigation and holding a hearing, didn't believe the employer. It determined that Duval had been fired for trying to organize a union. Duval won, but it took five years for the Board to make a final decision, in part because management dragged its feet every step of the way. Duval had to get another job to support his family, and, because his pay at King David was so low, the pay at his new job was about the same. The Board awarded Duval a total of $1,797. While Duval won in theory, the real winner was his employer. They got rid of Duval, kept the union out, and got off with a slap on the wrist.

Other violations of the NLRA carry no penalty at all. Common practices include management's interrogating workers about their union sympathies, surveillance of workers' organizing activities, and threatening to retaliate against workers who vote for the union. Since these do not cost the workers any money, there is no penalty. All the Board does is tell the employer to stop. If the violations are extreme and numerous, the Board sometimes finds that a vote about unionizing which the employer won is invalid and requires another one. Since there is no union while the process is repeated, this, too, is an employer victory. In theory, the Board can find that the intimidation was so severe that a fair election is impossible and order the employer to bargain with the union. But the Board almost never exercises this authority.

Reinstatement also turns out to be of little help. An employee whom the employer has been forced to rehire is a marked man. It is only a matter of time before the employer will find some excuse to fire him that can't be proven to be retaliation. In the meantime, the employer makes his life as difficult as possible. Most employees who are reinstated because of an NLRB decision don't last a year. The benefits are so small that most people who are offered reinstatement turn it down and look for another job anyway.

Because the penalties are so small, it makes financial sense for employers to break the law. The National Labor Relations Board found employers involved in organizing campaigns nine thousand times in 2008 alone. This includes the 34 percent of employers who fired employees for trying to organize a union. Employees who belong to unions make about 20 percent more than nonunion employees in the same job. In a large company, this pay difference can amount to millions of dollars. Firing the employees who are leading the organizing drive not only disrupts the campaign, it intimidates enough other employees that the campaign fails. Paying a few thousand dollars in NLRB penalties is a small price to pay to keep wages and benefits down. Professor Matthew Finkin of the University of Illinois Law School concludes, "Purely from a cost-benefit perspective, an employer would be stupid to obey the law."

One-Sided Elections

Employers can also defeat organizing drives unfairly without breaking the law. The National Labor Relations Act provides for an election once 30 percent of the employees in a unit of the company sign cards saying they want to join a union. The election looks very much like a political election. Every worker casts a secret ballot indicating whether or not he or she wants to be represented by a union. If the majority of the employees voting say they want a union, then the union represents all the employees. If not, there is no union.

For an election to be fair, both sides have to have the opportunity to present their arguments to the voters. But that's not the way it works in union representation elections. Employers run campaigns to convince their employees that would be the envy of most politicians running for office. Employers hold "captive audience" meetings that all employees are required to attend. At these meetings, employers present a sales campaign against the union, and management invariably makes dire predictions about what will happen if employees unionize. Employees are told that the company may shut down or move its operations to another location if there is a union.

The intent and effect of these statements is to make employees afraid of joining the union. Technically, the employer cannot make threats, but it is allowed to make "predictions." Essentially, employers are allowed to make threats as long as they word them carefully. Management attorneys and anti-union consultants can easily teach employers to make threats without crossing the line. Supervisors follow up by pulling employees aside to ask how they feel about the union and twist their arms if they are thinking of voting "yes." Employees receive a barrage of antiunion letters and memos from management. Management's statements in the campaign can be misleading or even untrue. In political elections, the law allows candidates to say virtually anything they want and lets the voters decide what to believe. The same is true in union representation elections.

Meanwhile, the union has almost no access to the employees. Representatives of the union are not allowed onto company property to make their case. They can't even stand at the back door and try to talk to employees as they leave work. They have to stand on the street by the company's driveway in the futile hope that someone will stop her car and get out to talk to them. The only other thing the union can do is send information to the employees' homes. In a case called *Excelsior,* the NLRB ruled that the employer must give a list of the the the home addresses of the employees in the bargaining unit to the union. Employers have been known to drag their feet, not giving the list to the union until the election is half over, and play other games. But even if the employer follows the rule, the ability to communicate with people by snail mail isn't worth much, especially in today's world. When employers hold meetings, the union isn't allowed to attend.

Even the employees themselves are hamstrung if they want to talk about a union. The most efficient way for workers who want a union to spread the word is by e-mail. E-mail has become the predominant method of business communication, far surpassing the U.S. mail and even the telephone. Employers use e-mail to send antiunion messages. But the employer can block employees from sending pro-union e-mail.

The NLRB recently ruled in the *Register Guard* case that employers can ban union-related e-mail messages even when it allows employees to send personal messages unrelated to work. Employees are even restricted in their ability to speak to each other. Employers can ban employees from talking about the union, or even the issues that make them want one, during working hours. It can also restrict such discussions to nonworking areas, such as the cafeteria. You may be able to talk about politics, the weather, or baseball while you work, but you can't talk about a union. Employees can't even speak about unionizing at the meetings the company calls to discuss the issue. Any employee who speaks up and disagrees with the employer's antiunion spiel can be legally fired.

Professor Gordon Lafer of the University of Oregon says that NLRB elections "resemble what happens in rogue regimes abroad rather than anything we call American."

Teksid Aluminum in Dickson, Tennessee, is an example of how employers can exploit the NLRA's weaknesses. When employees started to organize, the leaders, Bobby Felts, Steve Forcum, and Gary Johnson, were fired. Another union supporter, Randy Crowell, was given a written warning for taking his asthmatic two-year-old son to the hospital, even though he notified his super-visor five hours before his shift started. Bobby Dickens forgot to take an inex-pensive file out of his back pocket when he left work and was fired for theft. In the face of such intimidation, the union lost the election. Two years later, the National Labor Relations Board ruled that the company's actions had been illegal. But it was too late. The employees had lost the fight and didn't want continue. The union withdrew.

Teksid Aluminum's actions aren't unusual. The National Labor Relations Board received 23,080 complaints in 2006 of employer violations of the right to organize. Over 8,500 of these complaints were found to be valid.

Even if the union wins the election, the fight isn't over. Management can appeal the decision to the NLRB. For the length of the appeal process, the company can act as if the union doesn't exist. This might be reasonable if the employer had strong evidence that the election was flawed in the union's favor. But even if the appeal is completely frivolous, the employer can legally act as though it won. Appeals within the NLRB, like appeals in court cases, take years to resolve. Even if the employer's appeal is completely unsuccessful, put-ting the union on ice for a year or two is frequently enough to kill it.

Labor Law "Reform"

Even these flimsy protections proved too much for the business community to tolerate. As soon as World War II was over and the Republicans had con-trol of Congress, the Taft-Hartley "reforms" of the NLRA were introduced. President Truman vetoed the bill, but his veto was overridden.

One of the most pernicious provisions of the Taft-Hartley Act was the authorization of state "right-to-work" laws. You might think that such legisla-tion would have something to do with the right to a job, or at least some pro-tection against arbitrary firings. But it doesn't. Right-to-work laws allow employees to accept the benefits of a collective bargaining contract negoti-ated by a union without paying any of the costs.

When a union wins an election, it represents every worker in the bargain-ing unit, not just the workers who voted for the union. ("Bargaining unit" is a technical term that refers to all the workers in a company whose interests are sufficiently similar to be protected by a single representative.) There are no clear rules for determining which workers are included in a single bargaining unit. The National Labor Relations Board considers the similarity of the work, how the workers are compensated, whether they work in a single location, and having the unit include enough workers to justify the administrative costs. The only clear rule is that managers can't be in the union.

Every worker in the unit gets the benefits of the collective bargaining agreement the union negotiates with the employer, including better pay and better benefits. They also get greater job security. Even if you voted against unionizing, you are no longer an employee at will. Your job can be taken away only if the employer has just cause to fire you. If you are fired (or seriously disciplined) and think it was unfair, the union will file a grievance on your behalf and negotiate with the company. Sometimes a union can get the employer to rescind the penalty, or at least make it lighter (like turning a termination into a suspension). If this doesn't work, and your case has some merit, the union will take it to a neutral arbitrator for a decision. About half the time unions appeal terminations to arbitration, the worker gets his or her job back.

All of this costs money. The money comes from dues paid by each worker. A worker whose case goes to arbitration does not have to contribute to the arbitrator's fee or to the legal fees. They have paid for these services by paying their dues. Since everyone benefits from the union contract, it's only fair that everyone contribute to the expenses. But under Taft-Hartley, states are allowed to pass laws (so-called "right-to-work" laws) that allow employees who have received the higher pay and other benefits of the union contract to refuse to pay their share of the costs.

Supporters of right-to-work laws say they are needed to protect workers from being forced to join unions against their will. They argue that it's unfair to force someone to join a group they don't want to belong to. This is absolutely true. It is also what the National Labor Relations Act provides where there is no right-to-work law. As former general counsel to the NLRB Fred Feinstein explained to the New Hampshire legislature when it was considering a right-to-work bill, "Workers in a unionized company already have the right not to join the union. All they have to do is pay their share of the costs of the benefits they receive." Claire Ebel, executive director of the New Hampshire ACLU, called the claim that the right-to-work bill protected freedom of association "baloney." She added, "There's no constitutional right to get something for nothing."

What right-to-work laws actually do is weaken unions. About 8 percent of employees who work in union shops in right-to-work states take the benefits without paying dues. When a union is legally required to spend money on workers from whom it cannot collect dues, it can't do its job as well. That means the union won't be able to file as many grievances on behalf of its members. It won't be able to take as many cases to arbitration. It won't be able to bargain as hard in negotiations over salary and benefits with the employer because it doesn't have the financial resources for a fight.

Right-to-work laws could even allow an employer to get rid of the union completely. Many unions don't have a lot of money because their members can't afford to pay much in dues. If 8 percent (or more in some cases) of the "customers" of a business whose financial situation was already weak stopped paying their bills, the company (in this case the union) could go bankrupt. If the union's financial weakness prevents it from filing legitimate grievances, disgruntled workers, with the employer's help, can call for a new "decertification" election to get the union thrown out.

Since only employers gain from right-to-work laws, it's not surprising that employers are the ones behind them. They try to hide it. Every state campaign is run by the National Right to Work Committee, which is an arm of the U.S. Chamber of Commerce.

Right to Strike

The systematic unfairness of our labor laws extends to employees who have overcome all these obstacles and successfully organized a union. Employees' leverage in negotiating a contract comes from the right to strike. Avoiding a shutdown and the resulting loss of profits is what motivates employers to compromise with employees.

In theory, the right to strike is protected by the NLRA. But in practice this right is just as illusory as the right to organize. In the *Mackay Radio* case, the Supreme Court ruled that while an employer may not fire employees for striking, it may "permanently replace" them. The difference is something only a law professor could find significant. If you are "permanently replaced," you are entitled to get your job back if the person who replaced you quits or is fired. Since most people stay in a new job for at least a year or two, by the time this opportunity arises, it will be too late to do you any good. The bottom line is that exercising your right to strike can get you fired.

Employers do not hesitate to use this power. The United States General Accounting Office found that 25 percent of employers involved in strikes threaten to fire the strikers and 15 percent carry out this threat.

Not-So-Independent Contractors

Other bad decisions have denied many workers even the little protection the NLRA provides. For example, in order to be protected by the act, you have to be an "employee." Independent contractors are not protected.

On the surface, this makes sense. If an employer calls up a plumber to fix a broken sink, the plumber doesn't really work for the employer. It wouldn't be right for all the plumbers in the area to form an organization to fix prices. That's why we have antitrust legislation.

But the National Labor Relations Board has ruled that many people who are really low-wage employees are actually independent contractors who are not allowed to form a union. For example, in the *St. Joseph News-Press* case, the Board held that workers who deliver newspapers are independent contractors. These individuals worked full-time for a single newspaper that dictated virtually all the significant terms of their work, including the area in which they were allowed to operate and the price they charged for the papers. The Board found that they were independent business owners, largely because they had the ability to solicit new customers in their territory (giving them the ability to influence their income). They also used their own equipment (i.e., their cars).

Even if true, these represent only two of the many criteria which determine independent contractor status. All the other factors point to the opposite conclusion. More important, the paper deliverers didn't have the ability a true business owner enjoys to solicit customers anywhere it likes, set its own hours, or determine what price to charge for its product. To equate them with an independent plumber or the owner of a small store is absurd.

Supervisors in Name Only

Last year, at least a million more workers lost their right to organize because the NLRB issued a decision that turns rank-and-file employees into supervisors. Managers and supervisors can't organize a union. There is some logic to this. How can you negotiate and enforce a contract with management if you're part of management?

But once again, the Board took a reasonable rule to ridiculous extremes. In *Oakwood Healthcare*, it held that Linda Bennett and the other "charge nurses" were supervisors who couldn't unionize. A charge nurse is basically a traffic cop. There is almost always more than one nurse on duty in a ward. Someone has to divide up the work. If one patient's bedpan needs emptying and it's time for another patient to take her medication, the charge nurse decides which nurse does which job. A charge nurse doesn't have the power to hire or fire. He or she can't promote anyone or initiate discipline. Charge nurses have nothing to say about who gets a raise. Yet the Board found that they were supervisors. The new rule the Board fashioned to reach this absurd result is that any employee who is responsible for the work of another employee is a supervisor. By this standard, a teacher with an aide, a welder with an apprentice, and an executive secretary with an assistant are all supervisors.

Real Reform

Congress is currently considering the most dramatic change in labor law since the creation of the National Labor Relations Act. Under the proposed Employee Free Choice Act (EFCA), workers could join a union the same way they join any organization, by signing a membership card. If a majority of the workers at a company signed cards, the employer would be required to recognize the union. The voting process would be eliminated.

My first visit on Capitol Hill to talk about EFCA was to Senator Herbert Kohl, a moderate Democrat from Wisconsin who, before running for office, was a very successful businessman (owner of the Kohl's department store chain). Kohl had declined to become a cosponsor of EFCA. I met with his staff expert on labor issues, but I didn't get far into my explanation of the many serious defects in the NLRB election process before he interrupted me.

"I know the NLRA election process is a joke," he said. "Why don't we fix it instead of eliminating elections? Isn't that the more democratic thing to do?" This was a legitimate question, and I had to admit that I didn't have an answer. I was told to come back when I had an answer, but not before. When I went down the hall to visit Senator Jim Jeffords, a moderate Republican from Vermont who had become an independent, it was like an instant replay.

Kohl's and Jeffords's question was hard, but fair. Elections are the gold standard of democracy. Why was EFCA abandoning elections instead of fixing the obvious flaws in the system? But when I tried to construct a system for union elections that would work, I found it was impossible. One of the bedrock principles of fair elections is that both sides must have equal access to the voters. But how can you achieve this in the real world? It would be easy, at least in theory, to say that union supporters have to be given equal time to speak when management holds a meeting to lay out its arguments against unionizing.

But this is only a fraction of the effort to convince worker/voters. During an NLRB election campaign, management, from the CEO to the first-line supervisors, is constantly communicating its arguments. Every casual conversation on the factory floor is an opportunity for supervisors to lobby a worker. It's impossible to give the union the same opportunity to gets its message across. No outsider can walk into a factory and wander around talking to anyone he wants to. At a minimum, it would disrupt production. At worst, it would be a safety hazard. You can't walk up to a worker pouring molten metal or running a high-speed machine, tap him on the shoulder, and ask him how he feels about the union.

It's also impossible to run a truly fair election in a dictatorship. In the United States, you could campaign for Barack Obama without being concerned about the consequences to you if he lost. We live under a system of laws, and the government can penalize you only if you've broken the law. Even if he had wanted to, a victorious President McCain could not have punished those who campaigned against him. That's not true in Zimbabwe. If you campaign for Morgan Tsvangirai's opposition party and it loses the election, President Mugabe will send goons to beat you up and throw you in prison. You might even be killed. Several opposition members have already been killed and Tsvangirai's wife was killed in a car accident under very suspicious circumstances. In this kind of atmosphere, no election is truly fair.

Sadly, the American workplace is more like Zimbabwe than the United States. If you support the union, and it loses the election, you are a marked man in an employment-at-will relationship. You won't get beaten up or killed, but you are almost certain to be fired. Having this threat hanging over every worker makes it impossible to have a truly fair election.

We put our analysis in writing and took it back to the senators. Both said they found it convincing. Senator Kohl changed his position and became a cosponsor. (I'd like to think NWI's work had something to do with this.)

Because of the weakness of the NLRA, and the way employers exploit it, most people who want a union don't have one. A 2005 poll by Peter Harris Research Associates found that 58 million Americans want to join a union. But only 16 million employees actually belong to one. The rest have few ways to protect themselves from abuse.

11

The Judge Is Not Your Friend: Obstacles to Justice Even When the Law Is on Your Side

The Lord giveth and the Lord taketh away.

—JOB 1:21

The legislature giveth and the court taketh away.

—PROFESSOR AL BLUMROSEN, RUTGERS UNIVERSITY

Even when there is a law to protect your rights on the job, you often won't receive justice. Judges work overtime to find ways to take away, or water down, the rights given by the legislature.

Some of these decisions involve only individual statutes. For example, the Supreme Court ruled in *Sutton v. United Airlines* that employees who are legally blind are not disabled because they can see while wearing glasses. The Americans with Disabilities Act states that a person has a disability if they have a condition that "significantly limits them in major life activities." Being blind certainly seems to fit that definition. There is nothing in the act that says, "unless the disability can be significantly reduced by a medical device." There is nothing in the legislative history that supports this exception. When Congress enacts a new law, it doesn't do it in a vacuum. There are thousands of pages of documents demonstrating how Congress reached its conclusion. The Senate and House committees that approve the bill and send it to the entire body each write a detailed report explaining the problem and how the bill deals with it. Every speech by a member of Congress for or against the bill is included verbatim in the federal record. The testimony of every witness before each committee is recorded along with the questions asked of the witness by the members of the committee and the answers the witness gave.

If Congress had any intent to qualify the definition of disability to mean only disabilities that could not be cured or reduced by a medical device, it would have appeared somewhere in this voluminous record. But it's not there. In fact, the opposite is there. The Senate report on the ADA specifically stated that whether someone was disabled should be determined *without* the effect of mitigation. Congress never intended to take away protection for the millions of disabled people who are helped by a medical device. The Supreme Court just made it up.

Fixing the Supreme Court's Mistakes

Unfortunately, cases like *Sutton* are not an aberration. The Supreme Court issued so many bad decisions misinterpreting federal antidiscrimination laws that it forced Congress to pass a series of new civil rights acts just to fix the mistakes. In 1988, Congress passed the Civil Rights Restoration Act (CRRA), overriding President Reagan's veto, to correct the Supreme Court's decision in the *Grove City* case. In *Grove City*, the Court ruled that recipients of federal funds could practice discrimination without losing funds as long as they didn't discriminate in the specific program receiving the funds.

Congress obviously intended to use the financial leverage of federal support to get recipients to eliminate discrimination. While it is illegal for colleges and universities to discriminate on race, gender, and other categories covered by federal law, these laws don't enforce themselves. Some institutions comply only when the cost of discrimination is high, which isn't always the case. Not everyone who is a victim of discrimination files a claim. Not everyone who files a claim can prove his case. And many of those who file and win receive relatively modest damages. It is often possible for an institution to continue to practice discrimination because the cost isn't high enough to make them stop.

Congress recognized this problem and decided to cut off federal funding to any college found to be illegally discriminating. This penalty is often much greater than the damages involved in the private cases brought against the institution. Allowing institutions to continue to receive federal aid while practicing discrimination so long as they play fair in the single program receiving federal funding obviously defeats the purpose of the program. The financial incentive to stop discriminating under this interpretation is small to nonexistent. All dollars are identical. Once they go into the institution's treasury, there is no way to say which dollar went to support which program. Institutions might be able to continue discriminating just as before by claiming that the federal funds went to a program that didn't discriminate. CRRA made clear what Congress had intended all along: institutions that receive federal support cannot discriminate in any aspect of their operations.

In 1991, Congress passed a second civil rights act to fix four cases in which the Supreme Court interpreted the Civil Rights Act of 1964 in a manner that undermined what Congress had intended. The most notorious of these was *Patterson v. McLean Credit Union*. In *Patterson*, the Court ruled that victims of workplace racial harassment could not sue for damages under the Civil Rights Act of 1866, now called Section 1981.

Section 1981 has largely been replaced by the Civil Rights Act of 1964 (called Title VII), which provides much more comprehensive protection against racial discrimination. But Title VII covers only companies with fifteen or more employees. Victims of employment discrimination by smaller companies still rely on Section 1981.

Section 1981 says that all citizens, regardless of race, have the same right "to make and enforce contracts." The Supreme Court held in the 1976 case of *Runyon v. McCrary* that Section 1981 prohibits discrimination by private parties such as employers. In *Patterson*, the Court held that it was a violation of Section 1981 for an employer to refuse to hire someone because of his race, but not a violation to harass him because of his race after he had been hired. This distinction makes no sense and was clearly not what Congress intended. Justice Kennedy's majority opinion said that "making and enforcing contracts" covered only hiring, not conduct after a person is hired.

The phrase "making and enforcing contracts" is rather vague, and could be interpreted in a number of ways, including Justice Kennedy's interpretation. But the Court is supposed to interpret a statute to mean what Congress intended unless there is no reasonable way to interpret the words of the statute in this manner. Making and enforcing contracts can be read to include posthiring discrimination as easily as it can be read in Justice Kennedy's more narrow view. Since Congress clearly intended the broader interpretation, the Court should have chosen it.

Almost as bad was *Ward's Cove Packing v. Antonio. Ward's Cove* involved a type of discrimination known as "disparate impact." When most people think of discrimination, they think of an employer's deliberately not hiring someone because of his or her race or gender. Lawyers call this "disparate treatment." Disparate impact cases do not involve this kind of conscious prejudice. In disparate impact cases, the employer creates an unnecessary job qualification that disproportionately excludes women or minority applicants.

The first disparate impact case involved the Duke Power Company, which had a company policy requiring a high school diploma for every job. In 1971, when the Supreme Court heard this case, relatively few black people in North Carolina (where the company was located) had a high school diploma. While the rule was neutral on its face, it had a discriminatory effect.

Having a discriminatory effect doesn't automatically make a policy illegal. If the qualification is something that you need to do the job, the policy is legal, despite its discriminatory effect. (This is what lawyers call a "bona fide occupational qualification," or BFOQ for short.) But if the requirement has a discriminatory impact on women or minorities and isn't needed to do the job, the requirement is illegal.

In the case of Duke Power, the Court held that the requirement of a high school diploma was legitimate for any job involving reading or writing. Even though there are some high school graduates who (alas) can't read and write, and some people who haven't graduated who can, the Court concluded that no test was perfect and the relationship between literacy and a high school diploma was close enough to be reasonable.

But there were jobs at Duke Power that didn't involve reading or writing. Some employees did nothing but manual labor, such as shoveling coal into furnaces. An illiterate person with a strong back and a good attitude could do this job just as well as a high school or even college graduate. Requiring a diploma for these jobs was unnecessary and had a disparate impact on blacks. The Court ruled it illegal, rejecting the employer's claim that discrimination required proof of employer intent to discriminate.

Ward's Cove involved an employer who ran a salmon cannery. Most of the jobs were on an assembly line gutting fish. These were backbreaking jobs in rooms full of fish guts that paid very little. Most of the workers in these jobs were Filipino immigrants. There were also some higher-level jobs that were much easier and paid better, most of which went to whites.

The way the company went about filling openings when a good job became vacant made it difficult for the Filipinos in the bad jobs to move up. First, the company gave preferential treatment to relatives of people who held these positions. Since most of the incumbents were white, this tended to keep the Filipinos out. The company also gave first preference to people who had previously worked for it in these positions. This also tended to keep the upper-level jobs white. Unlike many companies, Ward's Cove didn't post notices of openings for the good jobs in the cannery, so the Filipinos on the line didn't know they existed and didn't apply.

The end result of these practices was that the upper-level jobs stayed predominantly white. The plaintiffs argued that these were not BFOQs, and this meant the employer was violating the disparate impact rule from *Duke Power*.

But the Supreme Court held that even if the plaintiffs could prove that some of the requirements were arbitrary and that the combined effect was discriminatory, it wasn't enough. The plaintiffs would have to show the discriminatory effect of each individual requirement.

This may sound fair in theory, but in practice it's a nightmare. The employer's records will contain the names of all the applicants and the names of those who met the requirements to be considered for employment. But the records often will not show which of the requirements caused an individual applicant to be disqualified. Without this information, it is impossible for the plaintiff to meet the Supreme Court's requirement.

Moreover, even if the employer's records do have the needed information, it may not be feasible to conduct the analysis the Court demanded. Even a case involving a single requirement (or the total impact of several) involves complex statistical analysis that requires each side to hire an expert witness. If every factor in the hiring process has to be independently analyzed, the amount of statistical work is multiplied. This increases the cost of what was already an expensive case. Many legitimate disparate impact cases are never brought because the number of employees and their financial damages are too small to justify the expense of hiring a statistician. After *Ward's Cove*, the cost went up much higher and even more legitimate cases couldn't be brought. According to Professor James Pope of Rutgers University Law School, *"Ward's Cove* was a get out of jail free card for all but the largest employers."

Finally, in 2009, Congress had to act to change the absurd result of the *Ledbetter* case, in which the Court held that a female employee who had been paid less because of her gender was precluded from filing a claim because she didn't file in time. The reason she didn't file sooner was because she didn't know she was being discriminated against; she didn't know that men doing the same job were paid more. It wasn't her fault she didn't know. Not only did the company not tell her how much the men were paid, they refused to release this information even if an employee asked for it. Her employer deliberately kept her in the dark about the facts she needed to file a case and then argued that because she didn't file the case in time it should be dismissed.

In the end, Congress had to pass three federal statutes, not to increase protection for human rights, but simply to repair the damage the Supreme Court did in these cases and get the law back to what it should have been all along.

Dismissing Employment Cases

In other situations, judges have created rules that deny rights to employees, not just under a single law, but under all laws. The most notorious example is summary judgment. In our system, juries are supposed to decide factual disputes and the judge decides the law. If the jury believes one party's version of events, that party is victorious.

Before a trial begins, both sides have a right to see all the evidence the other side intends to introduce. If you know what evidence the other side plans to introduce, you can get the evidence you need to counter it. Without this, your opponent could introduce a fraudulent document by surprise and get away with it because you wouldn't have the evidence to prove it was fraudulent. In theory, the judge could stop the trial to give you time to get this evidence. But as a practical matter this is impossible. Once trials start, they have to continue until they are done. It's hard enough to get all the parties and witnesses in the courtroom at the same time once. If judges had to juggle several trials simultaneously, while attorneys went out to get additional evidence, the whole system would break down.

To avoid trial by ambush, the parties engage in a process called discovery. During discovery, each party must reveal to the other the witnesses and other evidence that they plan to produce at trial. Sometimes after discovery one party will argue that even if the jury were to accept the other side's evidence, it would not be enough to legally justify a decision in their favor. Such an argument is made in a motion for "summary judgment." If the motion is granted, the case is dismissed without a trial.

There is nothing wrong with summary judgment in principle. If one party doesn't have enough evidence to justify a verdict in its favor (even if the jury believes all of it and rejects everything the other side says), there is no point in a jury trial.

The problem is that judges frequently grant summary judgment when they shouldn't. An example is the Florida case in which an employee claimed she was fired by Jackson Memorial Foundation because of her age. She had evidence that the employer had said he needed "someone younger" at the meeting when he fired her. The employer's stance was that it fired her because of poor job performance, and had evidence of its own to back that assertion up. The employee argued that her performance problems were minor and weren't the real reason she was fired. Whether she was fired because of her age or her job performance is an issue of fact, something the jury is supposed to decide, since there is evidence to support both positions. The judge should have given the evidence to a jury and had them decide the real reason for the firing.

But that's not what happened. Instead, Judge Joan Lenard decided the case herself. She decided that the employer had fired the employee because of her job performance, not because of her age. Whether she was right or wrong isn't the issue. The issue is that the judge shouldn't have decided the case herself. She should have given the evidence to the jury and let them decide.

Cases like *Jackson Memorial* happen all the time. In fact, the majority of employment discrimination cases (60 percent) are decided by summary judgment. When cases are decided by summary judgment, the employer virtually always wins. NWI looked at the results of the 20,514 employment discrimination cases decided by summary judgment by the federal courts for an entire year. Employers won 98 percent of these cases; employees won only 2 percent. There were undoubtedly some cases in which a plaintiff's attorney had completely misjudged a case, and spent a year or more getting a case ready for trial when they had no evidence. But the vast majority of cases were like *Jackson Memorial*: there was conflicting evidence and, rather than submit the case to the jury, the judge decided the facts herself.

The bottom line is that judges throw out over half of all employment discrimination cases, many, perhaps most, of which should have gone to a jury. This does even more harm than the high-profile cases in which the Supreme Court misinterprets federal statutes. Wayne Outten, one of the country's leading plaintiff's employment lawyers, calls summary judgment a stealth weapon used by employers to deny employees their day in court.

Understanding Judges

This comes as a shock to many people, including most new lawyers. We think of judges as wise and impartial. That's what the courts want us to think. It's the purpose of the black robes and other courtroom trappings. But judges aren't like that. They are politicians.

There are two ways to become a judge. The first is to run for office in an election. To get on the ballot you need the support of one of the two major parties. There aren't any primary elections or caucuses. The head of the party in your city or state decides whom he or she wants to nominate. The other way, optimistically referred to as "merit selection," is to be appointed to a judgeship by a government official who is a member of one of the two major parties. Either way, politicians decide who gets to be a judge and who doesn't. It doesn't get much more political than that. Moreover, it's not even conducted in the open. Lawyers who want to become judges court party leaders, usually by doing work for the party for free. Eventually, behind closed doors, the party leaders decide which of these petitioners to appoint, without a word of explanation. I will never forget a conversation I once had with a close friend who was a judge, one whose term was up. She described how she had to go on bended knee to the head of the local party and beg to be renominated.

Because judges are politicians, they respond to political pressures. They favor prosecutors over defense attorneys in criminal cases because the public wants them to be tough on crime (even if they have to bend the law to do it). And they favor employers over employees because employers have more political influence than employees.

We can't change the fact that judges are political. There isn't a way to select judges that isn't political to some extent. Nor should there be. We live in a democracy, where the ultimate political power lies with the people. Judges, like everyone else, ought to be selected by someone who draws his authority from the electorate.

But there are two things we could do to improve the situation. The first is to give judges longer terms of office. Supreme Court justices are appointed for life. They can be removed from office only if a majority of the House of Representatives votes for impeachment and two-thirds of the Senate votes the same way. No justice of the Supreme Court has ever been removed by this process. In 1805, the House of Representatives voted to impeach Justice Samuel Chase. The Senate refused to impeach because the effort was motivated by disagreement with his judicial decisions, not his conduct. Justice Abe Fortas was forced to resign in 1969 because of financial misconduct. Fortas accepted a $20,000 per year "consulting contract" from Louis Wolfson, a Wall Street financier who was under investigation for violating securities law.

But no Supreme Court justice has ever been removed from office because of his or her judicial decisions, no matter how controversial. Earl Warren was probably the most controversial chief justice in American history. There were thousands of billboards across the country saying "Impeach Earl Warren." But it didn't happen. Congress didn't even consider impeaching Warren, even though many members disagreed violently with his decisions. Right or wrong, Supreme Court justices "call 'em like they see 'em." If we want lower court judges to be less political, we should give them longer terms of office.

But by far the best way to get judges who will enforce workplace rights instead of undermining them is to elect public officials who care about human rights, officials who will go on to appoint judges who share their concerns. Professor Drew Westen, a psychiatrist at Emory University, has conducted groundbreaking research into human decision making. Westen has found that facts and logic have very little to do with people's beliefs and decisions. Emotion, not logic, rules the human brain. For example, Westen and his colleagues were able to predict people's opinion about the impeachment of President Clinton, the Supreme Court decision making George Bush president, and whether or not torture had occurred at Abu Ghraib prison, over 80 percent of the time with a five-minute questionnaire regarding their feelings about the major political parties. They studied public opinion regarding the relative merits of paper ballots and voting machines. This is a highly technical subject about which virtually no one knew anything before it became a decisive issue in the 2000 presidential election. Then we were inundated with information on the subject for the first time in our lives. Westen was able to predict people's opinion about this subject 84 percent of the time, based on their general political beliefs.

We'd like to think that judges are different from the rest of us. We see how people around us make decisions and want to believe that judges are more intelligent, more unbiased, and more rational. Unfortunately, they're not. Judges make decisions the same way other human beings do. Professor Westen was able to predict the votes of eight of the nine Supreme Court justices in *Bush v. Gore* before they heard any of the evidence.

This doesn't mean we can't get judges who will enforce workplace rights laws. But it means that the only way to do so is to elect public officials who value human rights and who will appoint judges who do as well. The Senate must approve all nominations to the Supreme Court. Nominees hide behind the claim to be impartial, but this pertains to the facts of the case, not to important issues. Senators should examine nominees' views on important issues like human rights before approving them.

12

Tell It to the Arbitrator

In suits at common law, where the value in
controversy shall exceed twenty dollars,
the right of trial by jury shall be preserved.

—UNITED STATES CONSTITUTION

An employee can be required to give up
their right to sue their employer in court
in their employment contract.

—UNITED STATES SUPREME COURT,

GILMER V. INTERSTATE/JOHNSON LANE CORPORATION (1991)

Meg Olson's boss called her a "bitch," threw condoms on her
desk, said women had no place on Wall Street, and walked around the office
with a riding crop. Olson couldn't sue her boss for sexual harassment because
she had previously agreed to take any complaints to arbitration. After hearing
the evidence, the arbitrator found that Olson's boss had done nothing wrong.

Olson is not alone. Thousands of employers have turned to private arbitration as a way to resolve employment disputes. According to a study conducted
by the General Accounting Office, at least 20 percent of American employers
now use arbitration.

The United States Constitution guarantees all Americans a fair trial before
a neutral judge and a jury of their peers. But this right, too, disappears when
you go to work. Employers are allowed to require employees to use private
justice systems when they have a discrimination case or other employment

dispute. In these companies, you cannot take your case to court, even if you can prove that your boss broke the law.

In employers' private courts, there is no jury. An arbitrator decides your case, someone who does not have to be a lawyer or have any legal training. They do not have to follow the rules of evidence, they do not have to follow the law, and they do not have to give any explanation of their decision.

To make matters worse, arbitrators can be biased. In some arbitration systems, most of the arbitrators are former corporate executives or management lawyers. Those who might tend to sympathize with the employee are usually kept off the list, no matter how qualified they might be. In others, the arbitrators get most of their business from a single employer. Such arbitrators are financially dependent on the employer and know they will be penalized by losing business if they rule for the employee. Lest the message be unclear, some arbitration providers drop arbitrators from their roster if their decisions upset the employer. In a particularly egregious example, the National Arbitration Forum dropped Harvard law professor Elizabeth Bartholet from its roster after she made a large award against one of the banks that was involved in a case she handled. Not only did NAF refuse to refer any more cases to Professor Bartholet, they even dropped her from cases to which she had already been assigned.

Some arbitration systems are little better than kangaroo courts. In most arbitration systems, there are requirements an arbitrator must meet before being added to the roster. These generally include a minimum number of years of legal practice, experience in handling arbitrations or at least formal training, and the absence of any ties to the company that could affect their independence. In the system set up by the Hooters restaurant chain, there were no required qualifications to be an arbitrator. Management unilaterally selected arbitrators with no requirement that they be qualified or even impartial. The president of Hooters could literally appoint his wife or golf partner as an arbitrator. Employees had no say in the process.

Fair Arbitration

Arbitration doesn't have to be unfair. In 1994, the American Bar Association created a national task force composed of leading members of the corporate bar, employment attorneys, unions, civil rights leaders, and arbitration experts. Their assignment was to create a system of rules for arbitration that would make it fair for both parties, especially employees. I served on that group as a representative of the ACLU. After a year of work, we published the *Prototype Agreement on Job Bias Dispute Resolution,* generally referred to as "The Protocol." The Protocol provides the following protections to ensure fairness:

Neutral Arbitrator

Under the Protocol, the arbitrator must be neutral and unbiased. Individuals who have any business or social relationship with a party to the case, or with any of their attorneys, are disqualified from handling a case. A relationship with a potential witness in the case is also a disqualification. Prospective arbitrators are required to disclose any relationship that might be considered such a conflict of interest. Failure to do so is grounds to have the decision overturned.

The arbitrator is also required to have knowledge in the legal issues involved in the dispute.

Rosters of arbitrators are required to be open to all qualified applicants. An arbitration provider cannot maintain a roster of arbitrators who are all former executives or corporation lawyers. Qualified lawyers who represent employees must be admitted as well, along with lawyers from unions and the civil rights community. Rosters of arbitrators must also be open to women, members of racial minorities, and other groups necessary to create diversity.

The employee also has the right to participate in the selection of an arbitrator from the roster in the same manner as the employer. If the employer gets to strike two names from a list of five potential arbitrators, the employee has the right to strike two as well. Unilateral decisions by employers on which arbitrator to use are not allowed, even if the roster is fair and the arbitrator chosen has no conflict of interest.

Right to Counsel

Both parties have the right to the counsel of their choice. While most people would choose to have an attorney as counsel, if a party wants to be represented by someone who is not an attorney, they have the right to do so. This provision can be helpful to employees, especially when they do not have a lot of money. There are situations in which a paralegal, or someone else without a law degree, can effectively represent an employee for a lot less money than a lawyer would charge. For example, when workers who belong to a union have a dispute with their employer, the worker's representative in the arbitration is not always a lawyer. Unions train selected members of their staff to represent workers before the arbitrators. With training and experience, these union reps frequently become among the most effective advocates for workers. If I were a worker with a case going to arbitration, I would choose a union representative over most lawyers.

Discovery

Discovery is absolutely essential to employees in a dispute with their employer. The employee, as the plaintiff, has the burden of proof. As the plaintiff, you have the obligation to produce evidence that shows your legal rights were violated—it is not your employer's obligation to show that they were not violated. But without access to the relevant evidence, the employee loses. And in these cases most of the evidence is in the hands of your employer, or other parties beyond your control. For employees to receive justice, in court or in arbitration, they must have the ability to compel their employer to produce evidence in its control.

Meanwhile, discovery is very expensive. Disputes about what evidence is relevant, reviews of documents, and depositions of witnesses frequently require more time from the lawyers (i.e., money) than the trial itself. In a court case, the judge has the authority to control discovery and keep it from getting out of hand. For example, if one side is running up excessive costs by taking unnecessary depositions of minor witnesses (or people who may never be called as witnesses), the other party can complain to the judge, who can rule that these depositions not be held. Unfortunately, judges seldom use this authority. Listening to parties arguing about whether a particular witness is necessary or whether one party has asked for too many documents to be disclosed is extremely tedious. I have served as an arbitrator in a number of cases. I'd rather go back to boot camp than listen to another such argument. Since judges can handle a case any way they want, they typically decide not to get involved in these squabbles. While you can't blame judges for wanting to avoid this tedious work, the result is that discovery is virtually unlimited, driving litigation costs sky-high. Making arbitration affordable for employees requires reining in discovery.

The Protocol resolves this dilemma by giving the arbitrator the authority to require the production of as much (or as little) evidence as she needs to make a fair decision. There is nothing in the Protocol that forces arbitrators to get involved in resolving discovery disputes. But arbitration, like other professions, has a culture, an unwritten set of rules and expectations about how things are supposed to be done. An important part of the ethos of arbitration is that it is the arbitrator's responsibility to keep the costs to the parties down. Otherwise, your peers will view you as a failure. I've worked with many arbitrators over the years (some outstanding, some not so good), but I've never met one who didn't consider it part of the job to make the process faster and cheaper than going to court.

Full Legal Remedies

One trick unscrupulous employers often use in their arbitration systems is to limit the award the arbitrator can make. This can be accomplished by putting an absolute limit on the size of the award or, more often, by eliminating certain remedies altogether, such as punitive damages.

Under the Protocol, all such limitations are prohibited. An employee who wins her case is entitled to all remedies she would have received in court.

Written Decision

The Protocol requires arbitrators to issue decisions in writing, with an explanation of how they reached their decision. If an employee loses his case, he must be told why the arbitrator ruled against him. This is not only the right thing to do, it is also necessary to protect the employee's right to appeal. This doesn't (and shouldn't) mean that an arbitrator must write the sort of long formal opinion complete with dozens of footnotes that a judge would create. It merely means that the parties must be able to determine from the decision how the arbitrator reached her decision.

Allocation of Fees

Arbitrators, unlike judges, are paid by the parties. Traditionally, the parties split the arbitrator's fee equally. But if the plaintiff is a rank-and-file employee, paying half of the arbitrator's fee can be a serious burden. In such cases, the Protocol gives the arbitrator the authority to require the employer to pay more than half, even up to the entire amount.

Appeals

The Protocol does not create rules for appealing an arbitration decision. In part, this is because the circumstances under which an arbitration decision can be appealed are a question of law that is established by the legislatures and courts. The parties cannot change these rules, even if both would like to.

The Protocol also omits the subject of appeals because there is no consensus on what the rules should be. Some people, including the majority of the plaintiffs' employment bar, favor broad grounds for appeal. That way, if the arbitrator rules against you incorrectly, you have more opportunity for a court to correct the mistake. The flip side of this coin, however, is that this also makes it easier for the employer to appeal. Employers who lose in court frequently file appeals, even if they know they'll be unsuccessful. They then offer to settle the case for much less than the jury awarded the employee. Most people have bills to pay and waiting another year or more to get their award is a hardship, so they accept the offer. Many, including virtually all unions and the National Workrights Institute, think employees are better off under a system in which, when they win, the victory is final and they can get their money quickly.

The actual legal rules make it very difficult to appeal an arbitrator's decision. A decision by a court can be overturned by a higher court for any significant failure to follow the law. The grounds for appealing an arbitrator's decision are much narrower. Under the Federal Arbitration Act (FAA), a court will overturn an arbitrator's decision under only three conditions:

- Lack of Jurisdiction. Unlike judges, arbitrators have the authority to resolve legal disputes only when the parties have agreed to give them this authority. If an arbitrator rules on a dispute that the parties have not agreed to submit to arbitration, a court will vacate the decision.
- Bias. If the arbitrator has a relationship with one of the parties that creates a conflict of interest, a court will overturn his decision.
- Manifest Disregard for the Law. If the arbitrator deliberately refused to follow the law, a court will overturn his decision.

For other types of mistakes by the arbitrator, there is no recourse. For example, if the arbitrator doesn't follow the law because he doesn't know the correct legal rule, a court will let the decision stand. If the arbitrator rules in favor of one party when all the evidence shows that the other party is right, the decision will stand. If the arbitrator rules in favor of a party based on evidence that would have been inadmissible in court, the decision will stand.

The fact that it is so difficult to appeal an arbitrator's decision makes it absolutely essential that the rules of arbitration be fair.

Response to the Protocol

Leading arbitration agencies, such as the American Arbitration Association and JAMS, immediately endorsed the Protocol and changed their rules where necessary to comply with it. If an employer's arbitration plan was not consistent with the Protocol, AAA refused to handle the cases, even if the employees "agreed" to the different rules. I personally witnessed AAA refuse to accept cases unless the employer changed its system to comply with the Protocol.

Studies by several leading researchers have found that employees generally do as well in arbitrations conducted by AAA as they do in court. Several major studies have been conducted comparing the results of jury trials and arbitrations, including studies by Professor Theodore Eisenberg of Cornell and by Professor Lisa Bingham of Indiana University. An analysis of these studies, conducted by the National Workrights Institute, found that juries ruled in favor of employees 57 percent of the time, while arbitrators ruled in the employees' favor in 62 percent of cases (a difference which is not statistically insignificant).

But not every employee who files a case in court gets to a jury. Judges dismiss about 25 percent of employment cases without a trial. This is extremely rare in arbitration. When you look at all employment cases (not just those that reached the jury), the employee win rate in court is only 43 percent, much lower than the 62 percent who win in AAA arbitration.

Access to Justice

Litigation has become extremely expensive. Legal fees alone in a typical employment case are at least $25,000, and usually much more. Few people are able to pay such a large fee, especially if they have just been fired. Because of this, employment litigation is usually handled on a contingency fee basis, in which the plaintiff's lawyer receives a percentage (generally 33 percent or more) of what she recovers for her client. But in order for an attorney to take a case on this basis, she must be confident of winning, since she gets nothing if she loses. The employee's damages must also be large enough for the attorney's share of them to pay for the time they spend on the case. This means that employees must have both a very strong case and potential damages of at least $75,000. Some experts estimate that the minimum damages an employee must have to get a lawyer is over $100,000.

This means that many employees with legitimate claims can't file a claim because they can't afford a lawyer. NWI has received hundreds of complaints from employees over the last twenty years. The majority had no legal case; their employers may have been unfair, but had broken no law. But at least twenty people had solid evidence that the employer had violated their legal rights. In each case, NWI called employment attorneys, many of whom we knew, to try to get the person a lawyer. Only once did we succeed. Every other time, the employee never got a lawyer, never saw the inside of a courtroom, and never received justice.

I recently spent many hours trying to get a lawyer for a man from Indiana named Jerrold Hatchins. Jerry was a factory worker for Crescent Plastics. He was fired for failing a drug test. Knowing that he didn't use drugs, he immediately took another test at his own expense to show he was innocent. After he passed, he took two more tests and passed them both. Hatchins took the three test results to his employer, who refused to look at them. Clearly there was a problem with the first test. Either the company or the laboratory had been negligent. In addition, Hatchins was one of the few black employees at the company and had continually been subjected to low-level harassment. I personally spoke to six different employment lawyers. I told them the facts and why Hatchins had a case. All six lawyers agreed that Hatchins probably had a viable case, but not one of them would take it. Hatchins didn't make a lot of money, so his lost wages would have been only about $30,000, even if he was out of work for a year. The legal fees would have been one third of this, or $10,000. All six lawyers decided that the case would require too much work to earn this fee. The end result is that Hatchins never got a lawyer.

There are a lot of people in Jerry Hatchins's situation. The average employee in America today is paid about $30,000 a year. Based on my experience, and the numbers, I believe that the majority of people in America today with legitimate legal claims against their employer are unable to file a case. While 90 percent of terminations are legitimate (not necessarily fair, but not in violation of any law), the remaining 10 percent represents 150,000 people every year, most of whom will never receive justice.

Arbitration is generally less expensive than going to court. This not only saves the employee (and the employer) money, it frequently means the difference between being able to afford bringing a complaint and just giving up. In 2003, NWI conducted a study in which we looked at the size of employment cases handled by the American Arbitration Association for an entire year. We found that the majority of cases involved less than the minimum amount needed to get an attorney and go to court. Many cases (26 percent) involved less than $25,000 in damages. Clearly, there are literally thousands of people with a legitimate employment claim who have the courthouse door slammed in their face and who could get justice in arbitration.

Arbitration Isn't Perfect

Even the best of arbitration systems, however, have their problems. The most serious problem is the size of arbitration awards. Most employees who are wronged have only economic damages. They have lost money because they lost their job. This is stressful, but most people don't need a psychiatrist's care to get by. In cases like this, arbitrators award the same amount as does a jury.

But some cases involve more. Sometimes the employer's conduct is so outrageous that a court would award punitive damages to the employee to teach the employer a lesson. In other cases, the employee requires medical care to cope with losing her job and being unable to support herself and her family. Juries are much more likely than arbitrators to award noneconomic damages to punish the employer or compensate the employee for her suffering. When it comes to awards for emotional distress and punitive damages, arbitrators' awards are only about half of what employees receive in court.

Class Actions

Class actions are generally prohibited in arbitration. Class actions are filed when an employer (or other party) violates the rights of many people in a single act but each individual has relatively modest damages. For example, if an employer with one thousand employees closed the plant and gave the employees only thirty days' notice instead of the sixty days' notice required by federal law, the total damages would be substantial, but the loss suffered by an individual employee would be small (about $3,000 on average). In this situation, if the employees had to file suit individually, the employer would get off scot-free, because the cost of bringing the case would be more than an employee would recover. The employee would win the case, but lose money.

To enable employees in such situations to receive justice, courts have established class actions, in which a large number of people with the same claim against the same company can file their case as a group.

Many of the most important employment cases in recent years have been class actions. In 1997, Boeing was found to be discriminating against its fifteen thousand female and minority employees. At Mitsubishi, in 1998, three hundred female employees not only faced employment discrimination, but were groped and forced to have sex to get jobs. A study by NWI of five major employment class actions (including Boeing and Mitsubishi) found that none of the more than fifty thousand employees involved in these cases could have afforded to seek justice on their own.

Many employers seek to take advantage of this by including a provision in employment contracts in which the employee "agrees" that they will not participate in a class action against the company (called a class action waiver). The major providers of arbitration services honor these provisions and refuse to handle a case as a class action if the employer's arbitration procedures don't allow them. This prevents many people with legitimate cases from ever filing a claim, which is exactly what the employers intended.

The justification offered by the providers is that courts frequently enforce class action waivers. To some extent, this is true. Several courts have held that class action waivers are enforceable. Employees in these jurisdictions are no worse off by being in arbitration. But most courts have not yet ruled on this issue. Employees whose cases are in these courts at least have the opportunity to argue that the "no class action" clause is unenforceable. In arbitration, no one can raise the issue.

Repeat Player Effect

One potential problem that has received much attention is the "repeat player effect." The concern is that a large corporation involved in an arbitration may have the opportunity to use the same arbitrator again in future disputes. If the arbitrator rules against the company, they may not use him again. Since arbitrators are paid by the case, the potential financial loss to the arbitrator is significant. The likelihood of an individual employee's having the opportunity to use the same arbitrator again is virtually zero. This can create a powerful conflict of interest in the employer's favor.

Whether this is actually a problem depends on the number of arbitrators and parties in the specific system. AAA, for example, has several hundred employment arbitrators on its roster. (These are not AAA employees, but independent arbitrators and lawyers who accept cases from AAA.) Literally thousands of employers bring cases to AAA. The chances of an arbitrator for AAA seeing the same employer twice are so small they might as well be zero. I have arbitrated several cases a year for AAA for the last fifteen years. (This hands-on experience is very helpful when wrestling with legal and policy issues.) I have never seen the same employer twice except for a single situation in which a large corporate merger flooded AAA with cases. Except for this once-in-a-lifetime exception, I have never had to worry that ruling against an employer was going to hurt me financially. Even in this situation, there was no unfairness in the results. I ruled against the employer in several of the cases, yet they continued to agree to use me as an arbitrator.

Other arbitration systems, however, are quite different. The National Arbitration Forum (NAF) handles credit card disputes for most of the country's major banks. The number of banks in America is small, especially after the recent consolidations. Because credit card disputes are so common, each bank generates thousands of cases every year. NAF arbitrators are virtually guaranteed to see the same bank over and over. I served on NAF's arbitration roster briefly in 2006 before resigning because I was uncomfortable with aspects of their system. In that brief time, I handled six cases, five of which involved the same bank.

Public Citizen reports that twenty-eight NAF arbitrators in California handled thirty thousand cases in a single year, over a thousand for each arbitrator. Each of these arbitrators saw the same bank over and over, possibly hundreds of times. Ruling against a bank in this system could cost the arbitrator a lot of money, and they are well aware of it. As mentioned before, one NAF arbitrator, Harvard law school professor Elizabeth Bartholet, was dropped from the NAF roster after issuing a large ruling against a major bank. Repeat-player corporations obviously have a huge advantage in a system like this.

Legal Protection

You might think that, because of these problems, there would be laws protecting employees. But there aren't.

The United States Supreme Court has ruled that employees can be forced to "agree" to give up their right to go to court as a condition of getting a job. In *Gilmer v. Interstate/Johnson Lane Corporation,* the Court held that Robert Gilmer could be forced to use his employer's arbitration system even though the company admitted that he was forced to agree to arbitration in order to be hired. The Court's opinion, written by Justice Byron White, reasoned that Gilmer had not given up any rights by "agreeing" to arbitrate. After all, he could raise all the same claims in arbitration that he could have in court, including his claim that his employer fired him because of his age (a violation of the Age Discrimination in Employment Act).

But while Gilmer had not lost any *substantive* rights, he had lost *procedural* rights. He lost the right to have his case heard by a jury. Instead, he got a panel of three arbitrators, two of whom came from the financial industry. Since Gilmer worked as a stockbroker, these two arbitrators were much more likely to sympathize with Gilmer's employer. Moreover, the financial executives sitting in judgment on Gilmer's boss knew that Gilmer's boss could be sitting in judgment of them in the future.

The Court's failure to recognize the importance of procedural rights is staggering. Any student of the law knows that substantive rights are only as good as the procedures that enforce them. The Russian and Chinese constitutions provide for a wide variety of rights, all of which are ignored by the judges. The judges work for the government and rule the way they are told. The laws of most countries give employees the right to organize a union. But that right is meaningless in many countries, such as Colombia, where thirty-nine union organizers were murdered in a single year and the government refuses to prosecute the murderers (and in some cases is involved in the crimes). To say that only the substantive rights of employees are important is dangerously wrong.

Justice White also missed the point on whether Gilmer's "agreement" should be legally binding. He recognized that Gilmer didn't want to sign the agreement, but argued that employers set terms and conditions of employment on "take it or leave it" terms every day. If you don't think your job pays enough, go find one that pays better. This is true, but not when fundamental rights are involved. An employment contract that says you can never sue your boss, even if he fires you because of your race or sexually harasses you, isn't enforceable. An employer who argued, "She agreed not to sue me for harassment," would be laughed out of court. The right to a fair hearing, before an impartial jury, is not something a person should have to give up to get a job.

Due Process

Nor does the law protect your rights once your case goes to arbitration. While the Protocol has been widely recognized and praised by legal scholars and judges, not a single court has adopted it. In extreme cases, courts will strike down unfair aspects of an employer's arbitration program. In the Hooters case, a federal court of appeals refused to enforce the arbitration agreement and allowed the employee to take her case to court because the method of selecting arbitrators was so biased. But this was an extreme case. The Hooters arbitration system was so biased that George Friedman, vice president of the American Arbitration Association, testified as an expert witness for the employees.

Many times, however, courts turn a blind eye to injustice. In the case of *Great Western Mortgage v. Peacock*, the federal court of appeals for the Third Circuit upheld an employer arbitration program that provided a shorter deadline for filing a case than provided by law. Employees who filed a claim in arbitration within the time period provided in the law but after the expiration of the date in the employer's plan would have their case dismissed. In *DeGaetano v. Smith Barney, Inc.*, the court upheld the agreement and forced the employee to arbitrate even though the arbitrator was precluded from awarding punitive damages or attorney's fees, both of which were authorized under the law. A Connecticut court ordered an employee to take his case to arbitration even though there were members of the accounting firm he was suing on the arbitration panel.

Judicial Expedience

Why do judges allow unfair arbitration decisions to stand? Largely because it makes their lives easier. The number of cases filed in court has increased dramatically in recent years. To make matters worse, cases are generally more complicated and time-consuming than they used to be. Judges are struggling to keep up with the caseload and are willing to embrace almost any technique to bring it down. Some of the steps courts have taken are very constructive. For example, in many states, including New Jersey, parties in civil cases are required to participate in mediation.

Mediation

Mediation is a unique method of resolving disputes. Instead of having a third party (judge, jury, or arbitrator) deciding the case and the parties' having to accept the results, mediation involves helping the parties resolve the case themselves. Most civil cases (over 90 percent) eventually settle. That's good, because it spares the parties the trauma and expense of a trial. Unfortunately, the settlement usually takes place on the courthouse steps. By this time, the parties have already spent two years with their lives disrupted while paying lawyers to file motions and take depositions. Most cases could be settled earlier, but most people (and their lawyers) don't get serious about evaluating their case until they have a trial date looming.

A mediator sits down with the parties early in the case and tries to help them find a mutually acceptable solution before they pour time, money, and sweat into the case. Sometimes the mediator points out to the parties weaknesses in their cases that make the plaintiff willing to take less money and the defendant to offer more, enabling them to settle. Sometimes the arbitrator can find a creative solution to the dispute that the parties have overlooked.

One of the most remarkable mediations took place not in the business world but in international diplomacy. The Sinai peninsula was a serious bone of contention for Egypt and Israel. The Sinai had been part of Egypt for centuries before they lost it to Israel in wartime. Egyptians could not accept having another country, especially Israel, take it away from them. It was a matter of national pride. They didn't want to go back to war (they had lost the Sinai by attacking Israel and were soundly defeated). But they would start fighting again before they would give the Sinai up.

The paths to a resolution are limited only by the imagination of the mediator. The Israelis had been attacked more than once by Egyptian troops based in the Sinai. By keeping it, Israel created a buffer zone to protect its citizens. It was prepared to go to war to keep the Sinai. The mediator, Henry Kissinger, realized that the two countries' goals were not really at odds. Egyptians wanted to keep Sinai part of their country. The Israelis didn't want the Sinai to be part of Israel; they just wanted to keep the Egyptian army from using it as a launching area for attacks. The solution was to give Sinai back to Egypt, but as a demilitarized zone with monitors from the United Nations on site to make sure neither country's troops entered. The arbitrator's creativity prevented what looked like certain war.

Mediation is remarkably successful. Most parties come to the mediation angry at the other side and willing to "fight all the way to the Supreme Court" to get their way. But when the mediation is over, about 75 percent of the time the parties find a resolution they can both live with. Some top mediators, such as Edward Bergman of Princeton, New Jersey, who teaches dispute resolution at Wharton Business School, have success rates approaching 100 percent.

But sometimes judges are so determined to get rid of cases that they make mistakes, like forcing employees and consumers into arbitration that isn't fair. They see the imperfections in many arbitration systems (if they don't, the employee's attorney points them out). But they find a way to convince themselves that the problems aren't that serious. Perhaps if they were required to participate in arbitration as plaintiffs themselves, their vision would improve.

Roadblocks to Reform

A man hears what he wants to hear and disregards the rest.

—PAUL SIMON

Frequently, as this book illustrates, reform of employment law comes from the state legislatures. Unfortunately, that avenue is blocked when it comes to arbitration. Under the preemption doctrine in the Constitution, if there is a conflict between a federal law and a state law, the federal law takes precedence. There can also be preemption in the absence of a direct conflict. If Congress passes a law on a subject which says (or even implies) that the federal statute represents the exclusive rules, even state laws that are not in conflict are barred.

The federal government acted on arbitration in 1925. At that time, courts were openly hostile to arbitration. Judges didn't consider arbitrators capable of resolving legal issues correctly and saw them as a threat to their authority. Agreements to arbitrate were almost never enforced. Even where two sophisticated corporations of equal bargaining power both wanted an arbitration clause in a contract, courts refused to enforce them if one party wanted to back out after a dispute arose.

The federal government disagreed. Congress and the president didn't consider arbitration to be second-class justice. If both parties agreed to arbitrate disputes, that agreement should be enforceable. The Federal Arbitration Act (FAA) provides that agreements to arbitrate must be treated equally to other contracts. If there is a general rule that applies to all contracts, it can be applied to arbitration contracts. For example, every state has laws against fraud. If one party uses fraud to get the other party to sign a contract, the contract is unenforceable. This includes arbitration contracts. But there can be no rules that single out arbitration contracts for special treatment.

For example, Montana enacted a law stating that arbitration clauses in contracts had to be typed in uppercase letters, underlined, and placed on the first page of a contract. No other type of clause had these requirements. The Supreme Court, in *Doctor's Associates v. Casarotto*, found that making arbitration agreements harder to enforce than other types of contracts violated the FAA. But the courts have taken this legitimate principle to an absurd conclusion. Any law that establishes a rule for how arbitration must be conducted applies only to arbitration. A state law that says people have a right to counsel in arbitration has no meaning in a contract that doesn't involve dispute resolution. Yet the courts have consistently held that any state law making arbitration fair is unenforceable because it is preempted by the FAA. This might be understandable if the federal government had established its own set of rules for arbitration. But it hasn't. The federal government is, in effect, saying, "We won't make any rules to ensure arbitration is fair and you can't either."

The Minnesota attorney general recently developed a new way to attack unfair arbitration that may circumvent the preemption doctrine. He sued the National Arbitration Forum (whose headquarters is in St. Paul) for fraud, claiming that NAF had deliberately made false and misleading claims about the fairness of its system. Rather than fight, NAF decided to stop conducting consumer arbitration.

Using antifraud laws against unfair arbitration may have a great impact. It may also have virtually none. Most consumer and employment arbitration today is not voluntarily chosen. The individual must "agree" to arbitrate as a condition of employment (or of doing business). Under these conditions, even if a biased system was completely honest in describing its process, employees and consumers would still have to use it.

Reform

Congress is considering legislation that would change the law of arbitration. Under the proposed Arbitration Fairness Act (AFA), agreements to arbitrate would be enforceable only if they were entered into voluntarily by both parties after the dispute arises.

This sounds like a good idea, but may not be. To begin with, it doesn't create any due process standards. If an employee voluntarily signs an agreement to arbitrate after she has a dispute with her employer, the agreement is enforceable, no matter how unfair the arbitration system is. The bill's authors, primarily trial lawyers, assume that no one will agree to participate in an unfair system because their lawyer will tell them not to. That's true, for employees who have lawyers. But, as we've already seen, most people with an employment dispute don't have lawyers. Who is going to protect these people from signing a one-sided arbitration agreement that makes it almost impossible to win? Also, what happens to the employee who has a lawyer, but signed an unfair arbitration agreement first? Nothing in the AFA says you can change your mind after you talk to a lawyer and find out you made a mistake.

The AFA would also have the effect of virtually eliminating employment arbitration. Today, almost all arbitration is forced on employees at the time they sign their employment contracts. This unfair practice would be eliminated by the AFA. But there is nothing in the AFA that requires an employer to agree to arbitrate when the employee wants it. Employers don't want to arbitrate every case. They know that cases too small for the employee to take to court will show up in arbitration. From an employer's standpoint, that's a loss. Employers accept this loss because it allows them to get cases that might have multimillion-dollar awards for emotional distress or punitive damages away from juries.

If the AFA passes, the small number of employees with million-dollar cases will be better off because they will get a jury trial. But what about the rest? The AFA's authors assume that employers will voluntarily agree to arbitrate the cases private lawyers don't want to take to court. They won't. Why would any corporate lawyer agree to arbitrate a claim when he knew that the amount of money at stake was so small that the employee would never be able to take the company to court? If you agree to arbitrate, you have to spend money defending yourself, and might have to pay a judgment at the end. If you refuse to arbitrate, the employee goes away and you don't lose a penny. It's not a hard decision. I've spoken to numerous corporate attorneys, and virtually all of them said they would refuse to arbitrate an employment dispute if they knew it was too small for the employee to get a lawyer.

This unacknowledged problem is also borne out by data. NWI analyzed every employment arbitration handled by AAA in 2001 and 2002 to see when the parties agreed to arbitrate. We found that, in 2001, 94 percent of the arbitration agreements were made before the dispute arose. Only 6 percent of the time had the parties sat down and agreed to arbitrate after the dispute arose. In 2002, it was even more lopsided, with only 3 percent of the arbitrations coming from postdispute agreements.

This data confirms what logic tells us; litigation is an adversary process. What's good for you is bad for your adversary, including whether or not to arbitrate, once both sides know the facts. Postdispute agreements to arbitrate are wonderful in theory, but that's not the way the world works in practice. In the real world, parties either agree to arbitrate in advance or they don't agree to arbitrate at all. The AFA's proposed rule invalidating all predispute agreements would have the effect of leaving the majority of wronged employees whose cases are too small to take to court even worse off than they are today.

Many distinguished champions of employee rights, such as Professor Theodore St. Antoine of the University of Michigan Law School, don't support the AFA. "The AFA would make things much better for employees with large cases involving emotional distress," St. Antoine told me in an e-mail, "but it would make a bad situation even worse for the majority of employees with small claims."

Real Reform

The AFA should read as follows: All agreements to arbitrate must be voluntary. If both parties want to arbitrate future disputes, they should be able to make a binding agreement to do so. If an employee doesn't want to sign an arbitration agreement because she wants to get everything she has coming to her if she encounters sexual harassment in the future, she should be able to. If she wants to sign the arbitration agreement to be sure she will get her day in court regardless of the size of her case, she should be able to make that choice instead. Neither choice is right or wrong; they just have different advantages. Competent adults should be allowed to choose for themselves. The law should say that arbitration agreements can be made either before or after the dispute arises as long as it is the voluntary choice of both parties.

And, of course, all arbitrations must be fair. The AFA should require all employment arbitration to comply with strict due process standards, including every point in the Protocol. It should also include points the Protocol doesn't address, such as the availability of class actions.

At this point, what will happen is anybody's guess. The trial lawyers support the AFA as currently drafted because this is the best option for the people they represent (employees whose cases are big enough to take to court). The business community likes the law just the way it is. The dispute resolution industry is showing signs of supporting due process reform. NWI alone is supporting both employment arbitration and changing the law to make sure it is voluntary and fair.

13

The Rights You Have

Even a blind pig finds a few acorns.

—ANONYMOUS

·**There is one area of American employment law** that is close to what it should be. This is the right to equal treatment. Whatever decisions employers make about you should be based on what you do, not who you are.

This principle was entirely absent from our laws until 1964, when Lyndon Johnson signed the Civil Rights Act of 1964, also known as Title VII. Before Title VII, it was completely legal for an employer not to hire you because of your race. Since 1964, we have expanded our antidiscrimination laws to include almost every form of identity-based discrimination. It is now illegal, anywhere in the United States, for an employer to fire, refuse to hire, refuse to promote, or discriminate in any other way against someone because of his race, religion, gender, age, national origin, disability, or genes.

The current battleground is sexual orientation. Twenty states and the District of Columbia now have laws prohibiting employment discrimination based on sexual orientation, and the list is gradually expanding. Many cities and towns have local laws against this form of discrimination too. But in most of America today, this activity is still legal. An employer can walk into court and literally say, "I refused to hire him because I don't like queers," and have the case dismissed.

Federal legislation has been pending for many years that would prohibit employment discrimination based on sexual orientation nationwide. The

Employment Non-Discrimination Act (ENDA) has attracted wide bipartisan support. But it is still not the law.

The only other major group that isn't protected is people who are fat. As discussed in chapter 8, if you are "morbidly obese" you are generally protected under federal and state disability discrimination laws. But if you're just overweight enough to turn people off or make an employer think your medical bills will be higher than average, you're out of luck.

This doesn't mean that employers can't discriminate in arbitrary ways. Your boss can still fire you because he doesn't like your politics, doesn't like something you said on your blog, or doesn't like the way you part your hair. Discrimination on the basis of what you do is still legal. But at least discrimination based on who you are is fading from the workplace. It's a start.

Employees need to be clear, however, about exactly what antidiscrimination laws do and don't mean. Laws against racial discrimination don't mean an employer can't fire a black employee for her politics or spy on her with a hidden camera. All the law says is that you can't treat people differently because of their race. An employer can still fire a black employee for an arbitrary unfair reason; it just can't fire her because she is black.

Enforcement

The biggest problems with antidiscrimination laws usually relate to enforcement. Most of these laws are enforced by the Equal Employment Opportunity Commission (EEOC). The EEOC received over 95,000 complaints in 2008, up 19 percent since 2000. Yet the EEOC's staff hasn't increased. In fact, it's been cut 23 percent. The number of investigators, the heart of the agency, has been cut even more. In 2000, the EEOC had 857 investigators. In 2007, the number of investigators was down by almost a third to 565. A typical EEOC investigator has to handle almost two hundred cases every year. To keep up, she would have to do an entire investigation almost every day. Conducting a thorough investigation into every complaint with this workload is impossible. Why did the Bush administration cut the number of investigators while the number of complaints went up?

A word to the wise, if you ever file a claim with the EEOC: don't expect them to do the legwork. Give them the names of the people in the company who can back up your story and what each of them knows. If possible, get written statements. The less work the EEOC investigator has to do to see that your claim is legitimate and the more she can see your commitment to the case, the better job she will do.

The federal courts are also notorious for throwing up roadblocks to enforcing civil rights laws. In the most recent travesty, Lilly Ledbetter sued Goodyear because for almost twenty years it paid her less than men doing the same job. The case should have been a slam dunk—Goodyear had been caught red-handed systematically discriminating against women.

But Ledbetter's case was thrown out. The reason was that she hadn't filed her case within the statute of limitations (the time period established by law within which a case must be filed). There's nothing wrong with having a statute of limitations. It wouldn't be fair to allow a plaintiff to sit on her claim for years and then file it when the defendant could no longer get the evidence needed to present its case.

But that's not what happened here. Ledbetter didn't sit on her case. She didn't file because she didn't know she had a case. Goodyear never told her that the male employees in her job were getting paid more. Nor was there any way she could have found out. Corporations virtually never tell one employee what other employees are making. They say it's a matter of privacy, which is partly true. It's also a good way to get away with illegal discrimination. Women who are getting less than men can't sue if they don't know what the men are getting. In essence, Goodyear deliberately denied Ledbetter the information she needed to know she had a case and then asked the court to throw her case out because she didn't file it in time.

You might not think that this sort of sleight of hand would get far in the Supreme Court. But it did. By a vote of five to four, the Court ruled that Ledbetter should have filed the case she didn't know she had. They weren't forced to this absurd conclusion by the law. There is a well-established line of cases holding that the statute of limitations doesn't start to run until a person knows (or at least has reason to know) that she has a case, even when the defendant hasn't deliberately withheld the critical information. The Court, however, ignored these cases.

This particular travesty is now in the past. One of the first acts of the Obama administration was to sign legislation reversing the *Ledbetter* decision. While this is a victory for justice, it comes at a price. The number of laws Congress and the president can create in four years is very limited. Every new law that has to be enacted to undo an injustice is one less law that can be passed to increase justice.

Wages and Hours

Another area where the law is reasonably good relates to wages and hours. Under the Fair Labor Standards Act, your employer must pay you for every hour you work. There are no exceptions. The company can't say your work was no good. It can't argue that you got the job by claiming to have education or experience you didn't have. It can't say that your workplace conduct was atrocious. An employer can fire you for these reasons (or for no reason at all) and it may be able to deny you unemployment compensation, but it can't deny you your pay. If you were on the job, the company has to pay you, period.

But just because something is legally required doesn't mean employers do it. While most people who work for commercial corporations get their paycheck every week, low-wage workers who work for small companies in construction, landscaping, and food service get cheated out of their wages all the time. Kim Bobo is executive director of Interfaith Worker Justice, which has helped create twenty-one centers around the country where low-wage workers can come for free legal advice and assistance. "Wage theft is by far the most common problem we see," Bobo says. "In some industries, wage theft is a fact of life." The U.S. Department of Labor found that 60 percent of nursing homes steal employees' wages. In poultry plants, the rate was 100 percent; every plant DOL looked at stole workers' wages. Bobo estimates that over a million workers are cheated out of wages every year. Almost all of them are low-wage workers who need every dollar to survive.

Wage theft takes many forms. One way to steal is to officially pay workers what they're owed but take illegal deductions from their pay or make them pay for the equipment and supplies they use in their work. One employer in Chicago made its employees bring their own toilet paper to work.

One reason wage theft is so common is that it's profitable. Most of the time, employers who cheat workers out of their wages get away with it. Many victims of wage theft have few, if any, job skills. They have a hard time finding jobs and will put up with almost anything to keep one. They know that if they complain about not getting all their pay, they'll get fired. So they say nothing and the boss keeps the money. Some say nothing because they are undocumented immigrants who are afraid (with good reason) that their boss will turn them in to Immigration and Customs Enforcement (formerly known as the Immigration and Naturalization Service) if they complain and they will be deported. Some workers are willing to stand up and fight for their wages, but don't know how to file a claim. The bottom line is that the vast majority of employers who steal employees' wages get away with it.

The other reason wage theft is so common is that the penalties for getting caught are a joke. If a worker steals $100 out of the cash register and gets caught, he will be criminally prosecuted and very possibly sent to prison. If an employer steals $100 in wages from a worker, the chance of criminal prosecution is virtually nonexistent.

Police departments don't treat wage theft as a crime. Even if the employer withholds a thousand dollars from an employee, or even a thousand dollars each from fifty employees, the police refuse to make an arrest for a theft amounting to fifty thousand dollars. The worst that can happen is that the state department of labor or a small claims court will order the employer to pay the workers what they were owed in the first place. From a purely financial standpoint, certain employers would have to be stupid not to steal workers' wages.

Overtime

Federal law also requires that most employees be paid one and a half times their normal pay for all work in excess of forty hours in a single week. There are logical exceptions to this rule. A doctor, lawyer, or CEO is supposed to work long hours. That's one of the reasons they get paid so much. It would be ridiculous to pay an executive making $250,000 a year overtime for working more than forty hours a week.

The major exceptions to this rule are professionals (doctors, lawyers, architects, and members of other recognized professions), executives, administrators, and employees who direct the activities of other workers. In addition to falling into one of these categories, an employee must make at least $23,660 per year to lose eligibility for overtime pay, and must receive a fixed salary. If the employer doesn't pay the employee her full salary on weeks when she works less than forty hours, it can't refuse to pay her overtime when she works more than forty hours.

Unless you are covered by one of these exceptions, the law requires your employer to pay you overtime. Your employer can't change your right to overtime by how it classifies the job, nor can you agree to work without receiving overtime pay. But this law is widely flouted. Employers routinely classify employees as overtime-exempt when they are qualified. Just as with wage theft, they do it because they can get away with it. The legal rules regarding who is eligible for overtime pay aren't all that complex by legal standards, but they are more complicated than the average person can understand, even if they knew where to find them. Jules Bernstein, the dean of litigation for federal overtime laws, says, "There are millions of Americans who are entitled to overtime pay who never receive it."

Unlike wage theft, violations of overtime law are frequently committed by large corporations. A big company can save literally millions of dollars every year by not paying overtime. And, just like wage theft, it's a smart gamble (for anyone without ethics). The Department of Labor is reasonably active in pursuing overtime violations, at least within the limits of its resources, and frequently exacts penalties in excess of simply paying the workers what they were owed all along. But DOL has limited resources and can't go after every employer that breaks the law. Cheating workers out of overtime is still the cost-effective thing to do.

Because there is so much money to be made and getting caught is unlikely, there is an epidemic of cheating on wage and hour laws. In 2007 alone, the Department of Labor successfully charged over 150 companies with violating the law, including such household names as Wal-Mart, Goodyear, Wackenhut

Security, Bell Aerospace, and CVS. Over 100,000 people were cheated. The amount of money employees were cheated out of was over $75 million. And the cases that the overworked DOL had time to pursue are just the tip of the iceberg.

Unless you are a doctor, lawyer, or executive, you should call your state department of labor if you regularly work more than forty hours per week without receiving overtime pay.

When you look at how many people are cheated by all these methods together, the numbers are astounding. Bobo estimates that ten million employees are paid less than they are legally entitled to.

Defamation

Your employer can lie to you, but it can't lie about you. When you are looking for a job, you almost always have to provide prospective employers with a job history listing all your past employers. There is a good chance that someone at the company to which you're applying will call your former employers to ask what kind of an employee you were.

Many companies today will only confirm the fact that you used to work for them, and the time period involved. But there is no law that says employers can't say more. The law explicitly allows former employers to talk to prospective employers about your work for them. If you did a good job, you probably don't have much to worry about. Even if you didn't do a great job, you probably won't get hurt. Most employers are reluctant to speak badly about someone who no longer works for them, even if they were fired.

But if your former employer doesn't like you, he can do you a lot of damage. He can share negative information about you, as long as it's true. If you were absent from work more days than company policy permits, for example, there is no law that stops your former employer from revealing this. Your former employer can also express a negative opinion about your job performance, such as "We weren't satisfied with the quality of his work." The only thing your former boss can't do is lie about you. He can say you were absent in excess of company policy (assuming you were), but if he says he thinks you had a drinking problem, he's crossed the line unless he has very solid evidence.

If your former employer crosses the line, the company can be sued for defamation (commonly known as slander) just like anyone else. A typical case of defamation by reference check is *Hobson v. Coastal Corporation*, in which Hobson claimed that his former employer told a prospective employer who called him for a reference that Hobson had filed frivolous charges against the company with the NLRB. Coastal admitted that they made this statement but claimed that it wasn't liable for slander because the statement was true (i.e., Hobson had filed frivolous charges with the NLRB). The court of appeals for the Tenth Circuit held that Hobson's charges weren't frivolous and allowed his suit.

But the courts give employers a great deal of leeway in defamation cases. If it's a close call, the employer virtually always gets the benefit of the doubt. An Arizona appellate court held that it was legal for an employer to tell a reference caller that a former employee was "unprofessional," "insubordinate," and "abusive." A federal court in New York found in favor of an employer who said a former employee had been fired because they "screwed up."

Can You Prove It?

This leaves you in a difficult position. Your old boss can often undermine your efforts to get a new job without saying anything illegal. Companies are very careful when hiring new employees because the cost of making a mistake is very high. HR employees are extremely risk-averse. If they hire someone who doesn't work out (for any reason), they look bad. If everything in the file at the time of hiring was positive, it's hard to blame the HR staffer who made the decision. But if there was anything negative in the file of an employee who doesn't pan out, the Monday-morning quarterbacking can be devastating to the recruiter's career. An HR staffer will turn down the person they think will do the best job if there is something negative in the file, and hire someone with a spotless file that they know won't perform as well. You can't really blame them. If the company rewards HR for playing it safe (with no penalty for mediocrity) and punishes HR for taking risks, what else would you expect them to do?

Even if your employer crosses the line, you may not be able to do anything about it. To begin with, you don't know what someone says when you're not around. And it's unlikely that anyone will tell you. If your ex-employer is black-balling you, they're certainly not going to tell you. You might think you could ask the company that seemed so interested in you why they changed their minds. But they won't tell you either. If they tell you it was because a former employer gave you a bad reference, you might sue your former boss. The company that turned you down will be subpoenaed to come to court as a witness. Nobody wants to go to court unless there is something in it for them, and there is absolutely no payoff for them for getting involved in this litigation.

If you keep getting to the reference-check phase of getting a job and then having the company suddenly lose interest, you can hire an investigator to call your old employer and do a "reference check." It's best to do this through a lawyer.

If your former boss really has it in for you, he can damage your prospects for getting a new job with virtually no risk. Instead of giving out negative information about you during reference checks, he can do it informally. People in the same field bump into each other all the time, and they frequently talk, even if they are competitors. One place this happens most often is at trade shows and conferences. If your boss says something bad about you over a beer at a trade show, it's likely to be repeated. Soon it may be all over the industry, and you'll never be able to learn how it happened, much less prove it.

The difficulties involved in bringing a defamation action against a former employer can be seen in how rare such cases are. There are only about ten reported cases a year in the entire country in which someone sues a former employer for defamation during a reference check, of which employers win about 75 percent.

Name, Rank, and Serial Number

Even though very few employers ever face liability because of something they said in a reference check, most employers have responded to the possibility of liability by refusing to provide references. Corporate lawyers all tell their clients to limit their response to reference inquiries to confirming that the former employee worked for them and the dates of employment and the position that he held (often referred to as "name, rank, and serial number").

Corporate lawyers are in much the same position as the human resources department. They get little credit when things go right, but lots of blame when things go wrong. Smart corporate lawyers advise their clients against doing anything that might create liability, even if the risk is minuscule. If a lawyer tells a corporate client not to give references, there is no potential for the lawyer to have problems down the line. But if a lawyer tells the client that the risk of getting sued is tiny, and the company is later sued for defamation, the company will probably get itself a new lawyer.

This can work in your favor, especially if your work record is lackluster. Not only will your former employers not reveal the negative aspects of your performance, but you will get the same neutral reference as employees who did a better job.

If you've worked hard and done a good job, however, the policy of refusing to give references hurts you. How can you show your prospective employer how good your work is if your previous employers won't say anything?

Ironically, this closed-mouth policy hurts employers too. For a corporation, nothing is more important than finding the right person for each job. How well HR evaluates potential employees and matches their abilities to the requirements of the job can spell the difference between success and mediocrity, or even failure.

This job is difficult under the best of circumstances. A résumé can reveal whether a person has the education and background that you're looking for, but it tells you very little about how well she performs. A series of promotions is an indication that the person is a strong performer, but a smart (or slightly dishonest) résumé writer can make an average career look stellar. Interviews help, but how much can you really learn about someone in an hour?

What you really need to know to make the right decision is what the applicant did in his previous jobs and how well he did it. Former employers are by far the best potential source of information about a person you are considering hiring. Hiring someone based only on a résumé and interview is like deciding to marry someone after exchanging letters and going on a single date. Without this information, employers frequently hire the wrong people.

They aren't necessarily bad performers, they just aren't right for that job at that company at that time. This costs the employer a great deal of money in diminished productivity. The employee, stuck in a job that doesn't fit her talents, doesn't do her best, and her career suffers.

Why do corporations listen to their lawyers when they give such bad advice? Mostly, it's because lawyers rank higher in the corporate pecking order than the head of HR. In most companies, when the senior executives meet, the head of HR isn't even at the table. She (it usually is a woman) reports to another executive, not directly to the CEO.

It's also because HR has abandoned its original mission. The human resources department is supposed to be a voice for employees. CFOs think it's all about money. People who run research and development think technology is most important. Vice presidents of sales and marketing believe success comes from taking care of customers. All of them are right and none of them are right. In a well-run company, the CEO listens to all of them and makes a decision that strikes a balance between these perspectives. HR should be making the case that the company's most important asset is its employees.

But HR executives don't do that anymore. In most companies, HR has become a department that carries out decisions made by others. It seldom points out the implications of new policies for employee morale, turnover, or recruitment. It's not that HR executives have pointed out the harm of eliminating reference checks but the CEO decided that the advantages of reducing the risk of liability were worth it. In most companies, the head of HR has never brought this issue to the CEO's attention.

The end result of the widespread refusal to give references is that employers can't get the information they need to make good hiring decisions. They don't often hire incompetent people, but they hire people whose skills aren't what the job requires. Instead of excellent job performance, they get mediocrity. This is the most expensive mistake an employer can make, especially in a highly competitive economy in which companies that can't keep up go out of business.

Several years ago, I had the opportunity to debate the head of a large midwestern bank at a conference in St. Louis. Needless to say, he disagreed with virtually everything I said. But then I got to the point about the harm employers inflict upon themselves by refusing to give references. "I never heard that before," he said. "You're right. I'm going to change our policy. If we start giving references to other banks about our former employees, maybe they will respond by talking more candidly to us when we call them." His HR department had never told him about this problem.

Helping Yourself

You can successfully navigate the reference-check minefield if you know how. If you did a good job for your previous employers and want your prospective employer to know about it, start by ignoring HR. They will never give out more than name, rank, and serial number. They wrote the policy (after the legal department told them to) and are in charge of enforcing it. They're not going to break it themselves.

Sidestepping human resources is also a good idea because they don't know much about your work (unless you worked in HR). All they know are the contents of the performance appraisals your supervisor wrote for your annual reviews. The only other thing they know is your disciplinary record, which can't help you, but can hurt you.

If you want your prospective employer to know what a good job you did for your last company, have them talk to the person who really knows: your former supervisor. He or she is the one who saw your work every day and knows how good it was. What's more, they will probably talk to the company you're applying to, if you handle it right. But remember, it isn't whether you think you did a good job that counts, or even whether you really did a good job. All that counts is whether your former boss thinks you did a good job.

If you want your former supervisor to have this conversation, tell her. Do it in person if possible. If not, do it by telephone. Call her at home, not at the office. Tell her that you've applied for a job that you really want, and ask her if she would be willing to talk to the company about your work for her. Make it clear that you're not asking her to do anything but tell the truth. There is a good chance she will say yes.

In my corporate career, I ran an HR department. I also personally hired a number of senior executives. In each case, I called the applicant's former supervisor at every company they ever worked for. I called them at home, at a time the applicant suggested would be least disruptive. Not once did anyone refuse to talk to me. In fact, they talked at great length, usually for an hour or more. And they told me a lot. I never got any dirt about a candidate; that wasn't what I was looking for. But I learned a great deal about exactly what the candidate did for the former employer and how well they did it. All I had to do was see if the strengths the former employers told me the candidate had were the ones I needed for this job.

And, on the bright side, if your previous employment didn't always go well, you can generally sit back and know that the standard policy at your former employer will probably prevent anything from coming out.

The only time you have to worry is when your former boss has a grudge against you and will disparage your work if he gets the chance. If this is the case, you'll probably know it. This is most likely to happen in a small company that doesn't have an HR department.

If you're in this situation, the best thing to do is find someone else in the company who is willing to talk about you and your work. As long as they were above you on the organization chart and are familiar with your work, your prospective new employer will probably be satisfied, even if the person wasn't your immediate supervisor.

If you can't do that, your best option is to negotiate a statement. It's best to do this with a lawyer. Have your lawyer contact your former employer and say (not in these words): "My client doesn't want to sue you, but if you bad-mouth him and cost him a job, he will take you to court. Why don't we work out a statement we can agree on and avoid potential trouble?" Since your former employer has nothing to gain by giving you a bad reference, this often works.

The key point is to be active. Think about the people whom you used to work for and what they are likely to say about you. Then find a way to get your prospective employer to talk to the right people and neutralize the others.

Workplace Injuries

Every state has a workers' compensation law which provides that you are entitled to benefits if you are hurt on the job. It doesn't have to be the company's fault for you to collect. It can even be your fault. It doesn't matter. If you were hurt on the job, you collect, period.

The benefits are limited. You generally receive payment for your medical expenses and lost income (if you miss work). If the injury is sufficiently severe, you may receive an additional payment.

Workers' compensation systems are the result of a bargain in state legislatures many years ago. Before workers' compensation was created, you could sue your boss if you were hurt on the job. If you won, you could receive whatever damages the jury awarded you, probably much more than workers' compensation now provides. But to collect, you would have to prove that the company had been negligent. If it was your fault, or the result of another employee's mistake, or just an accident that was nobody's fault, you got nothing. Workers' compensation is a compromise under which everyone who is hurt on the job gets compensation.

The biggest problem with workers' compensation concerns occupational illnesses. If you break your leg at work, there is no room for argument about whether the injury is work related. But if you get sick, it's a different matter. If you get lung cancer, it could be from carcinogenic substances you were exposed to at work. But it could also be from something having nothing to do with work. Claims for occupational illness are often contested by employers. Both employer and employee generally retain medical specialists (sometimes called "dueling doctors") to argue that the illness was (or wasn't) caused by the job. Given the uncertainties in medical science, the results aren't always right.

While the law in these four areas is far from perfect, you usually have some rights. But when it comes to freedom of speech and other human rights, you usually have virtually none.

14

Exporting Human Rights:
The United States and the Third World

As the largest purchaser of goods and services in the world, the United States has a lot of leverage. Every country in the world wants to export to the U.S. and do it without paying any import duties. Eliminating import duties would lower the cost of the product to American consumers and increase sales, in some cases by a lot.

Some countries are already in this position. Canada and Mexico achieved it through the North American Free Trade Agreement (NAFTA). But other countries still have to pay import duties on at least some of the products they ship to the United States. They would be willing to take many steps to eliminate these duties. Many progressive organizations, including Human Rights Watch, Public Citizen (Ralph Nader's organization), Amnesty International, Americans for Democratic Action, and the National Workrights Institute, believe we should attach conditions to duty-free trade with the United States. Both President Obama and Secretary of State Clinton agree. The most commonly suggested requirements relate to protecting workers' rights and protecting the environment.

We theoretically did this with NAFTA, which contains "side agreements" regarding employment rights and the environment. But despite great pressure from unions and human rights organizations, the labor side agreement the Clinton administration created in NAFTA is absolutely meaningless. There is literally no requirement regarding workers' rights that any of the three countries have to meet to maintain their duty-free status. When you finally hack your way through the legalese, you find that the most a country needs to do is enforce whatever labor laws it chooses to enact. But there are no requirements a country must follow. If Canada or Mexico enacts a law protecting the right to organize, NAFTA requires them to enforce it. But if a country decides not to create any law protecting the right to organize, nothing in NAFTA requires it to create one. The same is true for all other employment rights.

Nor does a country have to do a good job of protecting whatever workplace rights it has on the books to maintain its duty-free status. As long as it makes a reasonable effort, that's good enough. And it doesn't take much to convince the officials in charge of enforcing NAFTA that you're making a reasonable effort.

Better Rules

We should do better in future trade agreements with other nations. There should be objective minimum standards that all countries should be required to meet to have free trade with the United States.

This isn't just a matter of improving protection for human rights, although that would be reason enough to do it. It's also a matter of economic fair play and genuine increases in the world's standard of living. If the United States is going to stop making sneakers and start buying them from Southeast Asia instead, Americans who make sneakers are going to lose their jobs. (One can hope they will get new ones created by increased American exports; economists disagree about whether this actually happened with NAFTA.) This loss of jobs can be justified only if the Asian companies are truly more efficient at making sneakers than we are, even if they achieve that efficiency by paying equally skilled workers less money. But Asian sneaker manufacturers should not be able to undercut American shoe companies when they lower their costs by violating human rights. This is not only morally wrong, but bad economics.

For example, the use of convict labor in making export goods should be outlawed. If Chinese workers are willing to do a job for less than American workers, there is no reason to stop them. But if the Chinese government puts people in prison and forces them to make sneakers for nothing, they aren't more efficient, they're just cheating.

The same is true of the right to organize. Workers in Cambodia are not going to get paid as much as Americans in virtually any job at the present time. But they ought to have the right to organize so that they can get the best deal they can for themselves and their families. To hold prices down by breaking unions, a common practice in the third world, is something we shouldn't enable. Our government should tell other countries that unless they protect the right to organize, they can't have duty-free trade with our country.

Child Labor

There is nothing wrong with child labor per se. Generations of Americans grew up helping their parents work on family farms. I started working weekend and summer jobs when I was eleven. It didn't hurt me a bit. In fact, it probably helped me. Looking around at today's youth, I sometimes think we could use more child labor.

But there is a world of difference between working when you're not in school and working instead of going to school. To have any chance of success in today's global economy, you have to have an education. As Terry Collingsworth, former executive director of the International Labor Rights Fund, puts it, "Taking away a child's education is taking away her future."

Prohibiting child labor isn't as easy as it sounds. For a family in Cambodia or Bangladesh that is struggling to get enough to eat, losing the wages a son or daughter can earn, no matter how meager, is not a small thing. But the price of allowing children to work full-time is too high. Instead of getting an education so they can have a better life than their parents, dropping out of school to work dooms them to relive their parents' poverty. Allowing child labor means an endless cycle of poverty.

It's difficult for a single country to ban child labor. If one third world country bans child labor and others do not, employers will migrate to the countries that permit it in order to hold down labor prices. The most effective way to end child labor is for all countries to ban it at once.

We don't have a world legislature that can pass such a rule. But if allowing child labor kept nations out of the international free trade club, it would have an enormous impact.

Making these rules mandatory for all countries that want free trade with the United States would not only help protect workers' rights in the rest of the world; it would help protect them here at home as well. In a global economy, all companies are under pressure to keep their prices down to what the cheapest producer is charging. It's more difficult for employers operating in the United States to follow the rules if companies in other countries are offering lower prices by breaking them. This is especially true when it comes to the right to organize. Employers know that having a union will raise their labor costs. They don't want this under the best of circumstances. But if competitors in other countries are offering lower prices by breaking unions, American employers have even more reason to fight unions.

Sweatshops

Many people think the best way to help poor people in the third world is to get rid of sweatshops and urge American consumers not to buy from employers that use them.

This well-intended belief is shortsighted. Working in a sneaker factory for a dollar an hour would be a nightmare for most Americans, but for many people in the world, an income of forty dollars a week would be a dream come true. Journalist Nicholas Kristof writes in *The New York Times* of watching people in Cambodia root through garbage dumps looking desperately for something to eat. Every year, at least eight million people starve to death in the world. Millions of women turn to prostitution in order to survive. Over a billion people live on less than a dollar a day. Denying people who are so desperately poor a job that will double or triple their income only makes their situation worse.

A better answer is to allow U.S. companies to build factories in third world countries but to do everything we can to help the workers in these factories make as much as possible. This is why the right to organize is so important. If third world workers in foreign-owned factories can form a union, they can negotiate substantially higher wages.

Another good idea is for all of us as American consumers to choose products certified as being made under decent conditions. These products may cost a little more, but if most American consumers started buying them, more producers would improve their wages and working conditions to get in on the market.

The United States can't eliminate every employment abuse in the world. But we can, and should, do more.

15

Capitalism and Freedom

If this legislation becomes law, what it will do to the economic stability of American society no one can predict.

—CONGRESSMAN WILLIAM CRAMER, DISCUSSING THE CIVIL RIGHTS ACT OF 1964

Why have Americans allowed this situation to exist? Why haven't we changed our laws to protect human rights at work?

Corporations Aren't People

We have a distorted image of who employers are. Americans tend to think of employers as entrepreneurs, rugged individuals who built a business out of nothing through hard work and taking risks. We feel uncomfortable telling such a person how to run his business. The law takes this feeling into consideration, and generally exempts small employers from laws protecting employee rights, even laws against illegal discrimination.

But this picture has nothing to do with the reality of most corporations in America today. The majority of Americans today work in large companies. Our economy is dominated by giant corporations like Wal-Mart, with over two million employees, and McDonald's, with almost half a million. They aren't run by entrepreneurs who built the company from scratch (even if there was one in the past). Corporations are generally large, bureaucratic organizations run by highly paid executives who (at least in theory) work for millions of stockholders. Treating the hired management of a huge corporation as if they were a character out of Horatio Alger who built the company from scratch doesn't make sense.

This is especially true when it comes to freedom of association. We all have a right to choose the people with whom we associate. If you want to be friends only with people of your own race or religion, you should be able to (however backward that attitude is). This may be true in professional life as well. If a lawyer wants a partner, she should probably be able to select whoever she feels most comfortable working with, however she makes the choice. A small employer who works intimately with his employees might be entitled to the same right, even though his views are biased.

But the CEO of a large corporation has no association with most of the people who work for him. He has literally never met most of them and never will. To speak about freedom of association in this context is absurd.

This doesn't mean that corporations shouldn't have legal rights. But thinking about them as if they were people, rather than organizations, warps our thinking and makes us hesitant to pass laws to protect our rights at work.

Ignorance: What You Don't Know Can Hurt You

Another reason we don't demand change is that employees frequently don't know what's going on at their workplace. Most people today know that their employer has the capability to monitor their computer and sometimes uses it. It's hard not to know this; we get a notice every time we turn on our computer. We may not read it, but we get the general message.

But we don't know how our employers actually conduct monitoring. Professor John Weckert, from Charles Stuart University in Australia, found that most employees don't mind computer monitoring because they assume their employer is doing it fairly. They assume that monitoring is done to investigate instances of possible computer misuse. They assume that their employer isn't using monitoring to pry into their personal lives. They have no idea that the employees who maintain the computer system are reading their personal e-mail for fun and that the boss lets them get away with it. If people knew how monitoring in their company really worked, they would object and demand laws to protect their privacy.

We also fail to demand laws to protect our rights because we mistakenly believe we already have them. I have spoken to literally thousands of people during the last twenty years about workplace human rights. I always ask about their reaction to Lynne Gobbell's boss's firing her over her bumper sticker. Virtually everyone says that it's not only wrong, but illegal. They are stunned to hear the truth. The same is true in other areas of workplace rights. Most people think they have legal rights that, in fact, are completely nonexistent.

Human Rights and Prosperity

But the main reason we haven't changed our laws is because we have listened to people like Congressman Cramer, quoted above. Every time someone proposes changing our employment laws to make them more just, organized business proclaims that we are undermining the free enterprise system and jeopardizing our prosperity.

Americans do not take this argument lightly, nor should they. We enjoy the highest standard of living in human history. This is not an accident. It is not because Americans are smarter than other people. It is not because we work harder. While Americans work more than most Europeans, there are many societies, especially in Asia, that make us look like slackers. Nor is it because of our natural resources. America is blessed with abundant resources, but there are many countries with even more that are not as prosperous. Russia, for example, has far more resources than the United States and its economy is in tatters.

What sets the United States apart from less wealthy nations is our economic system. More than any other country, we have embraced the market economy. People call it capitalism, but this is a misnomer. Capitalism is an economic system in which the means of production are privately owned. Our system is capitalist, but that is not what makes it so productive. What gives our economy its special dynamism is that it is a market economy. In a market economy, producers must compete against each other for business. Those that lose the race go bankrupt. This never-ending threat means that companies must constantly work at improving quality, reducing price, and creating new products just to stay alive.

No company, no matter how large and successful, can rest on its laurels. General Motors and the other U.S. carmakers once dominated the world. But when they became complacent, they went bankrupt and had to turn to the federal government to stay alive. It is this relentless competition, this industrial Darwinism, that produces our remarkable standard of living. Most of us are not economists, but we understand this process and are properly reluctant to tamper with a system that has served us well.

But we do not have to give up the benefits of our market economy to protect our human rights at work. There is no conflict between the needs of a market economy and human rights. A market economy requires that producers be compelled to compete for market share and that their managers be allowed to make the resource allocation decisions needed to compete. Managers need to be allowed to decide which products they will produce, where the facilities will be located, what processes to use, how many employees are needed and which are most qualified, and what wages and benefits they will offer. And they need to be able to change these decisions quickly when the market changes.

Employers can do all these things without violating employees' freedom of speech, freedom of association, due process, or privacy. Employers can make resource allocation decisions, but decisions about human rights should not be under employer control. Having a market economy does not mean turning every company into a banana republic whose only law is the whim of the current CEO.

The compatibility of market economics and human rights can be seen in the success of many companies that respect employees' rights. David Ewing, a professor of management at Harvard Business School, studied companies that gave up the right to hire and fire at will and adopted policies that require just cause to terminate an employee. These companies did not go bankrupt. Their sales did not decline. In fact, most of them exceed the national average in both growth and productivity. Many are industry leaders, such as General Electric and IBM. The leaders of these companies frequently say that their enlightened policies are one of the reasons for their success. John Donnelly, former CEO of the Donnelly Corporation, a world leader in producing high-tech glass products, whose remarkable employee discipline system was discussed in chapter 4, told me, "Our employees are more loyal, dedicated, and productive because they are treated fairly."

I saw the same dynamic at work in my corporate career. At Drexelbrook Controls, respect for employees was a fundamental value. We would never have dreamed of trying to tell employees what to do in their private lives, whether it was which politician to support or what unhealthy behavior to quit. We didn't monitor employee computers. We didn't have a drug testing program, even though we were in a very safety-sensitive industry. If you were terminated or put on probation and thought it wasn't fair, you could appeal to the head of HR and the company general counsel. Unless both of them agreed that the discipline was not only legal but fair, it was rescinded.

"You can't run a company that way," people told us. "Employees will take advantage. You need to be tougher." They were wrong. The company not only survived and was profitable, but it was much more successful than its more conventional competitors. The company grew an average of 20 percent per year, was highly profitable, and had virtually no debt. Drexelbrook did so well that a *Fortune* 1000 company made an offer to the controlling stockholder that he couldn't refuse. Another part of the owner's philosophy was that the financial well-being of all senior executives should be tied to the long-term performance of the company. Instead of receiving competitive salaries, we received more modest salaries plus stock in the company. When Drexelbrook was acquired, my stock was worth enough that I could afford to leave the corporate world and go to work for the ACLU without hurting my family.

One of the reasons the company was so successful was how it dealt with its employees. Drexelbrook's employees were treated with respect and had their rights respected. In return, they routinely went above and beyond the call of duty to help the company and its customers. The service manager, for example, installed a ship-to-shore telephone on his sailboat so customers with a problem could reach him when he was on vacation. What's more, he paid for the phone (which was expensive at the time) out of his own pocket. Such actions were common.

The experience of unionized companies also illustrates that companies can prosper while respecting human rights. In his classic work *What Do Unions Do?*, economist Richard Freeman found that companies with unions had higher productivity than their nonunion competitors. By reducing arbitrary firings and forcing managers to work with employees whose performance had slipped rather than discard them, unionized companies were able to retain productive employees rather than find and train new people.

The same picture emerges if one looks at the economic performance of countries where employers are required to respect human rights. Other industrial democracies have long had laws protecting employee rights. In the European Union, Canada, and Japan, your employer cannot fire you because you smoke or drink off the job. Your employer cannot fire you because of your politics. Your boss cannot read your personal e-mail. Laws protecting freedom of association are strong and vigorously enforced. The United States stands alone in its refusal to protect human rights at work. These companies have not suffered economically because of this decision. Industrial productivity and living standards in Canada, Western Europe, and Japan are generally comparable to our own.

This is not to say that the United States should blindly copy the economic systems of other countries. Other industrial nations have their own economic difficulties. France and other countries in Western Europe make it difficult for employers to fire people even when there is legitimate reason. This reduces productivity and makes employers reluctant to hire new people, causing high unemployment. But in general the success of other countries shows that respecting human rights at work is compatible with productivity and prosperity.

Our own history reinforces this lesson. When the Civil Rights Act of 1964 was introduced, Congressman Cramer was not alone in predicting that restricting employers' ability to hire whomever they wanted would lead to economic problems. Much of the business community made the same prediction.

That didn't happen. Requiring employers to hire and fire based on merit, not race, created opportunities for racial minorities and women to make greater economic contributions. The average black employee's pay increased from

60 percent of white employees' pay to 74 percent (in 1993). The average woman's pay increased from 60 percent of men's pay to 72 percent. Women and minorities began to appear in the executive suite. Prior to 1964, minorities and women in senior management positions were virtually nonexistent. Today, 15 percent of *Fortune* 500 corporate officers are women and 10 percent of the directors of large companies are from racial minority groups. While we have a long way to go before we reach Martin Luther King's dream of a country where each of us is judged by our character and not the color of our skin, employment opportunities today are far more equal than before, in large part because of antidiscrimination laws.

Nor did America's economy suffer. The decade immediately following passage of the Civil Rights Act saw one of the greatest surges in American history. Gross domestic product (GDP) more than doubled. While this growth had many causes, one was the increased contribution of millions of people who were no longer confined to menial jobs. Even former segregationists like Jesse Helms later admitted that recognizing the right of racial minorities to equal treatment was a step forward for America.

The truth is that employers have been pulling this argument out of their hats for decades. Organized business opposed the Age Discrimination in Employment Act, the Environmental Protection Act, the Occupational Safety and Health Act, the Employee Retirement Income Security Act, the Fair Labor Standards Act, and the recent Genetic Information Nondiscrimination Act. Every time, they've argued that the proposed new law would cause havoc and destroy productivity. Every time they've been wrong. Why do we still listen?

The argument that we will undermine our prosperity by protecting human rights at work is simply wrong. It is a red herring dragged out by those who want to maintain the status quo. The truth is that we can have both prosperity and freedom.

Why Liberals Hate Capitalism

Many people who believe in human rights are reluctant to embrace the concept of a market economy. It would be surprising if they didn't. It's hard to feel good about an economic system whose operating principle is greed. Even Adam Smith, the patron saint of market economies whose *Wealth of Nations* is the bible of free-market economics, freely admitted that a market economy is based on each person's getting as much as he can for himself. No one is trying to help anyone else. The social benefit comes not from unselfish behavior but because the "invisible hand" of competition forces companies to outperform their competitors to survive.

Choosing an economy for our country, however, is not a matter of aesthetics. The purpose of an economy is to produce the goods and services that people need. Market economies have outperformed economies that are owned or managed by the government throughout human history. The best measure of a country's economic efficiency is GDP per capita (the total value of all the goods and services a country produces divided by its population). According to this standard, the top ten economies in the world today are Austria, Denmark, Finland, Iceland, Ireland, the Netherlands, Norway, Sweden, Switzerland, and the United States. (This list leaves off Qatar, whose economy is simply awash in oil money, and Luxembourg, whose national population— 500,000—is less than that of thirty-four U.S. cities, including El Paso, Texas.)

All of these countries have a market economy. Some are more heavily regulated than the United States, but in all ten, major resource allocation decisions are made by the private sector.

State-Run Economies

Economies run by governments have performed poorly. For years, the largest government-run economy in the world was that of the former Soviet Union. Decisions were made by government bureaucrats and the results were terrible. The Soviet economy was a mess. At its strongest, in the 1980s, the Soviet Union's GDP was only half that of the United States, despite having a quarter more people. By the time the Soviet Union broke up in 1991, its economy had declined to as little as one quarter of ours. Food was rationed, consumer goods were rare and shoddy, and there were long lines to buy almost anything.

Since 1991, Russia has moved in the direction of a market economy. This has been an awkward process, with many serious mistakes. One of the worst was to privatize national industries and resources before establishing the rule of law. As a result, billions of dollars' worth of industrial capacity and natural resources were virtually given away to a few politically connected insiders. But despite all the mistakes, the Russian economy grew. Between 1991 and 2007, Russia's GDP almost tripled, rising from $500 billion a year to $1.3 trillion. Many factors contributed to this, including the rising price of oil (Russia is one of the world's largest oil producers). But it's hard to escape the conclusion that Russia is better off under even a half-baked market economy than under a government-run economy.

The same is true in China. Despite the best efforts of the party leaders in Beijing, China's economic growth after the Communist victory in the 1949 civil war ranged from unimpressive to disastrous. In 1958, Chairman Mao Zedong decreed the "Great Leap Forward," a five-year economic plan in which agriculture and industry would expand dramatically at the same time. The idea was to force China's farmers into large communes, which would be more efficient. The labor freed from farm work would be used to expand industry, especially steel production. Mao boasted that within fifteen years, Chinese steel production would surpass that of the United Kingdom.

The result was a great leap backward. The communes did not produce the projected increase in efficiency. When the "excess" farm workers were taken off for industrial labor, much of the next crop rotted in the field because there weren't enough people to harvest it. The result was mass starvation.

Nor did China achieve the planned industrial growth. Mao, who had little knowledge of metallurgy, decreed that steel would be produced in small backyard furnaces by peasants. The raw material was to be scrap iron. These backyard furnaces proved incapable of producing anything but lumps of pig iron of little economic value. Worse yet, to get the necessary scrap metal, peasants had to sacrifice their cooking pans and household utensils. To get fuel for the furnaces, peasants stripped the countryside of trees.

The Great Leap Forward caused the deaths of at least fifteen million people, one of the largest mass deaths in human history. Industrial production in China declined and did not recover to its previous level until 1964.

Most of the damage is directly linked to economic decisions made by government officials that would have been made differently in a market economy. If the farms had been privately owned and had to sell the food they produced in the open market, they wouldn't have sent workers needed for the harvest off to make steel. If the people making steel had to sell their steel to a willing buyer and had any choice over how they spent their working time, they would have quickly stopped making worthless pig iron that they couldn't sell. If China had a market economy, the so-called Great Leap Forward wouldn't have happened.

The turning point in modern Chinese economic history occurred in the late 1970s under the leadership of Deng Xiaoping. Deng instituted a series of reforms called *Gaige Kaifang* (Reforms and Openness), which he described as "socialism with Chinese characteristics." Most of these reforms moved China in the direction of a market economy. For example, Chinese farmers were now allowed to have small private plots of land (in addition to their work in the commune). On these plots, they could grow whatever they wanted and sell it in a free market. Deng created a series of "special economic zones" where foreign investment was encouraged and companies were permitted greater freedom in decision making. Perhaps most important, municipalities and provinces were allowed to invest in whatever industry they thought would be most profitable rather than have their investment decisions dictated from Beijing. If they made good decisions, they were allowed to keep the profits. This produced the shift to light industry that became the foundation of Chinese economic growth.

China's economic growth after Deng's reforms was nothing short of spectacular. In thirty years, China grew from a peasant society into an industrial superpower whose industrial output is exceeded only by that of the United States and Japan (whom they are rapidly overtaking). In recent years, as Deng's successors have instituted additional market-based reforms, China's economy has been growing at the astonishing rate of almost 10 percent annually.

Inequality

Our collective misgivings about market economies are based on more than emotion and philosophy. Many are also concerned about the social effects, and with good reason. We live in the wealthiest society in human history, yet we have people without homes sleeping on the streets and eating in soup kitchens (when they eat at all). Millions of bright young people have little economic future because they can't afford to go to college. There are 46 million Americans living without health insurance. This can be fatal. I will never forget hearing a colleague at the ACLU tell me how her mother hadn't been able to afford medical care when she developed breast cancer and, within a year, had died of the disease. Meanwhile, a small percentage of Americans have amassed vast wealth and fly around in private jets.

This economic disparity is obviously wrong, but the answer isn't to abandon the market economy, or even to tinker with it. The problem is not in the way we create wealth, but in the way we distribute it. There is no reason why we can't have both a market economy and universal health care. Perhaps we will see this in the next four years. There is no reason why we can't have a market economy and a welfare system that provides a decent life for those in need. There is no reason we can't have an educational system that financially supports all those with the ability and the desire to go to college. We actually did this once. It was called the G.I. Bill. Out of gratitude for the sacrifices they had made, the federal government provided financial assistance to any veteran who wanted to go to college. It turned out to be one of the smartest investments we have ever made. The number of college graduates in America boomed. So did the economy. The post–World War II years were among the greatest economic expansions in our history. And the federal government got it back in spades with the taxes they paid on their higher income. We can, and should, do the same thing today on an even larger scale.

All we have to do to make this possible is pay for it. This will require higher taxes, including higher corporate taxes. But we don't have to tell employers how to run their businesses. They can make whatever decisions they want (as long as they respect human rights); they just have to pay up at the end of the year. The Masai people of Kenya get their livelihood from their cattle. But they don't eat meat. Instead, they take good care of the animals and then collect milk (and blood, too). We could learn something from them.

The Environment

The other major reason progressives don't like market economies has to do with what economists call externalities. The most obvious example is the environment. In *The Social Costs of Private Enterprise*, K. William Karp explains that private corporations have no financial incentive to avoid polluting the environment. Every industrial process produces by-products that are harmful to the environment. Producing electric power from fossil fuels, for example, produces ash, nitrous oxide, and several other harmful by-products. These can be largely eliminated, but it is expensive. A privately owned power corporation has no incentive to pay for this. It can't charge any more for electricity if it cuts down on pollution, so the cost of pollution-control equipment reduces profits. The power company "externalizes" the cost of pollution by passing it off to the public.

My father used to tell me, "The assumption that gets you is the one you don't know you made." People who mistrust market economies because they externalize costs assume that producers would behave differently if they were owned by the public.

Public ownership, however, doesn't eliminate financial incentives for the people who run factories. The profit motive goes away, but others remain. The manager of a publicly owned factory still has personal financial goals. He wants to keep his job. He might want to get a better one. This requires that he do a good job in the eyes of his superiors. If the manager of a publicly owned power plant produces less than his quota of electricity, he is likely to be in trouble with his boss. Explaining that he did so by reducing the amount of pollution the plant produced is unlikely to help him if he did it on his own initiative. He has little to gain and a lot to lose by taking it upon himself to run his plant cleaner. The managers of companies in Russia and China that were owned by the government didn't act any more responsibly than managers in privately owned companies. They did whatever they needed to keep their bosses happy.

But won't the public demand that operators of "their" power plants reduce pollution? After all, nobody likes to breathe dirty air. Unfortunately, this is not how it works. No one would choose to breathe polluted air if clear air were free. But it isn't. Pollution-control equipment for a power plant doesn't become free because the public owns the plant. One way or another, people will have to either breathe air that isn't completely clean or pay slightly more for their electric power. Traditionally poor countries that are just starting to reap the financial benefits of industrialization often choose cheap power over clean air. The United States made the same choice until the 1970s. If a country's leadership has made this choice, a plant manager who chooses differently will not go far.

Anyone who believes that public ownership means better decisions on issues like pollution should visit China, which has some of the dirtiest air in the world and where many people are forced to wear surgical masks when they go outdoors.

Markets Aren't Magic

Some people, such as former president George W. Bush, think all economic problems will be solved by turning decisions over entirely to the free market. But America's economic history shows the fallacy of this simplistic view. The Great Depression occurred largely because the stock market at that time was unregulated. Irresponsible investment practices abounded. One of the worst was buying on margin, in which a person buying stock paid only part of the price (as little as 10 percent) and borrowed the rest. This worked like magic when markets were going up. You could buy ten times as many shares of stock, get ten times the appreciation, pay off the loan, and get rich. But when the market goes down, it all turns into a house of cards. When it comes time to repay the loan you took out to buy the stock, you don't have the money because the value of the stock has gone down. If you borrowed enough money, you can't pay the loan even if you sell all the stock. You have to sell other assets to pay the loan, even if you have to sell them at a loss. Soon you're bankrupt.

The damage is magnified when everyone else is doing the same thing. If all (or most) investors are buying on margin and the stock market goes down, everyone has to sell their shares when the margin loan comes due. But if everyone is trying to sell, there is no one to buy. The price of stocks goes into a death spiral and the economy falls apart. This isn't the only thing that caused the Depression, but it played an important part. One reason the United States went so many years without another depression is because Congress restricted buying stock with loans and created the Securities and Exchange Commission (SEC) to enforce this and other new rules.

The current recession is another painful reminder that markets need to be regulated. It will take years for economists to understand and explain what has gone wrong. But almost all the experts agree that the bursting housing bubble was the triggering event. When people can't afford their mortgage payments, traditionally the loss is limited to the homeowners themselves and the banks that lent them the money to buy the house (and a few additional banks that purchased mortgages from the original bank).

This time, however, it was different. In recent years, financial wizards on Wall Street found a way to buy up a large pool of mortgages and then sell a share in the entire pool like a traditional corporate stock or bond. Even though many of the individual mortgages were risky (because people borrowed more than they could realistically expect to pay back), the overall investment was supposed to be safe, since the odds were against too many mortgages going bad at any one time.

But something went very wrong. So many mortgages went bad at once that the securities representing shares in the mortgage pools became almost worthless. This affected more than just the banks traditionally involved in real estate, because virtually every major financial institution in America had invested in these new securities. It seemed like a great idea at the time; an investor could generate income from real estate without taking the risk of owning specific properties. Now even financial giants like Lehman Brothers and Goldman Sachs were in trouble. (Lehman Brothers eventually went out of business.) Some people (myself included) thought we would be relatively safe because we hadn't invested in these toxic securities, or even in any financial institutions that had. Even this turned out to be wrong. When the largest banks in the country become insolvent, corporations cannot raise capital. So even companies producing goods and services having nothing to do with real estate are hurt. John Wellemeyer, a former senior executive at Morgan Stanley (one of the country's most successful investment firms), explains, "Credit is the lifeblood of the economy. Without access to credit, even strong, profitable companies can't function."

While there is much we don't yet understand, one thing we know is that, unlike traditional stocks and bonds, the new real estate securities that turned toxic were largely unregulated. SEC regulation alone wouldn't have prevented the crash of 2008, but the lack of regulation made the situation a great deal worse.

The importance of government regulation of markets can be seen in a list of the world's most productive economies. Most of the top ten countries, such as Sweden, Denmark, and the Netherlands, heavily regulate employers to prevent abuses.

Determining when and how to regulate markets to prevent abuses and disasters without hurting economic growth is complicated and difficult. But rules requiring employers to respect human rights will not hurt our economy. The experience of unionized employers, progressive employers that voluntarily respect human rights, employers in other industrial democracies, and our own experience with workplace rights laws all show that we don't have to choose between freedom and prosperity. We can have both.

16

Taking Back Our Rights

I'm as mad as hell and I'm not going to take this anymore!

——HOWARD BEALE (PETER FINCH), *NETWORK* (1976)

There isn't much you can do alone to protect yourself. Legally, your boss holds all the cards. And unless you're an NBA star or a world-class neurosurgeon, your boss probably has all the economic leverage as well. But that doesn't mean you're helpless. There are a few things you can do.

Privacy

Reduce Your Chances of Being Monitored

Start by recognizing that your company is probably monitoring e-mail, even if it has never told you about it. Then take defensive action to minimize the likelihood that your messages will be the ones monitored.

The most important step in this process is to watch your language. Remember that most e-mail monitoring is done through keyword searches looking primarily for evidence of sexual harassment. Don't use any of George Carlin's seven dirty words or any anatomical words relating to sex. If possible, don't use profanity at all. This will feel unnatural, because it is. Standards of polite conversation have changed. Words like "damn" or "hell" aren't even considered profanity by most people today. But e-mail monitoring is stuck in a time warp back in the 1950s. If you want to keep your e-mail from being read, learn how to speak like your grandmother.

This doesn't mean you can't talk to your doctor or even send your spouse a romantic message in relative privacy. Just phrase your message to avoid verbal red flags. If it's your anniversary, promise your spouse a fantastic evening (maybe even a hot evening), but don't go into details. If you want to criticize someone, call them an "idiot," not as "ass." This doesn't guarantee that your message won't be read, but it changes the odds in your favor.

Ask Your Boss

If you're concerned about your employer's surveillance policies, ask about them. While relatively few companies tell employees how their monitoring program works, some will tell you if you ask.

Knowing how your company's monitoring program works can be very helpful. For example, if your employer monitors e-mails but not telephone calls (a common arrangement), you can use the phone to communicate about sensitive subjects. If the company monitors both e-mail and telephones, but not Internet access, you can sign up for a service such as theanonymousemail.com. With these services, you log on to their Web site and send e-mail from their server. But if your employer wants to, it can "open" your Internet connection and read the messages. This isn't easy or cheap. But, in the long run, most employers probably won't be foolish enough to set up an e-mail monitoring system and then sit idly by while employees bypass it.

You may also be able to find out something about how the monitoring system works. For e-mail monitoring, ask what kind of e-mail the company is concerned about. Your boss will never tell you what keywords cause your e-mail to be flagged and read. He may not even know himself. But if you know what the company is concerned about, you will have some insight into the type of vocabulary to avoid.

Before raising the subject, do a reality check. Is your boss the kind of person who is open to questions, or does he consider people who ask questions troublemakers? If your boss is the wrong type, don't ask. Also think about your relationship to your boss. Does he think highly of you and value your work? Or does he consider you a problem or a marginal performer? If your boss questions your value to the company, asking challenging questions is not a good idea. Have you been getting along with your boss recently, or have there been arguments or tension? If your boss thinks highly of you, but you haven't been hitting it off recently, now is not a good time to ask questions. Wait until you're back on his good side.

If you can't ask your boss, ask someone else. The people who run the company's computer system know whether monitoring occurs and how it works. The people in HR probably know too. If you have a friend in one of these departments, you may be able to find out about monitoring without engaging in a potentially risky discussion with your boss.

Finally, there may be a way to ask without revealing your identity. Many employers have set up systems for employees to ask questions or make comments anonymously. In the old days, it was the suggestion box, into which employees could slip a note. Today these systems are generally on the company intranet. While this has the advantage of being interactive, it is not anonymous. Your employer can easily determine which computer a message was sent from. If your company has a means of making suggestions that provides anonymity, take advantage of it.

Don't Use Your Employer's System

Last, but not least, you may be able to escape monitoring by texting. The employer has the legal right to monitor your computer because it owns the computer and the server. But text messages you send from your company-issued cell phone (if you have one) are different. Your employer owns the phone, but it doesn't own the equipment that transmits the message (there is no server). The federal court of appeals for the Ninth Circuit recently ruled (in the case of *Quon v. Arch Wireless*) that it was illegal for an employer to monitor text messages because it didn't own enough of the system. The Ninth Circuit is well known for being the most protective of individual rights, and other federal courts frequently don't rule the same way, so the ban on text messaging may hold only in California, Alaska, Arizona, Hawaii, Idaho, Montana, Nevada, Oregon, and Washington. But the argument that employers can't monitor text messages is strong and may prevail in other federal courts.

If the *Quon* decision stands up over time, it should also apply to e-mail you send from your BlackBerry or iPhone. But remember to set your device not to save messages. Your employer owns the device and can demand that you let him search it. If you want your messages saved, have the ISP save them.

One option that sometimes works is plug-in wireless Internet access. This is a cellular modem you can connect to your office computer that allows you to send e-mail wirelessly. Since this e-mail doesn't go through the company server, the company can't read it. However, if the employer's monitoring equipment is looking at your computer at the moment your message is transmitted, you're busted. Also, some employers continuously monitor. In this case, plug-in wireless is useless.

Remember, however, that employers constantly upgrade their monitoring systems. A technique that protects your privacy today may not do so tomorrow. Also, it's very difficult to learn enough about the monitoring system to know whether a particular tactic will work even now. With the possible exception of BlackBerrys and other PDAs, you always take a risk of being monitored when you use the company's equipment. Don't say something that could get you fired on the assumption that one of my suggestions will keep the boss from knowing about it.

There is a way to be completely safe. Buy your own smartphone or other PDA. Your messages won't go through the company server and the company won't be able to order you to let them examine it. The price of new electronic technology always drops over time. If you can't afford an iPhone today, there's a good chance you'll be able to afford one pretty soon.

Suggest Changes

Most employers give little thought to the way they conduct monitoring. They just buy a software program from a vendor and install it. If your employer's program is overly intrusive, it's probably not because the company made a conscious decision to pry. If you raise concerns about aspects of the program that seem too invasive and suggest alternative approaches that meet the company's needs, you may be successful.

One simple thing every employer should do is instruct the employees engaged in monitoring not to read messages for fun. You might think that every employer would have such a policy, but many don't. The Center for

Business Ethics at Bentley College surveyed employers and found that 25 percent of employers who monitor have no policy telling employees involved in monitoring to read coworkers' messages only for business purposes. Even among companies with such a policy, most have no method of enforcing it.

I've spoken to hundreds of employers about monitoring and have yet to meet one who wanted employees involved in monitoring to snoop. If your company doesn't have a policy against snooping, it's probably because they have never thought of it. Bringing this point to your employer's attention could lead to results.

If your employer is interested in learning how to do a better job of respecting employee rights (without hurting company performance), there is a model corporate privacy policy in appendix A on page 249.

Questions and suggestions are even more useful when they come from more than one employee. Most employers assume employees don't care about privacy. You can't really blame them. Very few employees ever raise the subject. Employees ask about pay, benefits, vacation, and a host of other subjects, but almost never ask about privacy. If more employees expressed their interest in privacy, employers would give it more priority.

Again, you have to do a reality check. Does your boss appreciate constructive suggestions, or does he resent them? If it's the latter, best keep your ideas to yourself.

Fair Discipline

The most important question when it comes to discipline is "Who makes the decision?" In the worst of all worlds, the person who wants to fire you has the first and last word. Some companies, however, give employees some right of internal appeal, at least for terminations. Sometimes this right is meaningless—the managers stick up for one another and no decision is ever changed. But don't automatically assume this is the case. In some companies, employees sometimes win internal appeals. Find out if your company has such a system and what has happened to the employees who have used it. If employees occasionally reverse a decision, use the system yourself.

If your company uses outside arbitrators, you're probably better off. Arbitrators are inherently more independent than anyone inside the company. But not all arbitration systems are created equal. Find out which organization provides arbitration services to your company. If your employer is using AAA or JAMS, you will probably get a fair shake. If your employer uses a different provider, check it out online. Do a search, and look at its Web site and the other information that pops up. You don't need a degree from Harvard Law School to get a good sense of what kind of organization it is.

If your employer's arbitration provider doesn't look entirely fair to you, consider suggesting that the company make a change. But be especially careful. While most employers with overly intrusive monitoring systems haven't given the issue much thought and may be open to changes, the odds are much greater that a company that chose a biased arbitration provider knew exactly what they were doing. If you have any friends in HR or the legal department, see what you can find out about how the provider was chosen before you say anything.

Join a Union

Employees who belong to unions are protected against most workplace abuse. Union members can be fired only for "just cause." This prevents your boss from firing you because of your politics or your off-duty behavior. Your employer would have to negotiate with the union about its surveillance policy, drug testing program, and anything else involved in your "terms and conditions of employment." This doesn't mean that the results will be completely fair, but they will be much better than a unilateral decision by the company.

Organizing a union, however, entails risk. As discussed in chapter 10, employers frequently retaliate against employees who try to organize. But if the abuses in your company are serious, it may be worth that risk.

If you're interested in joining a union, the best way to start is by contacting one of the two national labor federations, the AFL-CIO (aflcio.org) or Change to Win (changetowin.org). They can direct you to the appropriate union representatives in your area. It's important to take this step early. Even though you have a legal right to join a union, your employer isn't going to take it kindly. There is a good chance that there will be retaliation, including firings. In order to withstand this pressure and organize successfully, you will need the help of an organized union. Unions, like every other organization, do not have unlimited resources. As much as they would like to, they can't try to organize every employer at the same time. Before you stick your neck out, find out how much support you can expect to receive.

One way to improve your workplace without taking big initial risks is to work with unions on specific issues, like health and safety or making sure every employee who is entitled to overtime receives it. Unions have a great deal of expertise in many areas and are usually happy to share it for free. To them, it's both the right thing to do and a smart investment. By helping workers in a nonunion plant, unions can demonstrate their capabilities and build relationships that may eventually lead those workers to join the union.

Interview Wisely

You don't have much choice about your employer's policies. But you can choose to work for a company that respects the rights of employees. When changing jobs, don't ask just about compensation and benefits. Ask about your prospective employer's privacy policies, drug testing program, and termination policies. Then talk to people who work there about what it's like.

You can also learn a great deal about a company through research. A number of good books have been written about what specific companies are like as employers. The most famous of these is *The 100 Best Companies to Work for in America*, by Robert Levering and Milton Moskowitz. *Fortune* also publishes a list of the best companies to work for and updates it every year. These references tell you not only the best places to work in general, but also how the companies rank on specific issues. If you want to know which companies have the best work/family balance policies, or offer the best opportunity for advancement to women, this information is available. There are also Web sites about which companies are the best employers, including the Great Place to Work Institute (greatplacetowork.com). There is also a lot of information available about which companies are bad to work for, much of it on the Internet at sites like wanderlist.com.

More important than anything else, talk to some people who work at the company you're considering. They know better than anyone what their employer is like. And they will probably tell you if you ask, both the good and the bad (and maybe the ugly). Some people seem to think this is unethical in some way. Nothing could be more wrong. Your employer is asking the people you used to work for what kind of employee you were, so why shouldn't you ask about what kind of employer they are? If the company objects to your asking (assuming they ever find out, which is unlikely), they probably have something to hide. You should look for another company to work for, one that's proud of the way they deal with employees.

If you have more than one job opportunity, you may be able to choose a company that respects your rights. At the time I'm writing this book, that probably isn't the case for most people. The economy is in a severe recession and no one knows when it will end. Most people are happy just to have a job and want nothing more than to keep it.

But this isn't always the case. More often than not, the American economy is strong. Finding a job isn't always easy, and getting more than one job offer is more difficult. But it's often not impossible if you try hard enough. One key is to look for a new job while you still have your old one. It's not a bad idea to keep your eyes on the job market, even if you love your job. (You never know what might happen.) If you don't like your job, start looking for a better one now. That way you won't be forced to take the first offer that comes along just to pay your bills.

I ran a corporate HR department in my previous career and was always astonished at how little our employees knew about us when they joined the company. We read their résumés thoroughly, planned the questions we wanted to ask in the interview, and talked to everyone they had ever worked for. Sometimes we had more than one HR employee take the same steps just to get a second opinion. We did all this because it's expensive to hire a person who isn't right for the job and we didn't want to make a mistake. But employees have much more at stake. We had lots of employees; if we made a mistake and hired the wrong person, it was an expense, but not a catastrophe. Going to work for the wrong company is a nightmare, and it can leave a mark on your résumé that will follow you for the rest of your working life. How ironic that those who have the most to lose do the least homework. Don't be one of them.

Buy Wisely

Not every employer behaves badly. Some companies do a good job of treating employees fairly. If enough people stopped buying products from companies that don't deserve your business and started buying from companies that are good employers, things would change. Consumers have had an impact on the working conditions of American subcontractors in the third world. They could have the same effect here at home.

Three sources of information about which companies are good employers are ResponsibleShopper.org, ShopUnionMade.org, and FairTradeFederation.org.

Change the Law

We have met the enemy, and he is us.

—POGO THE POSSUM

The real answer, however, is to change the law. As long as the law fails to protect freedom of speech, privacy, and other human rights at work, there is no way to protect yourself.

Fortunately, we live in a democracy. If Americans tell their elected representatives that the law needs to be changed, they generally respond. In 1964, Americans decided that it was no longer acceptable to discriminate against people because of their race. Congress got the message and enacted the first Civil Rights Act. When we decided that it was wrong to discriminate based on disability, Congress passed the Americans with Disabilities Act.

When we decided that it was wrong to discriminate based on genetics, Congress passed the Genetic Information Nondiscrimination Act.

The reason Congress has not acted to protect other human rights is because we have not asked them to. In the last twenty years, three bills to protect workplace privacy were introduced into Congress. Despite the fact that these bills had powerful sponsors and the support of many civil rights and labor groups, not one ever reached the House or Senate floor for a vote. All but one died in committee.

Congress didn't act on these bills because their constituents didn't ask them to. Members of Congress receive hundreds of letters, e-mails, and telephone calls asking them to take action on various issues. The silence surrounding the privacy bills was deafening. Most members of Congress did not receive a single letter from a constituent asking them to support the privacy bills. Can you blame Congress for turning its attention elsewhere?

But if Americans were to tell Congress that they want laws protecting freedom of speech, privacy, and other human rights on the job, the outcome would be different.

What You Can Do

You don't have to be a lawyer to help create new laws. No matter who you are, there is something you can do.

Write Your Elected Representatives

Many people think that Congress doesn't pay attention to mail from voters. Nothing could be further from the truth. Members of Congress don't read the mail themselves, but they have staff people review every letter, e-mail, and telephone call and tell them which issues constituents are communicating about and their position on these issues. This is a major factor in deciding which of the hundreds of bills introduced every session get their attention and priority. It's not the only factor. On most bills, the leadership of the party (whether Republican or Democratic) takes a position and determines its priority among the hundreds of bills before Congress at any given time. Members of Congress are not required to vote the way the leadership wants, but they are generally expected to do so and there are penalties for those who stray too often (such as not receiving much financial support from the party when their term is up and they must run for office again). But constituent input counts too.

Constituent input is critical for legislation to protect workplace human rights. This is especially true if your representative is a Democrat. You don't have to be a Democrat to support a bill to help employees—Orrin Hatch, a conservative Republican from Utah, worked hard to help Ted Kennedy get the Polygraph Protection Act through Congress, and Democrats can be lukewarm on employment issues. But in general Democrats are supportive of greater rights for employees. It is highly unlikely that the party leadership is telling Democratic members of Congress to reject a bill to improve your rights as an employee. The real question is how high a priority your representative places on such a bill. This will be heavily influenced by how much mail constituents send supporting it.

In a speech to the Americans for Democratic Action, Congressman Barney Frank quoted FDR as saying, "I'll do the right thing, but only if you make me." Frank explained that members of Congress constantly receive pressure from employers and other powerful groups to do the wrong thing. If they ignore this "advice," there are consequences (such as losing a big corporation's financial support in the next election). It's a lot easier for them to withstand this pressure if constituents are pushing them to do the right thing.

If you want to write to your elected officials, but aren't sure what to say, you can begin with the template in appendix C on page 254 of this book.

If you are especially concerned about a specific issue, such as workplace surveillance, you can learn about pending legislation at the National Workrights Institute's Web site, workrights.org. The Web site also contains sample letters supporting specific bills.

You don't have to send an actual letter. Every member of Congress has an e-mail address and their staff keeps track of the messages. An e-mail doesn't have as much impact as a letter, but it still counts. Just Google your representative or senator's name and you will find his or her Web site, where you can leave a message. You can also communicate your views by telephone. The congressional switchboard at (202) 225-3121 can connect you to the office of any member of Congress.

While you're at it, don't forget your state representatives. Many employee laws are state laws, and there are bills pending in virtually every state legislature to improve employment law at any given time. Moreover, a state legislator has far fewer constituents than a member of Congress. A state legislative district is about the size of a county, sometimes even smaller. They get much less mail and your message will have more impact. Unlike members of Congress, state senators and representatives are not difficult to meet with in person. If you call them and ask for an appointment to talk about a specific bill (including one you'd like them to introduce), there's a good chance they will sit down and talk to you. This is usually a good experience for everyone concerned and can have the most impact of all.

Tell Your Friends

There are now millions of blogs and personal Web sites in the United States. Most of them belong to people like you. If everyone who is concerned about the lack of human rights at work were to talk about it online, the message would spread like wildfire.

Send a Letter to the Editor

Most cities and towns in America have a newspaper (although, sadly, the number is diminishing), and all publish letters from readers to the editor. Sending such a letter will tell many other people about the issue. It's not hard to get a letter published, especially in a small-town paper. Sample letters on a variety of subjects are on the NWI Web site.

Write to Other Human Rights Organizations

Large human rights organizations could do a lot to help improve legal protection for human rights at work. Sometimes they do. The ACLU, for example, played a major role in passing the Polygraph Protection Act and the Americans with Disabilities Act. It has also fought in the courts random drug testing for more than twenty years. But the ADA and the Polygraph Act are now two decades old. Other than drug testing, the ACLU doesn't give much priority to workplace human rights. You can't be too hard on them for this; they've been busy trying to prevent the federal government from locking people up forever without a trial and creating DNA data banks. But workplace rights are important too. If the ACLU can oppose the federal government's programs for reading our e-mail, it ought to be able to make an effort to protect e-mail from employer snooping.

Human Rights Watch, the other giant in the field (by nonprofit standards), published an excellent report in 2000 called *Unfair Advantage* about the failure of the United States to protect the right to organize, written by Professor Lance Compa of Cornell. HRW also recognizes the weaknesses in NAFTA's labor side agreement and pushes for better provisions in subsequent free trade agreements. But they have done very little on other workplace issues. Again, HRW is fighting against a multitude of abuses without the staff and resources they really need, so they can't be expected to put too much into efforts to expand other workplace human rights. But even a little effort from an organization with Human Rights Watch's resources and credibility would go a long way.

If you belong to one of these, or any other, human rights organizations, write the president and tell her that workplace human rights are important and deserve more effort. There is a sample letter in appendix D on page 255.

Volunteer

If you have time, volunteer to help. Almost all public interest organizations, including employment rights groups, need volunteers for a wide variety of activities. No matter what your skills, you can make a difference.

Vote Smart

I'm constantly amazed at the number of people who complain about the American government but don't do anything to make it better. People in many other countries are going to prison and even giving up their lives to get the right to choose their leaders democratically. In the United States, most people don't even bother to vote. In the 2006 presidential election, only 48 percent of those eligible to vote went to the polls. And that was actually a good year. In the previous two elections, the turnouts were only 46 percent and 45 percent. Many people don't even register to vote. Of the 201 million Americans who were eligible to vote in 2006, 65 million never registered.

The situation may be getting worse. Only 22 percent of people under twenty-five vote. People over fifty-five are three times as likely to vote (63 percent). Some of these young people will start to vote when they get older, but they may never reach the rate of today's adults. "The Millennial Generation (those born in the mid-1980s and later) are different than their Baby Boomer parents," explains Sue Harless, executive director of College Excel, a nationally recognized school for helping young people make the transition to adulthood. "They are more self-centered, less willing to take responsibility, and less likely to care about making the world a better place." This suggests that even when they grow older, these young adults will be less likely to vote.

Some people say, "It doesn't matter who gets elected, all politicians are the same." That's very shortsighted. In some ways all politicians *are* the same. They spend too much time raising money and are too dependent on those who give it. They worry too much about what the next public opinion poll will say and not enough about what will be good for our country in the long run.

But different politicians take different positions on the issues. In the last presidential election, Senator McCain believed we should continue the war in Iraq. Senator (now president) Obama wanted to end it. McCain wanted to address our energy issues by drilling for oil in Alaska and offshore. Obama wanted to place more emphasis on developing alternative energy. McCain is pro-life, while Obama is pro-choice. No matter which side of these issues (and many more) you are on, the decisions President Obama makes will be very different from those Senator McCain would have made.

When you decide whom to vote for, remember who is on your side as an employee. Virtually every law in history that helped employees was initiated by Democrats and opposed by Republicans. This includes Social Security, the minimum wage, bans on discrimination based on race, gender, and other illegitimate factors, workplace safety and health standards, and many more. The Republicans even opposed child labor laws. I've been working in Congress for better employment rights for twenty years. I could count the number of Republicans who ever helped me on my fingers (and have a few left over).

This doesn't mean you have to vote Democratic. Employment isn't the only issue. If you are pro-life, believe that military action is the foundation of foreign policy, don't believe in gay marriage, don't want additional environmental regulations, or agree more with Republicans than Democrats on the issues overall, you should vote Republican. I used to myself.

When I was a young lawyer in Philadelphia, Frank Rizzo, a Democrat, was the mayor. Rizzo was a former police commissioner who thought more police and more prisons were the solution to the city's crime problems. (He wasn't as concerned about reducing unemployment or reducing drug addiction through treatment programs.) Rizzo once boasted that he would "make Attila the Hun look like a faggot." Needless to say, I voted for his Republican opponents. I was even a Republican committeeman and poll watcher who almost got beaten up by Rizzo supporters when I objected to illegal voting practices. So if you think Republicans are the best overall choice to lead our country, you have my blessing to vote for them (not that you need it). But before you do, ask yourself one question: "Do I feel strongly enough about social issues to vote for a candidate who is going to hurt my family financially?" Would you rather block gay marriage or have more money to provide health care for your family and send your kids to college?

If you don't vote Democratic, do it with your eyes open. Rich people know where their bread is buttered. They know that their taxes will be lower with Republicans in office than with Democrats (especially at the national level). That doesn't mean they always vote Republican (although they usually do). Sometimes they vote Democratic because they agree with the party's positions on choice, foreign policy, or other important issues. But when millionaires vote Democratic, they know they are hurting themselves financially. No millionaires ever voted Democratic because they thought it would help them financially.

Regular people, however, frequently get it wrong. They vote Republican without thinking about how this will affect them as employees, or even (believe it or not) thinking that it will help them as employees. This is foolish and harmful. You don't have to take my word for it. In the next election, check the positions of the candidates on employment issues and see for yourself.

The Forbes Phenomenon

Among the most glaring examples of regular people not knowing who their friends are was the presidential campaign of Steve Forbes. Forbes was a one-trick pony. His entire campaign was based on a single idea: the flat tax. Under a flat tax, everyone in the United States would pay the same rate of income tax, no matter how rich or poor they were. Forbes, one of the richest men in America, would have the same income tax rate as a janitor. Forbes tried to disguise this by giving a family of four an exemption on the first $36,000 of income. But then he took away most of their deductions, starting with their mortgage deduction. Then he eliminated all taxes on investment income. After the dust settled, the rich would have won under that plan. According to the Center for Public Integrity, Forbes himself would have cut his tax bill almost in half. According to the late Donald Alexander, who served as commissioner of the Internal Revenue Service for Republican presidents Nixon and Ford and Democrat Jimmy Carter, the flat tax "will increase the divide between rich and poor in America. The rich will become vastly richer and the poor, poorer." A flat tax makes as much sense for the average American as a flat earth.

Yet many ordinary people supported Forbes. In a CNN poll, 15 percent of registered Republicans supported Forbes. Even if not a single Democrat voted for Forbes, this means that almost 15 million people supported him. They weren't all rich; there aren't that many millionaires in the entire world. Several million ordinary Americans supported a presidential candidate whose platform was "Ordinary people like you should pay more taxes so rich people like me can pay less."

Regular people also hurt themselves by not voting. Rich people vote. Of Americans who make over $100,000 a year, 64 percent voted in the 2006 election. People who made $20,000 or less only voted 31 percent of the time. In other words, people with money are more than twice as likely to vote as people without money. The impact of this is enormous.

If poor people voted as often as people with money, four million more votes would be cast. If even two thirds of them voted for the candidate who cared the most about employees, the difference would be over a million votes. This would have changed the outcome of many elections, including the 2000 presidential race. If people without money voted as often as people with money, Al Gore would have been president.

Having a Gore administration would have been a blessing for employees. For starters, we wouldn't have had the Bush administration's tax cuts for the rich. President Bush called his plan a "middle-class tax cut" and claimed that everyone's tax bill went down. That wasn't true. The top 20 percent of Americans (in terms of income) got 60 percent of the tax cut, three times what they would have received if everyone shared equally. The poorest 20 percent got only 3 percent of the tax cut. They would have received seven times as much if the cuts were fair. Put another way, a taxpayer in the top 20 percent got over twenty times the amount of money from the Bush cuts that a person in the bottom 20 percent received.

But aren't regular people better off with lower taxes, even if the rich get more than their share? The answer is no. Lower taxes mean the federal government has less money to spend on programs that help people. For example, there are 46 million Americans without health insurance, including eight million children. The proposed Children's Health Insurance Program Reauthorization Act (CHIP) would have provided health insurance for four million additional children. Congress passed CHIP in 2007, but President Bush vetoed it, claiming that the government didn't have enough money to pay for it. The cost of CHIP ($35 billion over five years) could have been paid for many times with the additional $620 billion the federal government would have had without the Bush tax cuts.

The government also has less money to pay for Social Security and Medicare, both of which are now facing financial shortfalls.

The bottom line is that whom we elect to office matters. If more people voted, and voted for candidates who believe in employee rights, our laws would be much better than they are.

Join the National Workrights Institute

**If the National Workrights Institute didn't exist,
we would have to create it.**

——CONGRESSMAN RUSH HOLT

Most public interest groups have very few resources. The National Workrights Institute is no exception. Our opponents receive millions of dollars of support from corporations and other sources. It is the ultimate David and Goliath struggle. If even a fraction of the people who believe in human rights were to join NWI, we would be able to do much more. There is a membership form in appendix F on page 258.

If you want to learn more about NWI before making a decision, go to our Web site at workrights.org.

It's Our Country

The United States was founded on the belief that every person has fundamental rights that those in power should not be able to take away, including freedom of speech, privacy, equal opportunity, and a fair chance to defend oneself when accused. For over two hundred years we have protected those freedoms for ourselves and helped millions of people around the globe achieve them for the first time. We paid dearly for this freedom; our national defense budget over the years has been several trillion dollars. Many Americans gave their lives to protect these freedoms.

But we leave our human rights behind when we go to work. In the past, we could blame the country's founders for not including corporations in the Constitution and Bill of Rights. After two hundred years, however, we have no one to blame but ourselves for this injustice. It's time to act.

Model Corporate Privacy Policy

1. Personal Information

    a. The company will collect personal information concerning employees only when it is needed to perform a legitimate corporate function.

    b. Personal information concerning employees will be disclosed to other employees only when it is necessary for them to do their jobs.

    c. Personal information will be disclosed to parties outside the company only with the permission of the employee or when required by law.

    d. The company will maintain security systems to ensure that the above policies are followed.

2. Medical Information

    The company may conduct pre-employment medical evaluations to ensure that the individual is capable of performing the job for which he or she is being considered. No such evaluation shall be conducted until the company has made an offer of employment conditioned upon the results of the evaluation. Only medical information that is related to the prospective employee's ability to do the job will be acquired or considered.

3. Monitoring

    a. Computers

        Employees are permitted to use company computers for personal purposes so long as such use does not interfere with the employee's job performance or have an adverse impact on the functioning of the company's computer system.

The company will monitor employee computer use only when there is reason to believe that the employee has used the computer in a manner that violates company policy or to evaluate employee job performance.

The employee will be notified if his or her computer is monitored.

The contents of an employee's personal computer will be monitored only if:

i. the employee brings his or her computer to the workplace, in which it will be subject to monitoring under the same policies as company computers

or

ii. the company has reason to believe that the employee has information in his or her personal computer that is the property of the company.

b. Video

i. Security. The company may install video cameras for security purposes. All such security cameras will be clearly visible.

ii. The company may also install clearly visible video cameras in work areas. Such cameras will be used only when normal supervisory methods are not adequate.

iii. The company may install hidden video cameras as part of an investigation into theft or other serious misconduct. Such surveillance shall be conducted only when other investigatory methods are ineffective. Under no circumstances shall video surveillance be conducted in locker rooms or bathrooms.

c. Telephone

i. The company may conduct monitoring of work-related telephone calls as part of a program to ensure quality of service. Employees will be notified when such telephone service observation is taking place.

    ii. The company may conduct computer analysis of the telephone numbers called from workplace phones in order to determine whether excessive personal calls are being made.

    iii. Except as part of an investigation into serious misconduct, the company will not under any circumstances listen to the content of non-work-related calls.

d. Employee Location

GPS or other means of locating employees will be used only when there is a legitimate need to know the employee's location. It will not be used when all that is required is the ability to communicate with the employee.

Under no circumstances will GPS or similar technology be used to locate employees while they are off-duty.

4. Off-Duty Conduct

Employment decisions are based upon job performance. The company will not collect information concerning employees' legal off-duty behavior or use such information in making employment decisions.

5. Substance Abuse

It is a serious violation of company policy for any employee to come to work under the influence of alcohol or illegal drugs. If the company has reason to believe that an employee is under the influence of alcohol or illegal drugs, it may conduct an investigation into the employee's condition. Such an investigation may include testing of an employee's breath or bodily fluids.

6. Notice

Except as specifically provided above, employees shall be notified of all information collection or monitoring practices.

7. Enforcement

The company will periodically review the activities of employees involved in monitoring, especially monitoring of computers, to ensure that these policies are being followed. Any employee who has reason to believe that company privacy policies are not being followed is requested to inform management. Employees may choose any member of management to inform and may do so in confidence if they desire. No adverse action of any kind will be taken against employees for reporting what they believe to be a violation of this policy.

Appropriate disciplinary action will be taken against employees who violate this policy.

Guidelines for IBM Bloggers: Executive Summary

1. Know and follow IBM's Business Conduct Guidelines.

2. Blogs, wikis and other forms of online discourse are individual interactions, not corporate communications. IBMers are personally responsible for their posts. Be mindful that what you write will be public for a long time—protect your privacy.

3. Identify yourself—name and, when relevant, role at IBM—when you blog about IBM or IBM-related matters. And write in the first person. You must make it clear that you are speaking for yourself and not on behalf of IBM.

4. If you publish a blog or post to a blog and it has something to do with work you do or subjects associated with IBM, use a disclaimer such as this: "The postings on this site are my own and don't necessarily represent IBM's positions, strategies or opinions."

5. Respect copyright, fair use, and financial disclosure laws.

6. Don't provide IBM's or another's confidential or other proprietary information.

7. Don't cite or reference clients, partners, or suppliers without their approval.

8. Respect your audience. Don't use ethnic slurs, personal insults, obscenity, etc., and show proper consideration for others' privacy and for topics that may be considered objectionable or inflammatory—such as politics and religion.

9. Find out who else is blogging on the topic, and cite them.

10. Don't pick fights, be the first to correct your own mistakes, and don't alter previous posts without indicating that you have done so.

11. Try to add value. Provide worthwhile information and perspective.

Sample Letter to Elected Representatives

Dear Representative _____:

I am very concerned about the lack of legal protection for human rights in the workplace. Americans should not lose their right to freedom of speech, their right to privacy, or other fundamental rights when they go to work.

It should be illegal for an employer to fire employees because of their off-duty political speech, something they say in a personal blog, or other legal off-duty behavior. Employers should not have the right to control our private lives in an attempt to reduce their health care expenses. Steps must be taken to protect employee communications about personal subjects from being monitored by employers. Tracking employees with technology like GPS when they are off-duty should not be permitted.

Please introduce legislation to extend legal protection for fundamental rights into the working lives of Americans.

Please let me know where you stand on this important issue.

Sincerely yours,

Sample Letter to Human Rights Organizations

Dear Mr./Ms. _____:

I'm writing you to urge _____ to give higher priority to violations of human rights in the workplace.

As you know, the United States Constitution and Bill of Rights do not apply to private corporations, no matter how large and powerful they may be. It remains legal for an employer to fire employees because of their off-duty political conduct, to dictate whether they can smoke, drink, or ride a motorcycle in their spare time, and to deliberately read personal messages that employees send during the workday or even from a home computer. The growing use of GPS-equipped cell phones is creating a system that can track Americans every minute of their private lives.

The American Civil Liberties Union reports that it receives more complaints about violations of civil liberties by private employers than it does about all government agencies combined.

There are many abuses of human rights in the world and _____ _____'s resources to respond to them are limited. At present, however, we do very little to address the wholesale violations of human rights committed by private employers. Surely we can do more.

If you would like specific suggestions, I will be happy to provide them. The National Workrights Institute (of which I am also a member) would be happy to meet with you as well.

Sincerely yours,

APPENDIX E

Employee Bill of Rights

The Bill of Rights of the United States Constitution, adopted in 1791, protects the liberties of the American people from abuse by the government. The National Workrights Institute believes that liberties should also be protected from abuse in the world of work. Herewith, NWI declares the inalienable rights of all people at work to be:

1. Freedom of Speech

All employees shall have the right to freedom of speech. No employee shall be disciplined for expressing an opinion of which management disapproves, or for expressing disagreement with company policy, unless that expression demonstrably interferes with his/her job performance.

2. The Right to Organize

Employees shall have the right to engage in collective action, including the right to organize and strike. No employee shall be disciplined for engaging in such collective activity.

3. Privacy

All employees shall have the right of privacy, both on and off the job. No employer shall:

a. require any employee to submit to a search, including a drug test, unless there is reason to believe that the search will reveal evidence of job-related misconduct.

    b. require any person to reveal information about themselves that is unrelated to the performance of their jobs.

    c. discriminate against employees because of their off-duty conduct, unless that conduct affects job performance.

    d. engage in covert electronic surveillance of employees.

4. Fair Treatment

No employee shall be disciplined without just cause. Just cause shall be understood to mean unsatisfactory job performance, or failure to follow reasonable rules of workplace behavior. Employees who believe they have been terminated without just cause shall have the right to have the decision reviewed and overturned by a neutral third party.

5. Equal Treatment

All employees are entitled to be judged by the quality of their job performance. No employer shall discriminate against any employee on the basis of a characteristic that is unrelated to job performance.

6. Legal Protection

These enumerated rights shall receive full legal protection. Individuals who believe their rights have been violated are entitled to an adequate and affordable legal remedy.

National Workrights Institute Membership Application

NATIONAL WORKRIGHTS INSTITUTE

MEMBERSHIP APPLICATION FORM

❑ Yes, I want to join the National Workrights Institute and protect freedom of speech, privacy, due process, and the right to organize and prevent genetic discrimination.

First name: _____ Last name: _____

Address: _____

City: _____ State: _____ Zip code: _____

Phone number (will be kept confidential): _____

E-mail address: _____

All the information on this form will remain confidential.

I am making a gift of:

❑ $50   ❑ $500—Eleanor Roosevelt Society

❑ $75
              Membership for gifts of $500 or more
❑ $100
              ❑ Other _____
❑ $250

Make check payable to: NATIONAL WORKRIGHTS INSTITUTE

166 Wall Street, Princeton, NJ 08540

If you would like to use a credit card, please join online at www.workrights.org.

Tear out

Index

Abu Ghraib prison scandal, 174
ADA Amendments Act (2008), 130
Administrative Management Society, 45
AFL-CIO, 235
Age Discrimination in Employment Act
  (ADEA) (1967), 187, 221
Aguero, Isaac, 50
Alabama, drug testing and, 97
Alaska:
  privacy issue in, 232
  whistle blowers in, 9
alcohol, drinking, 2, 44–45, 55, 99, 100, 111
Alexander, Donald, 245
Allen, Pamela, 16–17
ALS (Lou Gehrig's disease), 109
Alzheimer's disease, 108, 109, 114, 121
American Arbitration Association
  (AAA), 181–82, 183, 186, 188, 235
American Bar Association, 29, 70
American Civil Liberties Union (ACLU),
  xii, xiii, 42, 55, 66, 85, 119, 219, 225,
  241–42
American Hawaii Cruises, 71
American Journal of Public Health, 51
American Management Association, 20,
  21, 36, 92, 111–12, 134
American Psychological Association, 51
American Psychologist, 87
Americans for Democratic Action, 210,
  240
Americans with Disabilities Act (ADA)
  (1990), 117–18, 123, 129–30, 137,
  166, 238, 241

America's Best Carpet Care, 71
Amnesty International, 210
Andler, Edward, 85
annualcreditreport.com, 78
Apple Inc., 144
Arace, Heidi, 26
arbitration, 159, 175–95, 234–35
  class actions and, 184–85
  cost of, 182–83
  due process and, 188
  judicial expedience and, 189, 190
  law and, 187–94
  mediation and, 189–90
  problems of, 184–91
  Protocol measures for, 177–82
  repeat player effect and, 185–86
  roadblocks to reform of, 191–95
Arbitration Fairness Act (AFA), 192–95
Archibold, Marge, 47
Arizona:
  free speech issue in, 12
  privacy issue in, 232
Arlt, Ame, 63
Arthur Andersen, 152
Associated Press (AP), 22
Atlas Cold Storage, 16–17
Austria, 222
Automatic Data Processing, 69
automobile accidents, 99
Avis, 59

background checks, 68–79
Bangladesh, 212

Bank of America, 146, 152
bankruptcies, 110, 139
bargaining units, 158–59
Barrett, Cameron, 11
Barry, Bruce, 5
Bartholet, Elizabeth, 176, 186
B. Dalton, 88
Bear Stearns, 144
Bebchuk, Lucian, 144
Bell Aerospace, 202
Bell Canada, 26
Bennett, Linda, 162
Bentley School of Business Ethics, 21, 22,
    25, 233–34
Bergman, Edward, 190
Berkshire Hathaway, 146
Bernstein, Jules, 201
Best Lock Company, 2, 44–45
Bhopal, India, xii, 101
Biggert, Judith, 125
Bill of Rights, 5–6, 6*n*, 247
Bingham, Lisa, 181
biometrics, 3, 32–35, 43
Blandin Paper Company, 62
Blocker, Tasha, 135
blogs, 10–12, 29, 241
Blue Cross Blue Shield of Illinois, 152
Bobo, Kim, 199, 202
Boeing, 185
Boisjoly, Roger, 8, 57–58
bona fide occupational qualification
    (BFOQ), 168–69
Bone, Janice, 46–47
Boston police strike (1921), 153
Boston Sheraton, 18, 27
Boyle, Howard, 31
breast cancer, 108, 114, 121
Brenner, Harvey, 63
Brown, Sherrod, 140
Brownback, Sam, 71
Brownell, Kelly, 46
Buddy Beacon, 32
Buffett, Warren, 146
Bush, George H. W., 74, 96, 99–100
Bush, George W., 5, 50, 126, 128, 151,
    174, 197, 227, 246
Bush v. Gore (2000), 174

California:
    drug testing in, 95

free speech issue in, 13
junk food regulation in, 46
privacy issue in, 17, 18–19, 42, 56, 231
psychological testing in, 85
Cambodia, 212, 213
Canada, 211, 220
cancer, 108, 114, 121
Canon, 39
Carlin, George, 23, 38
Carnival Cruise Lines, 39
Carolina Freight Carriers Corporation, 74
Carroll, Lee, 7
Carter, Jimmy, 245
Cayne, James, 144
CCS International, 19
cell phones, 3, 22, 31–32, 232–33
Center for Business Ethics, 233–34
Center for Public Integrity, 245
Center for Union Facts, 150–51
Centers for Disease Control and
    Prevention (CDC), 2, 92, 130
Century Camera decision (1981), 91
Cesaro, Michael, 102
Challenger disaster, 8, 57
Chamber of Commerce, U.S., 160
Change to Win, 235
Charles Stuart University, 216
Chase, Samuel, 173
child labor, 6, 212–13, 243
Children's Health Insurance Program
    Reauthorization Act (CHIP), 246
China, 223–24, 226–27
ChoicePoint, 78
cholesterol, 46, 120
chronic beryllium disease (CBD), 115
Citigroup, 144
CityWatcher.com, 36
Civil Rights Act (1866), 167
Civil Rights Act (1964), 58, 167, 196, 215,
    220–21, 238
Civil Rights Restoration Act (CRRA)
    (1988), 166, 167
CJW Inc., 50
class action lawsuits, 138–39, 184–85
class action waivers, 185
Cleveland, Grover, 153
Clinton, Bill, 74, 174, 211
Clinton, Hillary, 49, 210
Coalition for Genetic Fairness, 124–25
Coburn, Tom, 125–26

cocaine, 104
Cohen, Sidney, 98
collective bargaining, 143, 158–59
College Excel, 243
Collingsworth, Terry, 212
Colorado, privacy issue and, 56
Columbia University, 81
communes, 223
Communications Workers of America, 41, 42
Compa, Lance, 242
computers, surveillance of, 20–30, 36–40, 42, 43, 216–17, 219, 230–34
conflict of interest, 55
Congress, U.S.:
    arbitration reform and, 191–95
    background check issue and, 74–75
    discrimination issue and, 165–70, 172–74, 198
    employment at will doctrine and, 58
    genetic testing issue and, 118–19, 120, 123–26
    labor and, 151, 153, 158, 163, 164, 238–41, 243
    plant closing issue and, 136, 140–41
    privacy issue and, 42
    psychological testing and, 86, 87, 90
    stock market and, 228
    Supreme Court and, 172–74
    see also House of Representatives, U.S.; Senate, U.S.
Congressional Research Service, 34
Connecticut:
    drug testing in, 94
    privacy issue in, 42
Connick, Harry, 13–14
Connick v. Myers, 13–14
Consolidated Freightways, 18–19
Constitution, U.S., 247
    arbitration issue and, 175
    due process clause of, 57, 58
    employment at will doctrine and, 57, 60
    free speech issue and, 1, 5–6, 6*n*, 9, 14
    preemption doctrine of, 191–92
    privacy issue and, 16, 41
construct validity, 87–88
Contract with America, 87, 119
convict labor, 212
Corporate Library, 145

corporations:
    employment at will doctrine and, 2, 57–67
    employment law reform and, 215–29, 238–41, 247
    free speech and, 5–13, 15
    privacy issue and, 16–43
Countrywide, 146
Coxson, Harold, 123
Cramer, William, 215, 217, 220
Crane, Rob, 54
credit cards, 76–77
credit checks, 75–79
credit reports, 2, 77–79
Crescent Plastics, 182–83
Crick, Francis, 108
criminal defense law, xi–xii
Croom, Bert, 35
Crowell, Randy, 157–58
Cult of Personality, The (Paul), 83
CVS, 202
cystic fibrosis, 109

Darrow, Clarence, 108
Deal v. Spears, 41
Debs, Eugene V., 153
DeCandia, Maurice, 150
defamation, 202–4
DeGaetano v. Smith Barney, Inc. (1997), 188
Delaware, privacy issue in, 42
DeLay, Tom, 125
DeMark, Christine, 113
Deng Xiaoping, 224
Denmark, 222, 229
Depression, Great, 227, 228
Devine, Tom, 8
DeVry University, 10
Dickens, Bobby, 158
Dilbert, 10–11
disability, 58, 117–18
discovery, 171, 178–79
discrimination, 44–56, 196–99, 220–21, 243
    Congress and, 165–70, 172–74, 198
    gender, 170, 185, 221, 243
    obesity and, 46, 47–48, 129–30, 197
    racial, 40, 41, 58, 73, 168–69, 185, 196, 197, 220–21, 243
    religious, 44, 85–86

discrimination (*cont.*)
  sexual orientation and, 47, 51–52, 58
  Supreme Court and, 165–70, 172–74,
    198
diseases, 108–15, 118, 120, 121
disparate impact, 73, 168–70
District of Columbia, job discrimination
    issue in, 54
DNA (deoxyribonucleic acid), 35–36,
    108, 241
Doctor's Associates, Inc., et al. v. Casarotto
    (1996), 191–92
Dole, Robert, 136
Donahue, Phil, 19
Donnelly, John, 64, 219
Donnelly Corporation, 63–64, 219
Dow Chemical, 25
Drexelbrook Controls, 101–2, 219
Drug Abuse and Alcoholism Newsletter, 98
drug testing, xii–xiii, 2–3, 46–47, 69,
    92–107, 143
  airline pilots and, 105
  alternatives to, 100–102, 105–7
  bogus studies and, 98–99
  decline in, 107
  drug abuse "crisis" and, 99–100
  federal certification of, 93–94, 104
  incentives for, 96–97
  law enforcement and, 103
  laws on, 94–95, 96–97
  legitimate studies of, 95, 100
  privacy issue and, 95, 219, 236, 241
  reliability of, 92–93, 104, 105
  screening and confirmation stages of,
    93
  strip-search tests in, 94, 95
  urine samples in, 92–93, 95, 104, 106
  usefulness of, 95–96
due process, 57, 58, 188, 218
Duke Power Company, 73, 168–69
DuPont, 119
Duval, Ernest, 154

Ebel, Claire, 160
Eberling, Bob, 8
Edison, Thomas A., 124
Egypt, 189–90
Eisenberg, Theodore, 181
elections, U.S.:
  of 2000, 174

  of 2004, 1, 5
  of 2006, 242, 245
  employment law changes and, 242–44
  judiciary and, 172
Electronic Communications Privacy Act
    (ECPA) (1986), 41
electronic surveillance, 16–43, 230–34,
    242
  health issue and, 26
  productivity and, 27
Eli Lilly, 68, 75
e-mail, 2, 157, 240
  privacy issue and, 19, 21, 23–26, 28,
    36–40, 42, 43, 217, 230–31, 242
employee assistance plans (EAPs),
    100–101
Employee Free Choice Act (EFCA),
    162–63
Employee Retirement Income Security
    Act (1974), 221
employment:
  arbitration and, 159, 175–95, 234–35
  background checks and, 68–79
  blogs and, 10–12, 29, 241
  corporate lawyers and, 204–6
  credit checks and, 75–79
  defamation and, 202–4
  drug testing and, xii–xiii, 2–3, 46–47,
    69, 92–107, 143, 219, 241
  free speech and, 1–2, 5–15, 209, 218
  genetic testing and, 3, 108–32
  health care issue and, 45–50, 110
  job interviews and, 68–79, 236–38
  judicial decisions and, 165–74
  law reform and, 215–29, 238–41, 247
  morality issue and, 50
  negligent hiring doctrine and, 71
  obesity and, 46, 47–48, 129–30, 197
  overtime and, 200–202, 236
  personal life and discrimination in,
    44–56
  plant closings and, 133–41
  privacy issue and, 16–43, 216–17, 218,
    219, 230–34, 236
  psychological testing and, 3, 80–91
  recreational activities and, 46, 49, 55
  reference checks and, 203–8
  rights of workers in, 196–209, 218–19
  sexual discrimination and, 47, 51–52,
    196–97

smoking and, 2, 45–47, 48, 54, 55, 111, 130
unions and, *see* unions
wage theft and, 199–200, 201
workers' compensation and, 116, 209
world trade and, 210–14
yellow-dog contracts and, 153
employment at will doctrine, 2, 57–67, 164
changing law on, 63–67
contract exception to, 59, 65, 67
damage done by, 63
public policy exception to, 59–60, 65, 67
Employment Non-Discrimination Act (ENDA), 52, 197
Enron, 151–52
Environmental Protection Act (1970), 221
ePolicy Institute, 40
Epolito, Anita, 45
Epson America, 37
Equal Employment Opportunity Commission (EEOC), 73–74, 123, 127, 140, 197–98
Equifax, 78
Ervin, Sam, 86
Etienne, Franklin, 18
European Union (EU), 220
Ewing, David, 218
Excelsior Underwear Inc. decision (1966), 157
executive compensation, 144–46, 219
Experian, 76, 78
externalities, 226
Exxon, 152

Facebook, 10, 52, 53
Fair, Brad, 27
Fair Credit Reporting Act (FCRA) (1970), 72, 76
Fair Labor Standards Act (1938), 221
Fall River, Mass., 135
Faulkner, Peter, 7, 8
Federal Arbitration Act (FAA) (1925), 180–81, 191–92
Federal Aviation Administration (FAA), 105
Federal Bureau of Investigation (FBI), 35, 69, 72, 73
Federal Reserve Board of Governors, 76
Federal Trade Commission (FTC), U.S., 77

Feinstein, Fred, 159
Felts, Bobby, 157
Finch, Peter, 230
fingerprints, 32, 33–35
Finkin, Matthew, 155
Finland, 222
Firestone Study, 98
First Amendment, 5–6, 9
Fisher, Stan, 65–66
Florida:
free speech issue in, 11
genetic testing in, 119, 120
Flynn, Nancy, 40
Food and Drug Administration (FDA), 90
Forbes, Steve, 245
Forcum, Steve, 157
Ford, Gerald R., 245
Ford, Henry, 44
Ford Meter Box, 46–47
Ford Motor Company, 145
FOREWARN bill, 140–41
Fortas, Abe, 173
Forte, Patrick, 104
Fortune, 236
France, 220
France, Anatole, 61
Frank, Barney, 51, 240
Frank, Michael, 47–48
Franklin, Benjamin, 133
freedom of association, 216, 218
Freeman, Richard, 142, 220
free speech:
Constitution and, 1, 5–6, 6*n*, 9, 14
corporations and, 5–13, 15, 209, 218
government employees and, 13–15
laws on, 12–13
whistle-blowers and, 7–10
Fried, Jesse, 144
Friedman, George, 188
Fuld, Richard, 144
Fulmer, Nate, 11

Gaige Kaifang, 224
Geary, George, 7–8
gender discrimination, 170, 185, 221, 243
General Accounting Office (GAO), 134, 136, 137, 138, 161, 175
General Electric, 218
General Motors, 145, 218

Genetic Information Nondiscrimination Act (GINA) (2008), 36, 120–21, 122, 221, 238
  employer reaction to, 123–24, 127
  implementation of, 127–29
  passage of, 124–26, 127
  unintended acquisition issue and, 123–24, 127
genetic monitoring, 114–15
genetic testing, 3, 108–32
  avoidance of, 113–14
  criminal justice and, 131–32
  employment decisions based on, 115–17
  future issues in, 130–32
  genetic monitoring as, 114–15
  health insurance and, 121–22
  laws on, 117–30
  privacy issue and, 112–13, 123–24
  secrecy of, 112
Georgia, privacy issue in, 16–17
Georgia-Pacific, 152
G.I. Bill of Rights (1944), 225
Gibson, Paul, 68, 75
Gilmer, Robert, 187–88
Gilmer v. Interstate/Johnson Lake Corporation (1991), 175, 187–88
Glasser, Ira, xiii
Global Positioning System (GPS), 3, 30–32, 43
Gobbell, Lynne, 1, 12, 50
Goldman Sachs, 228
Goodyear, 170, 198–99, 201
Google, 10
Gore, Albert, Jr., 246
Gorman, Dave, 134
Government Accountability Project, 8
government employees, free speech and, 5–6, 9, 13–15
Great Leap Forward, 223–24
Great Place to Work Institute, 236–37
Great Western Mortgage v. Peacock (1997), 188
Green, Philloria, 58
Green v. Missouri Pacific Railroad, 74
Griggs v. Duke Power Company (1971), 168–69
gross domestic product (GDP), 222, 223
Grove City College v. Bell (1984), 166
Gruber, Jeremy, 125
Guastello, Stephen, 90

Harless, Sue, 243
Harvard Business School, 218
Harvard University, 110
Hastings Center, 119
Hatch, Orrin, 240
Hatchins, Jerrold, 182–83
Hathaway, Starke, 81, 83
Hawaii:
  privacy issue in, 232
  whistle-blowers in, 9
Health and Human Services Department, U.S., 93–94, 104, 128
health care, 45–50, 121–22, 225
  rising cost of, 110–11, 130
heart disease, 120
Helmerich & Payne, 144
Helms, Jesse, 221
hemophilia, 109
Hewlett-Packard, 38
Hillier, Glen, 5, 12, 50
HMOs, 110
Hobson v. Coastal Corporation (1997), 203
Hoffman-La Roche, 152
home computers, privacy issue and, 28–30, 43
homosexuality, 47, 51–52, 58
Honda, 144
honesty tests, 86–91
Hooters, 176, 188
Hopkins, Ross, 50
House of Representatives, U.S., 165, 173, 239
  genetic testing issue and, 125
  see also Congress, U.S.; Senate, U.S.
housing crisis, 228
Howard Beale, 230
Human Genome Project, 109
human rights, 1, 4, 209, 210–29, 241–42, 247
Human Rights Watch, 210, 242
Huntington's disease, 109, 113

IBM, 12, 218
Iceland, 222
Idaho, privacy issue in, 232
identity theft, 3, 33–35, 76–77
illegal immigrants, 6, 200
Illinois, University of, Law School, 155
Immigration and Customs Enforcement Agency (ICE), U.S., 200

impairment testing, 105–7
implants (chips), 36
independent contractors, 161–62
Industrial Coils, 59–60
Inherit the Wind (Lawrence and Lee), 108
In Search of Excellence (Peters), 102
instant messaging, 21, 23, 36–37, 42
Institute for Bioethics, Health Policy, and Law, 119
Interfaith Worker Justice, 199
Internal Revenue Service (IRS), 245
International Labor Rights Fund, 212
Internet, 19–20, 25, 26–27, 28, 29, 36–40, 42, 43, 50, 52–53, 231, 233, 235, 236–37, 240
Iowa:
  drug testing in, 94
  free speech issue in, 10–11
Ireland, 222
iris scans, 32, 33
Israel, 189–90

Jackson, Maggie, 22
Jackson Memorial Foundation case (2008), 171–72
JAMS (Judicial Arbitration & Mediation Services), 181, 235
Japan, 220, 224
Jeffords, Jim, 163
Jevic Corporation, 133–34
job discrimination, 44–56
  legal protection against, 51–52, 54–56
  universal health care and, 48–50
job qualifications, 55–56
Jobs, Steve, 144
Johnson, Gary, 157
Johnson, Lyndon B., 196
Johnson, Tim, 16–17
Johnson Controls, 72
Johnson County Community College, 2, 17
judicial system:
  arbitration and, 182–83, 187–89, 190
  cost of access to, 182–83
  discrimination issue and, 165–70
  politics and, 172–74
  summary judgment in, 170–72
junk food, 46
jury duty, 59

just-cause termination, 143, 218–19, 234–35
Justice Department, U.S., 72

Kansas, privacy issue in, 17
Karp, K. William, 226
Karrh, Bruce, 119
Kelly, Kimberly, 68, 75
Kennedy, Anthony, 167–68
Kennedy, Edward M., 125, 126, 240
Kenya, 226
Kerry, John, 1
keyword monitoring, 23
King, Martin Luther, Jr., 221
Kissinger, Henry, 190
Kobus, Michele, 47
Kohl, Herbert, 163, 164
Kowalski, Chris, 134
Kozinski, Alexander, 24
Kristof, Nicholas, 213

Labor Department, U.S., 151, 199, 201
Lafer, Gordon, 157
Lake, Daniel, 53
Lambert, Edward, 135
Lane, Frederick, 48–49
Lawrence Berkeley National Laboratory, 112
Lay, Kenneth, 151–52
layoffs, 134, 137, 140, 141
Ledbetter, Lilly, 198
Ledbetter v. Goodyear Tire & Rubber Co. (2007), 170, 198–99
Lehman Brothers, 144, 228
Lenard, Joan, 171–72
Lesnick, Howard, 57
Levering, Robert, 236
life insurance, 121–23
lockouts, 150
Loopt, 32
Louisville, University of, 119
Luxembourg, 222

McCain, John, 164, 243
McDonald's, 215
McGrorey, Mike, 69
McNealy, Scott, 16
McPherson, Ardith, 14–15
MacWorld, 21
Madoff, Bernard, 152

Maine, drug testing in, 94
MAOA gene, 131–32
Mao Zedong, 223
margin buying, 227–28
marijuana, 2, 95, 97, 98, 99, 100, 104
market economies, 217–29
    environment and, 226–27
    inequality and, 225–26
    shortcomings of, 227–29
Maryland, whistle blowers in, 9
Masai, 226
Massachusetts:
    privacy issue in, 17–18
    psychological testing in, 91
Mayfield, Brandon, 34–35
Mayo Clinic, 47
mediation, 189–90
Medicaid, 110
medical discrimination, 45–50, 108–32
Medicare, 110, 246
Medoff, James, 142
Mendel, Gregor, 108
merit selection (of judges), 172–73
Merrill Lynch, 152
Metzenbaum, Howard, 136
Mexico, 211
Meyer, Jacinda, 51
Michigan:
    free speech issue in, 11
    whistle-blowers in, 8–9
Michigan Chemical Company, 8–9
Minnesota:
    drug testing in, 94
    psychological testing in, 91
Minnesota Multiphasic Personality
    Inventory (MMPI), 80–83, 85–86
Minnesota Multiphasic Personality
    Inventory II (MMPI II), 86
Minority Report, 131
Missouri, free speech issue in, 12, 13
Mitsubishi, 185
MIT Technology Review, 33
Model Employment Termination Act
    (META), 65–66
Montana:
    drug testing in, 94
    employment at will doctrine in, 64
    privacy issue in, 232
Morgan, John, 92
Morgan Stanley, 229

mortgage-backed securities, 228–29
Morton Thiokol, 8, 57–58
Moskowitz, Milton, 236
Mozilo, Angelo, 146
Mugabe, Robert, 164
Multi-Developers Inc., 46
Murray, Thomas, 119
Myers, Sheila, 13–14
Myers-Briggs Type Indicator, 85
MySpace, 52–53

Nader, Ralph, 210
Naked Employee, The (Lane), 49
National Academy of Sciences, 95
National Aeronautics and Space
    Administration (NASA), 8, 57, 105
National Arbitration Forum (NAF), 176,
    186, 192
National Association to Advance Fat
    Acceptance, 47
National Consumers League, 54
National Employment Lawyers
    Association (NELA), 66
National Institute for Labor Relations,
    151
National Labor Relations Act (NLRA)
    (1935), 142, 153, 154–64
National Labor Relations Board (NLRB),
    153, 154–64, 203
National Right to Work Committee,
    160
National Workrights Institute (NWI),
    xiii, 18, 54, 55, 85, 118, 123, 125, 127,
    150, 164, 172, 181, 182, 183, 193,
    210, 240, 241, 247
Nees, Vickie, 59
Nelson, Gail, 17–18
Netherlands, 222, 229
Network, 230
Nevada, privacy issue in, 232
New Jersey:
    drug testing in, 95, 96–97
    free speech issue in, 12, 13
    genetic testing in, 120
    job discrimination issue in, 54
    motor vehicle inspection system in,
    149–50
newspapers, 241
New York:
    background checks in, 73

genetic testing in, 120
  privacy issue in, 56
New York Times, 85, 213
Niess, William, 13
Nixon, Richard M., 245
NLRB v. Mackay Radio & Telegraph Co.
  (1938), 161
Nobles, Jim, 149
North American Free Trade Agreement
  (NAFTA) (1994), 210–11, 242
North Dakota, privacy issue in, 56
Northern Telecom, 41
Norway, 222
Nuclear Services Corporation, 7

Oakwood Healthcare decision (2006), 162
Obama, Barack, 128, 164, 210, 243
obesity, 46, 47–48, 129–30, 197
occupational illnesses, 209
Occupational Safety and Health Act
  (1970), 221
Office of Technology Assessment (OTA),
  21, 68, 87, 118–19
Ohanian, Robert, 59
Oiler, Peter, 50
Olney, Richard, 153
Olson, Meg, 175
100 Best Companies to Work for in
  America, The (Levering and
  Moskowitz), 236
Oregon, privacy issue in, 232
Outten & Golden, 9–10, 138–39
overtime pay, 200–202, 236

Pacific Group Medical Association, 151
Painter, Nell, 153
palm prints, 32, 33
Parsons Engineering, 149–50
Partnership for a Drug-Free America, 98
Patriot Act (2001), 24–25
Patterson v. MacLean Credit Union
  (1989), 167
Paul, Annie Murphy, 83
Pennsylvania:
  free speech issue in, 11
  whistle-blowers in, 8
Pennsylvania, University of, Medical
  School of, 116
perceived disability, 118
Perrin, Towers, 146

Peter Harris Research Associates, 164
Peters, Tom, 102
Pfizer, 152
Pillsbury Company, 25–26, 36
PIRG Education Fund, 76
plant closings, 133–41
  WARN Act and, 136–41
Playboy, 50
PNC Bank, 26
pollution, 226–27
polybrominated biphenyls (PBBs), 8–9
Polygraph Protection Act (1988), 90, 91,
  120, 240, 241
polygraphs, 90–91, 120
Pope, James, 170
post-traumatic stress disorder (PTSD), 81
predictive validity, 88
preemption doctrine, 191–92
pre-existing conditions, 111
Preventing Tobacco Addiction
  Foundation, 54
Prince, Charles, 144
privacy issue, 1–2, 16–43, 56, 216–17, 218
  biometrics and, 3, 32–35, 43
  blogs and, 10–12, 29, 241
  chip implants and, 36
  Constitution and, 16, 41
  DNA and, 35–36, 108, 241
  drug testing and, 95, 219, 236, 241
  e-mail and, 19, 21, 23–26, 28, 36–40,
    42, 43, 217, 230–31, 242
  future of, 30–43
  genetic testing and, 112–13, 123–24
  GPS and, 3, 30–32, 43
  identity theft and, 3, 33–35
  Internet and, 19–20, 25, 26–27, 28, 29,
    36–40, 42, 43, 50, 52–53, 231, 233
  legal protection and, 40–43
  Patriot Act and, 24–25
  psychological testing and, 82, 86
  sexual harassment and, 37–39, 41, 175,
    185, 230
  telephone communications and, 21–22,
    31, 38, 41, 43, 231–33
Private Security Enhancement Act, 74–75
procedural rights, 187
productivity:
  electronic surveillance and, 27
  human rights and, 219
  unions and, 146–50, 220

Protocol (*Prototype Agreement on Job
     Bias Dispute Resolution*), 177–82
   appeals under, 180–81
   discovery and, 178–79
   elements of, 177–81
   fees under, 180
   full legal remedies and, 179
   neutral arbitrator in, 177
   response to, 181–82, 188
   right to counsel in, 178
   written decisions and, 179–80
psychological testing, 3, 80–91
   control groups for, 82–83
   defense of, 82
   employers and, 83–85
   history of, 81–82
   honesty tests and, 86–91
   laws on, 85–86, 90–91
   reliability of, 87–91
Psychology Today, 83
Public Citizen, 186, 210
Pullman Company strike (1894), 152–53

Qatar, 222
Quaker Fabric, 135

racial discrimination, 40, 41, 58, 73, 168–
     69, 185, 196, 197, 220–21, 243
Raisner, Jack, 138–39
Reagan, Nancy, 99
Reagan, Ronald W., 14, 74, 96, 99–100,
     104, 136, 166
Red Earth, 23
reference checks, 203–8
Register Guard decision (2007), 157
Reid, Harry, 126
religious discrimination, 44, 85–86
Research Triangle Institute (RTI), 98
retina scans, 3, 32–33
Revere, Paul, 6
RFID transmitters, 36
Rhode Island:
   drug testing in, 94
   privacy issue in, 17, 42
   psychological testing in, 85–86, 91
right-to-work laws, 158–60
Rizzo, Frank, 244
Road Less Traveled, The (Peck), 51
Robert Mondavi Winery, 39
Roosevelt, Franklin D., 240

Rothstein, Mark, 119, 120
Rudd Center for Food Policy and Obesity,
     46
Runyon v. McCrary (1976), 167
Russia, 223, 226–27
Rutgers University Law School, 170

St. Antoine, Theodore, 61, 65, 194
St. Joseph News-Press decision (2005), 161
Salem State College, 17–18
Saucier, Peter, 142
SCHIP program, 110
Schultz, Jerald, 59–60
SEARCH, 72
Section 1981, 167
Securities and Exchange Commission
     (SEC), 146, 228, 229
Senate, U.S., 165, 166, 173, 174, 239
   genetic testing issue and, 125–26
S.E. Nichols stores, 89
September 11, 2001, terrorist attacks, 69
Sergeant, Terri, 108
Service Employees' International Union
     (SEIU), 149–50
sexual harassment, 37–39, 41, 175, 185,
     230
sexual offenders, 132
sexual orientation discrimination, 47,
     51–52, 58
Shaya, Carol, 50
Shick, Dave, 58
Shoars, Alana, 37
sickle-cell anemia, 109, 112
Simon, Paul, 191
Skagerberg v. Blandin Paper Company, 62
Smith, Adam, 222
Smith, Sally, 47
smoking, tobacco, 2, 45–47, 48, 54, 55, 99,
     111, 130
Smyth, Michael, 25–26
Snodgrass, Sandy, 72
Snyder, Stacy, 52–53
Social Costs of Private Enterprise, The
     (Karp), 226
Social Security, 243, 246
Society for Human Resource
     Management (SHRM), 11–12
Soroka, Sibi, 80, 85
South Carolina, free speech issue and, 11
Soviet Union, 222

Spohn, Meg, 10
Sprague, Robert, 7
Starbucks, 34
state-run economies, 222–24
Stetson, John B., 44
Steward, Dave, 10–11
Stieber, Jack, 58
Stimson, Henry L., 20
stock market, 227–29
strikes, 150–51, 152–54, 160–61
strip-search drug tests, 94, 95
substantive rights, 187
summary judgment, 170–72
Supersize Me, 46
Supreme Court, U.S., xi, 6*n*
  arbitration issue and, 175, 187–88,
    191–92
  disability issue and, 118
  discrimination issue and, 165–70,
    172–74, 198
  disparate impact and, 73, 168–70
  election of 2000 and, 174
  free speech issue and, 13–15
  permanent replacement ruling of, 161
  sexual offender issue and, 132
Sutton v. United Airlines (1999), 118, 130,
  165, 166
sweatshops, 213–14
Sweden, 222, 229
Switzerland, 222

Taft-Hartley Act (1947), 158, 159
Target, 80, 85
taxes, taxation, 225–26, 245–46
Tay-Sachs disease, 109
TBG Insurance, 29
Teksid Aluminum, 157–58
telephones:
  privacy issue and, 21–22, 31, 38, 41, 43,
    231–33
  see also cell phones
Teresa, Sister, 88, 89
Texas, genetic testing and, 119
text messaging, 231–33
Thiemann, Ronald, 29
Thomas, Clarence, 74
Thompson, Becky, 92
Thompson, William, 17
Three Mile Island accident, 8
Time Warner, 34

Title VII, 167, 196
Tobacco Control Legal Consortium, 54
Tobacco Public Policy Center, 54
torts, 65
Toyota, 144
TransUnion, 78
Truman, Harry S., 158
TRW, 76
Tsvangirai, Morgan, 164
Turic, Kimberly, 50
Turner, Carlton, 99

unemployment compensation, 96–97,
  147–48
Unfair Advantage (Human Rights
  Watch), 242
Uniform Commercial Code, 64–65
Uniform State Law Commissioners,
  64–66
Union Carbide, xii, 101
unions, 3–4, 64, 66, 142–64, 229
  arbitration and, 159, 178
  benefits of, 142–43
  collective bargaining and, 143, 158–59
  corruption and, 150, 151
  criticisms of, 143–44, 150–52
  decertification of, 160
  dues paid to, 159
  elections for, 156–58, 160, 163–64
  employer resistance to, 152–61,
    235–36
  independent contractors and, 161–62
  just-cause provision and, 143
  law and, 142, 153, 154–64
  management cooperation and, 149–50
  productivity and, 146–50, 220
  right-to-work laws and, 158–60
  strikes and, 150–51, 152–54, 160–61
  world trade and, 212–14
United Nations (UN), 190
universal health care, 48–50
UPS, 31
urine testing, 92–93, 95, 104, 106
USA Patriot Act (2001), 24–25
U.S. Steel, 7–8

values-based organizations, 55
Vaughn, Libby, 134
Vaughn, Sam, 133–34, 135
Vermont, drug testing and, 94–95

video surveillance, 16–20, 42
Vietnam War, xi
violent behavior, 131–32
voice recognition, 32

Wackenhut Security, 201–2
wage theft, 199–200, 201
Wall Street Journal, 21, 75–76
Wal-Mart, 6–7, 201, 215
Walsh, J. Michael, 104
wanderlist.com, 237
Ward's Cove Packing v. Antonio (1989),
   168–70
Warner-Lambert, 152
Warren, Earl, xi, 173
Washington:
   background checks in, 77
   privacy issue in, 232
Watson, James, 108
Wealth of Nations (Smith), 222
Web access software, 39
Weckert, John, 216
Wellemeyer, John, 229
Westen, Drew, 174
Westin, Alan F., 7
West Virginia, drug testing in, 95
Weyco Corporation, 45
Weyers, Howard, 45
What Do Unions Do? (Freeman and
   Medoff), 142, 220
whistle-blowers, 7–10

Whistleblower's Survival Guide, The
   (Devine), 8
*Whistle-Blowing: Loyalty and Dissent in
   the Corporation* (Westin), 7
White, Byron, 14, 187–88
Wilkins, Maurice, 108
Winn-Dixie, 50
Wireless Communications and Public
   Safety Act (1999), 31
Wisconsin, free speech issue in, 13
Wisconsin, University of, 26
Wolfson, Louis, 173
Wong, Peter, 151
Wood, Horace, 61
Woods, Jerrol, 71
Woodworth, Robert, 81
Worker Adjustment and Retraining
   Notification Act (WARN) (1988),
   136–41
workers' compensation, 116, 209
World War I, 81
World War II, 81–82, 158
Wynn, Daniel, 44–45

Yale University, 46, 47
yellow-dog contracts, 153
Yetsko, Norma, 26

Zieminski, Robert, 29
Zimbabwe, 164
Zimmerman, Ross, 146